The Chosen Shore

The Chosen Shore

STORIES OF IMMIGRANTS

ELLEN ALEXANDER CONLEY

UNIVERSITY OF CALIFORNIA PRESS
Berkeley   Los Angeles   London

University of California Press
Berkeley and Los Angeles, California
University of California Press, Ltd.
London, England

Library of Congress Cataloging-in-Publication Data

Conley, Ellen Alexander.
    The chosen shore : stories of immigrants / Ellen Alexander Conley.
        p.   cm.
    ISBN 0–520–21882–5 (cloth : alk. paper)—ISBN 0–520–23988–1
(pbk. : alk. paper)
        1. United States—Emigration and immigration.   2. Immigrants—
United States.   I. Title.

JV6465.C73   2004
304.8'73'00922—dc22   2004002851

Manufactured in the United States of America
13   12   11   10   09   08   07   06   05   04
10   9   8   7   6   5   4   3   2   1

Printed on Ecobook 50 containing a minimum 50% post-consumer
waste, processed chlorine free. The balance contains virgin pulp,
including 25% Forest Stewardship Council Certified for no old growth
tree cutting, processed either TCF or ECF. The sheet is acid-free and
meets the minimum requirements of ANSI/NISO Z39.48–1992 (R 1997)
(Permanence of Paper). ♾

To the brave immigrants

To my family: Steve, Alexandra,
and Dalton Conley; Dan Leonardi,
Natalie Jeremijenko, Sylvia Alexander,
Al Rubin, Arthur Alexander

To the next generation: E, Yo, and Dante

In memory of Howard Alexander
and Ralph Landis

The big mistake I made was coming to America. But then again, it would have been a bigger mistake to stay.

Abdul Badsha

Contents

Acknowledgments

I would like to thank all the fine people and institutions whose combined intellectual and financial support made this book possible. It will not be possible to name and extend my gratitude to all the parties, but here I would like to express appreciation to the Center for Advanced Social Science Research at New York University, Borough of Manhattan Community College of the City University of New York, Pratt Institute, the Mellon Foundation, Aaron Major, Frances Goldin, Naomi Schneider, Lea Chartock, Farida Saed, and the Writers Group. Thanks also to my immigrant contacts: Tara, Michael, Johnson, Dan, Larry, Masha, Steve, Alyson, Sid, Myrna, and Francine.

Foreword

Not long ago, I was taking a car service to La Guardia airport. After settling in my seat, I complimented the driver on his luxury model vehicle.

"A lot of work and lonesomeness went into it," he replied. He was from Pakistan, and he decided "to take a chance" by coming to America when he could not get work back home. His first jobs were in little bodegas and convenience stores. Twice his bosses got shot—one fatally. "What was worse than the poverty, the hard labor, and the violence was the lonesomeness. Maybe it would be different if I had emigrated with a wife."

When I told him that I was thinking about writing a book on recent immigrants, he added, "May God bless you a thousand folds. You will be doing a wonderful thing, telling our stories." Much to my shame, I lost his dispatcher's phone number.

On the way back from that same trip, I had a Russian cab driver. Our route crossed lower Manhattan and the infamous Bowery. "He looks healthy. He looks healthy," the driver muttered every time we passed a homeless person or someone asking for a handout, his implication being that "the homeless" looked healthy so they should be working rather than begging on the streets. The cab driver was not interested in my sociological explanations for some of these men. The driver's mantra—"he looks healthy"—continued until we got to my destination.

I should have quoted from the novel *Being Here* (1997) by Jaime P. Espirtu. While sitting on a park bench, the main character, an immigrant, asks a homeless man, "You were born and raised here. Many people throughout the world could only wish that had happened to them. What happened to you?"

"Everybody has a different story," the vagrant tells him. He was once part of the middle class. "You have an America to go to. I don't. I'm already here!"

Soon after the airport trip, a young Haitian-American in my evening class revealed that she had been homeless for a year and a half while she attended school and gained a high office in the student government. Edeline was so articulate that I felt that this book might write itself if I could snatch up her wise words for a book on immigrants and their idiosyncratic experiences.

But after that wonderful start, I had to seek out other interesting stories. Snowball sampling was the organic methodology I used for finding most of the immigrants whose stories are told in this book. I was looking for absorbing tales that would maintain geographic representation and illustrate the different facets of migration. I soon learned about a whole segment of young immigrants who had been adopted by American families. I met Tommy, who was of a different race and culture from that of his adoptive family. Some of these testimonies come from immigrants who share the same country of origin, proving that although statistics might indicate patterns, upon closer inspection, individuals showed idiosyncratic differences, indicating that "God is in the details." When asked, the subjects in the book had the option to use their real name or a psuedonym. Their preferences were honored.

After working a few years on this project, I began to look with fresh eyes upon the people with whom I came in contact: colleagues, students, friends, the guys in the parking lot, the porters in the building, the green grocers, the bank tellers. It seemed that there was a plethora of newcomers and a browning of America. Some had slight accents; others enunciated their words perfectly, including the dental d's or t's. Many brought added flavor from their motherlands, a unique way of weaving their hair, an original outlook, a distinctive way of telling a story punctuated with expressive hand gestures, the ability to laugh long and out loud. I even saw one neatly dressed student carrying his heavy book bag on his head in the traditional African manner until his buddies ribbed him and told him in today's vernacular that he looked like he came right off the boat. Several months later he was garbed in the latest hip-hop clothes, camouflaged into the inner urban college scene. With all these recent émigrés, there were ideas to be examined, and stereotypes to be laid to rest. The people in the book have made a profound impact on me and I hope on the reader. Many have become my new friends.

An inquisitive mind might ask, Why should I devote time to a single individual's story? Barbara Laslett, a professor of sociology at the University of Minnesota-Twin Cities, provides an answer. In her 1999 essay "Personal Narratives as Sociology," from the journal *Contemporary Sociology,* she explains that in providing space for the words, the subjectivities, the discourses through which individual life histories are told, there is a particular promise for sociological analysis that remains largely unrecognized in the discipline. Personal narratives offer new analytic and literary forms for sociologists, while advancing theoretical debates on issues such as social reproduction and social change, and connections between personal life, social institutions, and social structure. Personal narrative in sociology often focuses on people largely ignored by society. Given that kind of interest, such books are engaging in ways that many of us have been taught not to be engaged: emotionally.

Pico Iyer, in his book *The Global Soul: Jet Lag, Shopping Malls, and the Search for Home* (1999), considers himself one of a growing number of "children of blurred boundaries and global mobility." He reflects on the contradictions and paradoxes built into multiple identities, the result of having grown up in three cultures, none of them exactly his own. He considers himself not quite an immigrant, not quite an expatriate, but a permanent alien.

Ironies and paradoxes abound in these narrations, such as parents moving to the United States for the sake of their children, who as teenagers "have become too fast-fooded, too MTV'd." A high priority for some newcomers to America was to earn money in order to build and own a house back home. "My mother already has some land; my father is building one. I am going to start sending money to my uncle little by little," states Rosemond about her future in Ghana. "I could never live there," she remarked later, "because I'm too Americanized."

There are many paradoxes in this book. One seemingly simple concept is that everyone should have a chance to come to our new land and life. But two of the immigrants, Rosemond from Ghana and Sarah from South Korea, encountered hidden, second families that they did not know about as younger girls. Each father had another wife and child. This was a chance for the dad "to do right" by all his children, to give them an equal shot at education and United States citizenship, so he collected the offspring from the other woman and included these children on his visa. In both cases, the new siblings did not fare so well in the already established family structure. In Sarah's case, her new half-brother kept to himself and eventually was "disowned" by the father for a not-to-be-mentioned infraction of the father's rules. Rosemond's new sibling found it hard to fit in and communicate because she spoke a different African dialect, could not learn English, and missed her biological mother.

From my casual observations I noticed some points of interest. The well-known saying goes, "I didn't know I was poor until I was told I was." Rosemond happily sold little sweets at the central market in Ghana at the age of five and thought her childhood was bucolic. As a five-year-old child, Tommy felt fortunate that he could hang out all night with other mixed-race children in Korea. He did not even have to attend school, which he thought was fine. It was only when the woman who he thought was his mother put him in the orphanage that he felt his troubles began. Even though she supposedly beat him and burned him, he did not think he was bad off with her. Yet some with higher economic and educational status thought they were doing poorly.

The stories abound with tales of culture shock. Topping the list are supermarkets, with their air-protective wrap. Except for the few who came from Western countries such as England or Australia, most of the subjects said they were used to going to markets and sampling the wares. "You got a taste of the yogurt," stated Tatyana, about her homeland, Russia.

Even though she came from a relatively affluent background in Korea, Sarah said she used to accompany her grandmother as she went from stall to stall, filling up with the food samples. In the United States, the meats and fish are sealed up, and immigrants not only do not know how to read the freshness dates, they would rather sniff and poke. For other items, from cereals to soups, they found it necessary to make their purchasing decisions based on the photographs on the container, which often do not correspond to the taste and appearance of the product. One woman said that she served dog biscuits at a cocktail party for doctors because they were whimsically labeled "human crackers." Proust had his madeleines that, when dipped in tea and tasted, brought him back by sensory mode to his childhood remembrances. The smell of charcoal fires and rotting oranges can instantly invoke Haiti. Turmeric and cardamom becomes the spicy air of India. The newcomers can sniff and use their senses in Texas or Pennsylvania, but they cannot recollect the sense of home that can trigger the circuitry for recollecting their history, which brings about connections. They are cast adrift without reference points of their flavors.

In the urban community college, my students wax eloquently about the warm globular mangoes on their neighbors' trees. I say, "There are a lot of mangos in the New York supermarkets these days."

"Oh no," comes the chorus of West Indian voices. "Not sun-ripened mangoes. The ones in the States are a different fruit. They have no scent of being."

Paradoxes abound and probably never will get resolved. Abdul Badsha, an Indian now living in snowy Wisconsin, told me in complete sincerity, "The big mistake I made was coming to America. But then again, it would have been a bigger mistake to stay."

One of the colleges where I teach is located quite close to ground zero in Lower Manhattan. When classes resumed after the tragedy, the buildings were bathed in a beautiful violet light caused by the fire, the dust, and the rescue workers' lights. Inside the main doors, a memorial table had been set up for the seven students and seven staff members who had been killed. Candles and photos crowded the small surface. People left flowers and small trinkets in a makeshift memorial. Two of the young deceased faces created a double poignancy: They were brother and sister, who were thought to have immigrated from India or Pakistan. Someone wrote on a small white paper bag filled with cookies, "I was in your accounting class and will miss you both."

In my creative writing classroom, I gave an assignment shortly before September 11. Students were asked to eavesdrop on a conversation and record what they heard. A student picked this up shortly after the Twin Tower attacks. I have removed the expletives:

FIRST MAN: Let's go over to Myrtle Avenue and beat up the Indian cabdrivers.

SECOND MAN: But they weren't the terrorists.

FIRST MAN: You know they had something to do with it. And while we're over there let's get the Koreans.

My student thought that one of the speakers was from Jamaica.

"Let's go beat up the Indians!"
"I was in your accounting class and will miss you both."
Which is the real America?

Context and Immigrant Identity

AARON MAJOR AND ELLEN ALEXANDER CONLEY

> My son was born here in Chattanooga, and
> he grew up in this community. He speaks
> Spanish with an American accent. I have my
> wife and my son. This is the only family I
> have, so this is my country now.

Sam Lizarraga, Bolivian-American

> It is impossible to know where I want to
> remain. In Iran, in a way it is much nicer
> because I had my station there, it was my
> home there, I was relaxed, and I had money
> to spend. I see the street, and I know every-
> thing. Iran is the same as it was twenty
> years ago. It's not like here—changing,
> always constant change. It is impossible to
> answer where I want to remain. My heart is
> split culturally.

Navid Daee, Iranian-American

Like the stories found within this collection, these sentiments reflect the
challenges faced and the choices made by recent immigrants. They have
tried to come to terms with their identity while simultaneously navigating the demands placed on them by living between two different cultures: that of their homeland and that of the host society. Some have

1

settled within one or the other, feeling at home, as adopted Korean-American Tommy said about his new national setting—"I am pure New Jersey American"—while others, like Isil Gundes, still yearn to return to their place of birth. Still others, like Navid Daee, remain unsure of their place and may never find an identity based on any one culture or nation but rather will always be living within—and apart from—two worlds. Through individual ethnographic narratives, the stories document this process of coming to America, negotiating a new cultural landscape, and trying to come to terms with one's identity.

Through these narratives a wide variety of contemporary immigrant experiences have been recounted by those most knowledgeable about them—the immigrants themselves. Some came for economic opportunity or education, while others have fled political upheavals or persecution. Still others come for reasons all their own. Some bring with them money and technical skills, with many years of education behind them, while others come with none of these resources. Some come as children who must enter the American educational system, while others come as adults confronted with the American labor market. Every immigrant's experience is shaped by the context of arrival to the United States and departure from their homeland.

While each narrative provides its own answers to the question of how immigrants negotiate culture, identity, and place, a complete understanding is not possible without considering the impact of reception and departure.

THE CONTEXT OF RECEPTION

The passage of the Hart-Celler Act of 1965 led to a new surge of immigration. It replaced the old system of national quotas, which had characterized U.S. immigration policy of the past, with a new system that favored family reunification and immigrants with special skills.[1] The passage of this landmark immigration bill coincided with the beginning of massive economic restructuring in the late 1960s and early 1970s that continues up to 2003, characterized by an increasingly global and multinational economy, deindustrialization and the rise of the service sector, and a widening gap between the rich and the poor.[2] The occupational skill and family reunification preferences of the 1965 Hart-Celler Act has contributed to the massive increase of immigrants from the Asia Pacific region, who had previously been banned from entering the country and to the influx of immigrants from all over the world with high levels of education and professional training.[3]

However, U.S. law is only one of many factors that affect the inflow of immigrants from a particular country or region. For example, over half of all immigration to the United States comes from Latin America—Mexico alone contributing between a fourth and a third of the total. Many of these immigrants begin—or remain—as undocumented workers in the agricultural sector—an area that has been relatively unregulated at the behest of American agribusiness. Proximity is an obvious factor, but other important factors include historical relationships (such as colonialism, as in the case of the Philippines), the legacy of active or covert military conflicts (as in the case of the Vietnamese, Koreans, Salvadorans, and Cubans), and trade relationships (such as with Mexico). The stories presented in this book provide ample evidence of the varied reasons for immigration, which cannot be reduced to the laws of 1965. In an ingenious twist, Manuel Ortiz let the U.S. immigration authorities deport him so he could get free transportation home from Texas to Mexico; he then reentered California. Some immigrants sought refuge because of war or its aftermath: Thuc Nguyen and My Le made their tortuous journey because of the Vietnam War. Azra Hodzic escaped the fighting in Bosnia. As a young boy Edel Rodriguez was part of the Mariel boat lift from Communist Cuba—fleeing the harsh conditions resulting from the cold war. Tatyana Lytkina from Siberia is another person who sought American soil during the cold war era.

The changing face of the economy has altered the context of reception for immigrants along several fronts, most notably in the labor market, the structure of cities, and the attitudes of native citizens. These can be broadly classified as the circumstances of reception, which define the social structures that all immigrants, no matter what their economic, educational, or cultural backgrounds, must navigate when they come to settle in the United States. Perhaps the most immediate framework that confronts the new immigrant is the urban metropolis.

Like the immigrants who came before them at the turn of the twentieth century, today's immigrants—despite their diversity in socioeconomic status, educational attainment, and country of origin—are highly concentrated within America's major metropolitan areas. In 1993, 43 percent of all legal immigrants lived within just six American cities: New York, Los Angeles, Chicago, Miami, Houston, and San Francisco. All told, less than 5 percent of legal immigrants lived outside of an urban environment.[4] By 1998, the share of total immigrants living in the top six cities for immigrant settlement had dropped to 36.2 percent, but by the year 2000 only 5.1 percent of the foreign-born were living outside of metropolitan areas.[5] Thus, while cities have always served as gateways and communities for incoming ethnic minorities, residential patterns of immigrants are becoming less concentrated in urban metropolises. Not only that, but the cities themselves are nowhere near the same type of cities that immigrant Italians, Poles, and Germans encountered almost a century ago.

Global economic restructuring and immigration have drastically altered the labor markets of the major reception cities for immigration, and since the foreign born now comprise 12 percent of the employed civilian labor force, they play a significant role in defining the demographics of American labor.[6] With manufacturing and heavy industry on the decline, and tens if not hundreds of thousands of immigrants with diverse levels of education, occupational skills, and credentials entering the country each year, these cities have become increasingly postindustrial, with a large segment of jobs being created in the field of international business services. This has created a labor market characterized by space both at the bottom, for low-paid, low-skilled menial service work, and at the top, for well-paid, high-skilled professional work.[7] According to the 2000 U.S. Census data, immigrants from Europe and Asia tend to do well in the labor market, as they find professional and managerial positions with high salaries and benefits; immigrants from Latin America have a more difficult time finding work, with success most often in lower-paid blue-collar occupations.

Selected Economic Characteristics of Immigrants Living in the United States, by World Region of Birth

	Europe	Asia	Latin America
Unemployed	2.3%	3.5%	6.6%
Living below poverty line (ages 18–64)	8.4	11.8	20.1
Employed in managerial or professional occupations	38.1	38.7	12.1
Employed as laborers, operators, or fabricators	10.2	12.0	24.8
With income < $20,000	16.2	22.4	50.3
With income > $50,000	33.2	29.5	8.5

Source: U.S. Census Bureau, *Current Population Survey*, March 2000

This polarized labor market can have a profound effect on how immigrants deal with their own ethnic identities. On the one hand, immigrants with high levels of education and professional skills may attempt to shed their ethnic identities if it means a greater chance at upward mobility.[8] Sarah Lee is from Korea and is a student in fashion design. She stated, "My goal is not to be stuck with one country or one culture." On the other hand, real or perceived barriers to upward mobility and integration into the labor market, be they outright discrimination or a lack of opportunity to acquire jobs with prospects for economic security or advancement, may make immigrants more aware of their distinctiveness relative to the native-born population. This could lead to a reinforcement of the cultures, practices, and customs of their homeland and a strengthening of their ethnic identity.[9] When Kamal Patel lived in Texas she was required to take an English as a Second Language (ESL) course because of her Indian ethnicity—this despite the fact that she already spoke English well—which had the consequence of reminding her that she was not only Indian, but different, and may have played a role in her continuing observance of traditional marriage customs and her decision to marry only within the Patel clan.

The structure of the economy generates its own mechanisms for channeling immigrants into either ethnic enclaves or the free labor market, depending on the nature of the economic base that served as a source of income in their home country and the opportunities to reproduce this base in the host society. In his comparative study of six historic Russian migrations, Tony Waters has found that those who were able to succeed in the free land and labor market were also able to assimilate more readily into the mainstream culture, while those who were dependent upon a restricted group of people who had emigrated with them were much more likely to reproduce old patterns of behavior within an ethnic enclave.[10] Of course today's immigrants are not the peasants of Waters's study. Nevertheless, immigrants still face the problem of transferring their mode of economic participation in the home country to a mode of economic participation in the new country, and depending on the skills and education they bring with them combined with the nature of the economic structure of the host society, this process will likely be a primary factor in determining immigrant identity.

Reception cities have also changed in the way that communities are residentially zoned and thus ethnically constituted. The post–World War II era has brought with it a massive decline in explicit race-based zoning policies and has brought in its place class-based zoning. This change has had the effect of creating multiethnic communities that can sometimes be sources of hostility between ethnic groups—as the boycott of Korean greengrocers by segments of the African-American community in New York City demonstrates—and can also provide exposure to other racial and ethnic groups that may either reinforce or contradict an immigrant's preconceived racial stereotypes.[11] Interviewee Sarah Lee explains how in Korea darker skin is associated with poor, uneducated farmers, and yet when she immigrated with her family to Queens, New York, she found herself in a highly diverse neighborhood, populated by Greeks, Italians, and Latinos, which provided quite a shock for her because she had "never even seen a white person in Korea, much less a black."

Immigrants with low incomes and a lack of transferable occupational skills, who find themselves in poorer communities where opportunities for economic advancement have largely vanished, may become part of an oppositional culture. This occurs particularly among younger segments of the population where authority, goals of achievement, and the general values of "middle-class America" are rejected, such as those of school administrators and other officials who are seen as oppressive authorities. Immigrants who find themselves in underprivileged neighborhoods will be confronted and influenced by this culture, which will no doubt shape how they perceive and interact with other segments of the American population.[12] This was perhaps the fear of Manuel Ortiz, a father of three who immigrated to Texas from Mexico. He tells his children to befriend the white Americanos and stay away from the Mexican kids, who he sees as just picking fights and causing problems.

Economic restructuring has not only had these kinds of direct effects on the economic and residential contexts of reception for immigrants. It has also had a severe effect on another, related context of reception: the attitudes of the native-born population toward immigrants. Economic restructuring, resulting in general wage stagnation for the bulk of the working population as well as a surge in corporate restructuring leading to sudden and massive layoffs, has created a widespread feeling of economic insecurity, which has fueled a fear of immigration and generated a new wave of strong anti-immigration and nativist sentiments. The dominant rhetoric characterizing this period of economic restructuring has promised economic prosperity for all, while actually giving it to very few. Thus, a scapegoat is needed when the promised benefits of the new economy do not materialize; structural problems in the economy are thereby blamed on immigrants.[13]

While it is true that immigrants have been viewed negatively since the nineteenth century, much evidence exists to support the claim that the last decade has witnessed a resurgence in anti-immigrant sentiment as strong as any other historical period of nativism.[14] On the public policy front, the passage of Proposition 187 in California bars illegal immigrants from receiving welfare benefits, and the passage of the Welfare Reform Bill in 1996 bars noncitizens from most forms of public assistance. Activists meanwhile are attempting to pass legislation making English the official national language. Groups such as the Federation for Immigration Reform (FAIR), the American Immigration Control Foundation (AICF), and the New York-based Tri-Immigration Moratorium (TRIM) have been very vocal in pushing to reduce or eliminate altogether both legal and illegal immigration into this country, while anti-immigrant books such as G. Palmer Stacy and Wayne Lutton's *The Immigration Time Bomb* (1988) and Peter Brimelow's *Alien Nation: Common Sense About America's Immigration Disaster* (1995) find both academic and popular audiences.[15]

After the terrorist attacks of September 11, 2001, on the World Trade Center and Pentagon, immigrants from the Middle East and South Asia have become the victims of increased levels of anti-immigrant sentiment. In New York City, a potential passengers might first ask where a cabdriver was from if he had a beard, dark skin and hair, or a turban. More than one thousand Arabs and South Asians have been thrown in jail for noncriminal violations, many of whom were turned in by friends, coworkers, and neighbors through the State Department's "Rewards for Justice" program.[16] Agents from the Immigration and Naturalization Service (INS, now called U.S. Citizenship and Immigration Services under the Department of Homeland Security) and the Federal Bureau of Investigation (FBI) have investigated the activities of Middle Eastern students at more than two hundred college campuses.[17] In the past, the INS attempted to implement a technologically advanced system of monitoring and tracking international students, although objections from academic institutions kept this program at bay. Since September 11, much of these objections have gone silent, and Congress has mandated the implementation of a Student Exchange Visitor Information System (SEVIS).[18] Other difficulties are also emerging for immigrant students in the wake of September 11. Fears raised by the terrorist attacks have forced the City University of New York to end its longstanding policy of granting in-state tuition to immigrants who lived in New York for at least one year before admittance.[19] Other limitations to the civil rights of immigrants include the suspension of habeas corpus, private hearings, and the limitation of legal council—all implemented under the guise of "national security" concerns. The creation of the Department of Homeland Security augurs that these changes may be institutionalized and thus made a permanent part of the American social landscape.[20]

While it will still take some time before we fully understand the impact of September 11 on immigrants and immigration policy, all immigrants, and some groups more than others, will likely enter this country under vastly different circumstances than those of even the recent past. The government has radically reconfigured its context of reception while taking a more active role in monitoring its immigrant population, and some immigrant groups will face increased nativist hostility. In looking at the tremendous consequences of these events on U.S. immigration, we do not want to overstate the case and ignore the longer-term changes that have been taking place in the context of reception. Nativist sentiments have also been driven by the size and composition of the new immigrant population. With massive numbers of people entering the country each year whose primary language is not English and who are categorized as being uniformly uneducated and unskilled, the native-born population has become fearful that their country will suffer a decline under the weight of multicultural pressures, and that new waves of ethnic minorities will take advantage of affirmative-action programs.[21] Furthermore, because many of the new immigrants come from conditions of poverty and bring no skills or education with them, there is the further fear that they will be a drain on public resources and thus generate more social costs than benefits.[22] Despite such sentiments and the effects of national security concerns, labor market conditions may trump. With an aging population that will be exiting the labor force in large numbers in the near future, the need for immigrants—particularly skilled immigrants—may increase and outweigh other concerns.

Faced with citizens' feelings, immigrants have responded by becoming more politically active and by naturalizing at increased rates.[23] As rates of immigration continue to be high, first- and second-generation immigrants continue to make up a large portion of the ethnic population and help maintain strong ethnic communities. These high rates of immigration, combined with high birth rates in immigrant communities, will cause nonwhites to soon become the numerical majority in the United States, shifting the balance of political power to ethnic minorities, as witnessed by successful attempts to make schools adopt bilingual education and multicultural education programs and by extremely high rates of voter participation among first- and second-generation immigrants in

California around anti-immigrant policies such as Proposition 187.[24] So long as the current economic structure continues to generate economic insecurity, conflicts over immigration, culture, and identity are not likely to go away.[25]

Of course, the economic structure is not the only context that new immigrants enter into since, as was hinted at earlier, many of today's immigrants come from parts of the world automatically inserts them into a predetermined racial and ethnic structure. Immigrants today mostly come from the Asia-Pacific region and Central and South America. Despite the wide diversity of immigrants' actual country of origin, be it China, Korea, Vietnam, Mexico, or Columbia, the government, researchers, and the mass media classify them as "Asian" or "Hispanic" upon arrival in the United States. As Jacqueline Stevens has argued, race and ethnicity are little more than political constructions based upon perceived physical characteristics and upon one's place of origin as defined through politically constructed geographical borders. "Rivers and mountains do not separate people. Governments do . . . 'Germany' exists because that is the place where 'Germans' live."[26] Whether a person is a native-born Chinese-American or a foreign-born Vietnamese immigrant, he or she will be forced to take on a predefined racial and ethnic identity based upon appearance ("You look Asian") and country of origin ("You are Vietnamese. Why? Because you were born in Vietnam.") as well as the rhetorical baggage that comes with it.

Unlike the fourth- or fifth-generation descendants of early-twentieth-century Western and Eastern European immigrants, whose outward physical appearance gives them great latitude in how they choose to acknowledge and express their ethnic identities, the predominantly non-European, nonwhite physical characteristics of the new immigrants enforce upon them an ethnic identity that they may or may not want. As Mary Waters has observed, white Americans of European decent have a wide array of "ethnic options" in how they construct and display their largely symbolic and voluntarily adopted ethnic identity. For people of African, Asian, or Latino decent, however, the identities that are ascribed to them offer little room for maneuver because their physical characteristics pin them down to a predetermined set of racial and ethnic constructions—despite any attempts made to adopt white American cultural practices and the English language. As Waters writes, "The social and political consequences of being Asian or Hispanic or black are not symbolic for the most part, or voluntary. They are real and often hurtful."[27]

Many of the immigrants in this book recall experiences of racism directed against them—something that was especially difficult for those who had no experience with racism in their countries of origin. Navid Daee, an Iranian immigrant, experienced racism when he and his black friend were denied service by the white owner of a local store. Puerto Rican schoolboys threw pennies at Sarah Lee and told her to go back to Korea. King Chan learned to tolerate the racial epithets flung at him by some students in his school. When Dianne Barker, from Barbados, was walking down the street in Bayonne, New Jersey, a white woman coming the opposite way cowered in a corner and clutched her purse as she walked by. As Dianne recalls, "Coming to this country I experienced racism, I mean to the max."

One of the most obvious ways that racism and racial constructions can have real consequences for immigrants is in the labor market, although not all of these effects are negative, depending on the immigrant group. While explicit discrimination based on race or ethnicity in job hiring has been illegal for several decades, employers are no doubt still held captive by cultural stereotypes of certain immigrant groups. Some, for instance, may be seen as better suited for highly skilled work—note here the "model minority" label that is often attached to immigrants from the Asia-Pacific region—while others may be viewed as uneducated, unskilled, or just plain lazy.

Tatyana Lytkina earned her doctorate in microbiology before emigrating from Russia, but she was unable to get into a physicians' assistant program at Kingsborough College because the chairperson did not trust her credentials and believed that all Russians were crooks and liars. "That's what he tells me," Tatyana says. "Now I'm ashamed to go see other people for my education. Americans look down on us. They think we are all criminals or communist terrorists, so I don't tell people where we come from." Now Tatyana must try and conceal her ethnic identity if she wants to pursue a professional career in the United States. Sam

Lizarraga, a Bolivian immigrant, had a similar experience when he was passed up for promotion at his job; the higher position was given to a less experienced worker. Unfortunately, these scenarios occur much more often than instances in which immigrants benefit from their ethnic identity; as Tatyana's story demonstrates, this can have severe consequences for an immigrant's outward presentation and self-identity.[28]

The level of skills and education people bring to the labor market often determine the kinds of jobs they obtain. However, for most immigrants, participating in a labor market where racial typifications are ubiquitous can have severe effects on their identity. Immigrants who are negatively stereotyped, and possess few or no skills or education, may find themselves excluded from the mainstream economy and forced to find work in ethnic enclaves. On the other hand, immigrants with higher skills and educational credentials may attempt to disguise their ethnic identity and refuse to be associated with the ethnic group of their homeland as a way of neutralizing labor market discrimination and increasing their chances for success, much as Tatyana Lytkina learned she had to do.[29] In both cases the racial and ethnic structure of American society can seriously affect the way in which immigrants view and deal with their own identities.

Beyond the experience within the labor market, racial and ethnic typifications disguise the differences that exist not only among various ethnicities, but between immigrant ethnics and native-born ethnics. Immigrants can be found among groups comprising both the highest and lowest rates of education, self-employment, home ownership, poverty, welfare dependency, and fertility.[30] Alejandro Portes and Rubén Rumbaut have compiled several different indicators that show not only a great diversity in the characteristics between ethnic groups, but also a great deal of difference between immigrants and the native-born population. In 1990 the proportion of the native-born population that had completed four or more years of college stood at 20.3 percent. In that same year, more than half of all immigrants born in India, Taiwan, and Iran had completed four or more years of college, while of those who had been born in Mexico, Portugal, and El Salvador, less than 5 percent had completed four or more years of college. During this same year, 65.3 percent of people born in the United States were in the labor force while more than 75 percent of those born in the Philippines, Hong Kong, and India and less than 50 percent of those born in the former Soviet Union, Italy, and Cambodia participated in the labor force. During the same year, the native-born poverty rate was 12.7 percent, while it was only 5.9 percent and 6.6 percent for those born in the Philippines and the United Kingdom, climbing up to 38.4 percent and 40.3 percent for those born in Cambodia and Laos.[31]

Immigrants are also distinct from native-born ethnics in that they are not a random group of individuals who left their homelands for America but rather a select group of individuals and thus not representative of either the population of the land they left behind or of the native-born members of the ethnic community with which they are defined when they enter the new society. Immigration to a foreign land is a very difficult process that requires not only many preparations and high expense but also a willingness to be prepared to make difficult sacrifices as one tries to live in a foreign land with an unfamiliar culture, language, and perhaps (as is the case with this country) a native population that greets you with hostility. Thuc Nguyen spent a day in the cold and rain, hiding from the Vietnamese military before taking a small boat with eighty-three other people on a five-day voyage to Malaysia as the first part of his immigration to the United States. Edel Rodriguez and his family had to give up everything they had before taking a boat from Cuba as part of the Mariel flotilla in order to start a new life from scratch in Miami. Given obstacles such as these, immigrants tend to be positively self-selected on such tangible characteristics as education and occupational skills and also perhaps by less tangible characteristics, such as ambition or a willingness to work.[32]

While evidence supports the education and occupational portion of this claim, ambition is less susceptible to easy quantification. Nevertheless, research does exist. One possible indicator of greater personal ambition or self-reliance is the rate of small-business ownership or other entrepreneurial activity. Although for most immigrants the most common form of economic participation is in the labor market, immigrants do display higher rates of entrepreneurship than do the native born.[33] The story of My Le, a Vietnamese monk, and his four brothers illustrates this well. While My Le spent several years after his arrival in the United States working at many jobs, including washing dishes at a Roy Rogers restaurant and delivering newspapers for the *Washington Post,* his dream had always been to open his own spiritual center. After seven years, during which he and his brothers pooled their money together, he not only got his fledgling spiritual center but also a martial arts studio, and he is also looking into a second one. His brother, who has helped him finance these projects, owns his own beauty parlor.

This discussion of the diversity of the new immigrants *within* racial categories underscores the point that popular generalizations about Asian "model minorities," for example, create an oversimplified view where inter- and intraethnic tensions are overlooked. For instance, when Sarah Lee moved with her family from Queens to suburban New Jersey, she suddenly found herself in a predominantly Korean-American neighborhood, but her identity as a native Korean who could still speak the language made it difficult for her to associate with the American-born Korean-Americans. As she describes it, she "couldn't hang out the way the Korean-Americans hung out, because whatever they did cost a lot of money . . . and they thought I was strange because I spoke Korean fluently." Sarah did manage to make friends, but among non-Asian peers, and this seems to have caused a lot of racial tension. Thus, immigrants are forced to navigate through a preexisting system of values, beliefs, and behaviors assigned to them on the basis of their outward racial and ethnic physical characteristics while trying to come to terms with their own sense of identity.

When an immigrant arrives in the United States, he or she is not simply entering a new geographical space, but rather a politically defined space with powerful, well-defined economic and cultural structures that shape and constrain the process of identity formation. And yet this is only half of the story, for there is still one other significant way that immigrants are different from the native born. Immigrants do not just arrive as empty vessels into the American economic, social, and racial structure, but rather "they are decisively influenced not only by events in the United States but by experiences of a whole life in a different country."[34] Thus, to understand all of the factors that make immigrant identity formation such a difficult and dynamic process we also need to understand the political and cultural context under which people emigrate—the context of departure.

THE CONTEXT OF DEPARTURE

Great diversity in political, economic, and social contexts push people to leave their homeland to create a new life in a foreign society and shape the ways in which they form their identity. Migrants come from countries that have had some sort of historical relationship to the host society, be it military, economic, political, or cultural. The relationships allow for the creation of both formal and informal, legal and illegal, systems of immigration between sending countries and the United States. As Rubén Rumbaut writes, "As the United States has become deeply involved in the world, the world has become more deeply involved in America."[35]

While many of the immigrants who arrived during the last great wave of immigration at the turn of the twentieth century came from parts of the world where the presence of the national government was not felt in the rural and peasant communities, the late twentieth century has seen the creation of a consolidated and expansive international state system "where most people today not only belong to a nation-state, but are aware of this fact."[36] For some, this can result in the creation of a strong national identity associated with a positive image of the society that they left behind, while for those driven out for political reasons, their home government continues to generate feelings of opposition. This effect is particularly acute in modern society where easy access to global communication and mass media can focus an immigrant's political attention on affairs taking place in the homeland and where the presence of trade officials and diplomatic representatives from their home country can influence immigrant communities in subtle, but important, ways.[37]

In a study of Iranian immigrants in a small town in Iowa, Mohammad Chaichan found that those who had immigrated after the 1979 revolution and the rise of Ayatollah Khomeini were less likely to want to become American citizens and were more likely to hold on to a strong Iranian identity.[38] The story of Navid Daee also shows how political events in one's home country can still be very significant, even if they occur after one has emigrated. While Navid had already left Iran when the revolution occurred, his leftist political views became a source of tension with his American family, who were pro-shah. This forced Navid to lie to them about his political views for fear of jeopardizing his place in their home. Refugees, whose entire reason for emigration came from the political and social turmoil in their homeland, continue to be politically active in opposition to their native government while in the host society—even if they never plan on returning. As Portes and Rumbaut write, "Politics is at the very core of refugee communities and is apt to remain so for many years. Militant opposition to the regime that expelled them and an enduring commitment to oppose is what sets refugees apart from other immigrants."[39]

Cubans, for example, represented one of the largest refugee immigrant groups in the United States during the early 1960s, and for several years the life of the community revolved around trying to overthrow the Castro government. While the failure of the Bay of Pigs invasion and the subsequent events surrounding the missile crisis eliminated any hope that these refugees may have had to overthrow the Communist government and return home, Cuban-exile political culture is still strong. Powerful radio signals broadcast anti-Castro propaganda from Radio Martí, political action committees made up of exiles still make large campaign contributions to sympathetic U.S. senators, and the year-long Elián González saga brought to the surface the strong anti-Castro sentiments still held by many Cuban immigrants living in the Miami area, as did Jimmy Carter's visit to the island nation in 2002.[40]

It is in this context that one can appreciate the story of Edel Rodriguez, who emigrated from Cuba as a young boy when his family decided to flee the Communist regime. While Edel was too young to fully appreciate the reasons for their leaving, the events surrounding the move—leaving his home, spending a week in an emigrant processing center, and the ten-hour boat ride into Key West—all feature prominently in his tale and thus define for him what it means to call oneself "Cuban." Azra Hodzic and her husband were fleeing the war in Bosnia in the early 1990s when they came to this country, and Edeline Decossard and her family left Haiti partly in fear of François "Papa Doc" Duvalier, who had killed several of her aunts and uncles.

While not every immigrant, or even most immigrants, are exiled from their homeland and forced to take up residence in a foreign land, the political context at the time of departure can have profound effects on an immigrant's identity. Even in cases where the political context is not so tumultuous, the simple fact of being a member of an internationally recognized political space creates a reference point that is often used by immigrants when dealing with issues of their own identity. This comes out strongly in the narrative of Jorge Murillo Meza, a Mexican immigrant who uses the geographical space of Baja as a reference point for his own identity. As he describes it, "We are the people born and raised in Baja. Lots of people or tribes do not tell the truth and act like they are from Baja. A lot of Mexicans that you see there, they come from the south, and they are telling you that they are from Baja, and they're not. We have our customs, our way of living, our believing, our everything." Zohra Saed is from Afghanistan. Her mother is quick to say that her daughter has never covered up by wearing a chador. "My daughter Zohra knows too much about Afghanistan because I get so burning because I think all the time of my country. To my daughter, I tell all the stories of my beautiful country. Sometimes I am crying." The eldest daughter has been carrying on the traditions, although her younger brother and sister have previously gone "native Brooklyn." After 9/11 there were hostile remarks and actions directed at the family from members of the community, which brought them closer as a family and ethnic group.

Just as the nature of immigrants' new residential environment can have a significant effect on their interactions with, and adaptation to, the host society, so too does the residential context of their homeland. Unlike the peasantry of the last great wave of immigration, today's immigrants are most likely to come from the city, and part of what defines many urban environments in other countries is the transmission of Western popular culture through the mass media, competing with their own nascent popular culture. As Herbert Gans has observed, American culture is a very powerful force for attracting immigrants, and its force is felt across every corner of the globe—thus partly explaining the vast diversity in the countries of origin of today's immigrant population.[41]

How can American culture have such a pull on today's immigrants? Despite the fact that many of today's immigrants are highly skilled professionals with many years of education behind them, the economic and social structure of their countries of origin may not provide sufficient opportunities for advancement. Western culture, however, provides a window—however distorted it may be—through which these educated professionals aspiring for more see a chance to improve their standard of living. This is not to say that today's immigrants are overly optimistic about the opportunities that await them in the United States. Portes and Rumbaut have argued that the educated and highly skilled are generally well informed about employment opportunities, and past research by Portes has shown that occupational aspirations are rationally assessed in terms of their skills and education.[42] However, the intrusion of Western culture into other nations can generate both a powerful pull for immigration and a preconception of American society that immigrants have to often reconcile with reality upon arrival.

In Ghana, the villagers from Rosemond Reimmer's tribe were so taken by anything American that when her father, who had emigrated to the United States, sent packages of shoes and clothes back to his family, all the neighbors would come to the house to take what they wanted. As Rosemond describes the feeling, "Anything from America was gold. Everybody wanted something from America, even if it's a piece of thread." When she lived in Korea, Sarah Lee and her friends believed that America was nothing but beautiful homes with swimming pools inhabited by tall, beautiful blondes. However, it didn't take long for the sight of graffiti on the New York subway and the dirt and bad smells of her neighborhood to change her perception. Navid Daee did not even have to land in the United States before his preconceptions of this country were challenged. On the plane trip from Iran, he "flew above misty, redwood trees. I never thought America would be like that. I always thought high-rises. I had a dream about America before I came, and the dream was totally a western movie, and that's what we envisioned."

Transnational mass media is not the only source of transmission of Western culture, for if the two countries are in close enough geographical proximity there is a good chance that Western culture is also being passed by word of mouth from earlier sojourner immigrants, who either travel back and forth between their home country and the United States on a fairly regular basis, or who have spent some time in the United States only to return to their homeland to stay. These are what Alejandro Portes has called "transnational communities."

> Transnational communities are dense networks across political borders created by immigrants in their quest for economic advancement and social recognition. Through these networks, an increasing number of people are able to lead dual lives. Participants are often bilingual, move easily between different cultures, frequently maintain homes in two countries and pursue economic, political, and cultural interests that require their presence in both.[43]

The information that immigrants bring upon their return to their homeland can both facilitate the journey of the next group of immigrants and generate a "cross-fertilization" of cultures where American culture is brought back to the homeland, which then influences and modifies the culture that the next group of immigrants takes with them when they leave for the host society.[44] Dianne Barker describes this process well in her narrative: "I always thought that this country was paved with gold because people came here and they came home all bedecked with jewelry, a ring on each finger, six earrings in one, six chains around their neck, and they always gave us that gold impression." Social networks can also serve as social capital by giving future migrants reliable information and support. Thus, over time, immigration patterns will become less selective of the most affluent, educated, or skilled.[45]

Between their exposure to Western popular culture through the mass media and the recounted experiences of those who went before them, immigrants bring a culture that is not a direct reproduction of their old cultural patterns but rather a mixture of their own cultural practices, family traditions, and local customs, with a certain degree of "pre-Americanization."[46] This is what Min Zhou has called "pre-immigration cultural attributes," and it is clear that these are profoundly shaped by the cultural and geographical distance separating the country of origin from the host society, as well as by the extent of the intrusion of American culture through the mass media.[47]

To understand how these "pre-immigration cultural attributes" interact with the host society, one must first keep in mind that immigrants not only bring a unique blend of traditional and Western culture, but they also select which portions of their homeland culture they choose to keep and which to discard, which ones to display, and which to keep private.[48] Some immigrants, especially those who can not—or choose not to—keep in contact with, or return to, their country of origin, may construct a simple and static vision of their homeland as a way of making sense of the new society and dealing with the problems they face, despite the fact that their homeland is also going through a constant process of modernization and change such that little may remain of the past reality that they left behind.[49] Other immigrants who are able to communicate with, or travel back to, friends and family in their country of origin will play an active role in creating a cross-fertilization of cultures and will have a more dynamic picture of their homeland that they will bring with them in their interactions with the host society.

CULTURAL INTERPLAY AND THE IMMIGRANT EXPERIENCE

The interaction between the context of reception and the context of departure is what defines the experience of immigrants in "transnational communities," and it is what defines the experiences of the immigrants in this book. While both the country of origin and the host society have their own unique political, economic, and cultural structures that immigrants have to navigate and contend with in the process of coming to terms with their place in society and their identity, these two contexts do not stand in isolation from one another, but rather are, now more than ever, interacting through transnational networks of people and media.

Just as the power and reach of Western media can Americanize immi-

grants before they even cross the border and pull them toward the myth-
ical "land of opportunity," so too does the sheer volume and diversity of
recent immigration alter the cultural landscape of America by bringing
new histories, cultures, and traditions that come to define a multicultural,
multiethnic society. In turn the experiences of immigrants are transmitted
back to their homelands either directly or indirectly, shaping the attitudes
and perspectives that the next group of immigrants bring with them
when they set out to make the journey to a foreign land. While all of the
waves of immigration have brought about this interactive dynamic
between the host society and the country of origin, contemporary immigration has most likely accelerated this process as countries become more
connected politically and economically and as improved communication
and travel technologies increasingly facilitate the exchange of information, ideas, and people.

The stories contained in this book speak to this interplay of cultures
that characterizes the dynamic of modern immigration by adding a personal element to this picture that is not captured very well in discussions
of structural forces and constraints. While it is true that the personal and
subjective experiences of immigrants can not stand alone, but rather
must be placed within a larger theoretical framework,[50] it is equally true
that without a cultural analysis situated at the level of the individual
experience of the immigrant, we are likely to attach our own meanings,
our own explanations, to the lives of the people that we study and
encounter on a regular basis.[51]

For some, like Jacinta Jones, it is the experience of growing up in
England within an unstable family environment that serves as the background to her eventual move to California. For others, like Navid Daee
from Iran, the "context of departure" takes on a whole new meaning as he
is nostalgic for his brick house and gardens, childhood games, and afternoon naps that remind him of old Persia. To speak only in terms of "structures" and "contexts" leaves out the fact that each immigrant's life is a
unique story that produces memories, cultures, traditions, and realities
that are different for each person who settles in another country. The
point, however, is not to abandon the importance of the contexts of reception and departure, but rather to emphasize they influence immigrant

identity through their interaction with the individual experiences of the immigrants themselves. As Meri Nana-Ama Danquah writes about her own life in the introduction to *Becoming American*, "America, for me, was nothing more than a journey, an adventure, a world that spun seductively around my world, around my home, which was still the center of my universe, which was still governed by the influence of my native culture."[52]

We hope these life stories will challenge the constructed notions of immigration and immigrants by presenting deviant or paradoxical cases that do not neatly fit into sociological theories, racial and ethnic topologies, or popular rhetoric. While no one, deviant or exceptional case should cause someone to rush out and abandon what he or she has already learned, the individual case, the individual life story, provides the necessary raw material to rethink, reconsider, challenge, and advance the understanding of the immigrant experience.[53] The words of Thomas Wheeler, written thirty years ago for an introduction to a book capturing the experience of immigrant writers, still ring true today.

> The writers, of various ethnic backgrounds, have no sociology to tell, but rather the stories of life lived and felt by particular people in particular places. None pretend to give a typical picture of an ethnic group. Rather, by describing human experience as each has seen it, the writers are able to say something about the human condition of America . . . [and] the nervous system of Americanization.[54]

The stories in this book, while perhaps not a random sample of modern immigration, are certainly representative of its character and diversity and are certainly indicative of the kinds of process that immigrants go through in navigating between two cultures, two identities. We hope that reading them, thinking about them, and appreciating them will lead the reader to a greater understanding of the ways in which modern immigrants negotiate the new culture of American society and the culture of their homeland, the realities of the present and the realities of the past.

NOTES

1. David M. Reimers, *Unwelcome Strangers: American Identity and the Turn Against Immigration* (New York: Columbia University Press, 1998).

2. George J. Sánchez, "Face the Nation: Race, Immigration, and the Rise of Nativism in Late Twentieth Century America." In *The Handbook of International Migration: The American Experience*, ed. Charles Hirschman et al. (New York: Russell Sage, 1999).

3. James H. Johnson et al., "Immigration Reform and the Browning of America: Tensions, Conflicts and Community Instability in Metropolitan Los Angeles," *International Migration Review* 31 (1997); Herbert J. Gans, "Toward a Reconciliation of 'Assimilation' and 'Pluralism': The Interplay of Acculturation and Ethnic Retention"; and Rubén G. Rumbaut, "Assimilation and Its Discontents: Ironies and Paradoxes," both in *The Handbook of International Migration: The American Experience*, ed. C. Hirschman et al. (New York: Russell Sage, 1999).

4. Alejandro Portes and Rubén G. Rumbaut, *Immigrant America: A Portrait* (Berkeley: University of California Press, 1996).

5. U.S. Department of Justice, "Immigrants Admitted by Selected Country of Birth and Selected Metropolitan Statistical Area of Intended Residence, Fiscal Year 1998," *1998 Statistical Yearbook of the Immigration and Naturalization Service* (Washington, D.C., 2000); U.S. Census Bureau, "Current Population Survey," Ethnic and Hispanic Statistics Branch, Population Division (March 2000), tables 3.7, 3.8, 3.10, 3.11, 3.15.

6. U.S. Census Bureau, "Current Population Survey."

7. Roger Waldinger, "Immigration and Urban Change," *Annual Review of Sociology* 15 (1989).

8. Stephen Steinberg, *The Ethnic Myth: Race, Ethnicity and Class in America* (Boston: Beacon Press, 1989).

9. Barry Edmonston and Jefferey S. Passell, *Immigration and Ethnicity: The Integration of America's Newest Arrivals* (Washington, D.C.: The Urban Institute Press, 1994).

10. Tony Waters, "Towards a Theory of Ethnic Identity and Migration: The Formation of Ethnic Enclaves by Migrant Germans in Russia and North America," *International Migration Review* 29 (1995).

11. Pyong Gap Min, "The Entrepreneurial Adaptation of Korean Immigrants," in *Origins and Destinies: Immigration, Race and Ethnicity in America*, ed. Silvia Pedraza and Rubén Rumbaut (New York: Wadsworth Publishing, 1996); Reimers, *Unwelcome Strangers.*

12. Min Zhou, "Growing up American: The Challenge Confronting Immigrant Children and Children of Immigrants," *Annual Review of Sociology* 23 (1997).

13. Sánchez, "Face the Nation."

14. Thomas J. Espenshade, "Unauthorized Immigration to the United States," *Annual Review of Sociology* 21 (1995).

15. G. Palmer Stacy and Wayne Lutton 1988, *The Immigration Time Bomb* (Monterey, Va.: American Immigration Control Foundation, 1988); Peter Brimelow, *Alien Nation: Common Sense About America's Immigration Disaster* (New York: Random House, 1995).

16. Chisun Lee, "In the Crosshairs," *Village Voice*, Jan. 22, 2002.

17. Mary Lord, "Student Scrutiny," *U.S. News & World Report*, Nov. 26, 2001.

18. Michael Becraft, "Tracking International Students in Higher Education: Policy Options and Implications for Students," statement before the House Education Committee, Subcommittee on Twenty-first Century Competitiveness and Select Education, 2001.

19. Sara Hebel, "States Take Diverging Approaches on Tuition Rates for Illegal Immigrants," *Chronicle of Higher Education* 48 (Nov. 30, 2001).

20. The government agency includes a completely restructured Immigration and Naturalization Service (INS). On April 17, 2002, Attorney General John Ashcroft and INS Commissioner James Ziglar announced a plan, fully supported by President George W. Bush, to break up the service and enforcement function of the INS, centralize authority and lines of command, create an Office of Juvenile Affairs, and finally to appoint a chief financial officer and a chief information officer to help run the agency more efficiently. All of these changes were discussed in the context of both the perceived failure of the INS to respond effectively at the time of the terrorist attacks and the desire to strengthen domestic security against possible future attacks. U.S. Department of Justice, "Immigrants Admitted by Selected Country of Birth."

21. Sánchez, "Face the Nation."

22. Rumbaut, "Assimilation and Its Discontents."

23. Sánchez, "Face the Nation."

24. Richard Alba and Victor Nee, "Rethinking Assimilation Theory for a Era of Immigration," in *The Handbook of International Migration: The American Experience*, edited by C. Hirschman et al. (New York: Russell Sage, 1999); S. Karthik Romakishnan and Thomas J. Espenshade, "Immigrant Incorporation and Political Participation in the United States," *International Migration Review* 35 (2001).

25. Johnson, "Immigration Reform."

26. Jacqueline Stevens, *Reproducing the State* (Princeton: Princeton University Press, 1999), p. 194.

27. Marcy C. Waters, *Ethnic Options: Choosing Identities in America* (Berkeley: University of California Press, 1990), p. 156.

28. Portes and Rumbaut, *Immigrant America*.

29. Ibid.

30. Rumbaut, "Assimilation and Its Discontents."

31. Portes and Rumbaut, *Immigrant America*.

32. Ibid.

33. Alba and Nee, "Rethinking Assimilation Theory"; Ivan Light and Carolyn Rosenstein, *Race, Ethnicity, and Entrepreneurship in Urban America* (New York: Aldine de Gruyter, 1995).

34. Alejandro Portes, Samuel A. McLeod, and Robert N. Parker, "Immigrant Aspirations," *Sociology of Education* 51 (1978): 242.

35. Rubén G. Rumbaut, "Origins and Destinies: Immigration, Race, and Ethnicity in Contemporary America," in *Origins and Destinies: Immigration, Race and Ethnicity in America*, ed. S. Pedraza and R. Rumbaut (New York: Wadsworth Publishing), p. 124.

36. Portes and Rumbaut, *Immigrant America*.

37. Ibid.

38. Mohammad A. Chaichan, "First-Generation Iranian Immigrants and the Question of Cultural Identity: The Case of Iowa," *International Migration Review* 31 (1997).

39. Portes and Rumbaut, *Immigrant America*, p. 112.

40. Ibid.

41. Gans, "Toward a Reconciliation"; Portes and Rumbaut, *Immigrant America*.

42. Portes and Rumbaut, *Immigrant America*; Portes et al., "Immigrant Aspirations."

43. Alejandro Portes, "Immigration Theory for a New Century: Some Problems and Opportunities," in *The Handbook of International Migration: The American Experience*, ed. C. Hirschman et al. (New York: Russell Sage, 1999), p. 812.

44. Portes and Rumbaut, *Immigrant America*; Nancy Foner, "The Immigrant Family: Cultural Legacies and Cultural Changes," *International Migration Review* 31 (1997).

45. Douglas Massey, "Why Does Immigration Occur? A Theoretical Synthesis," in *The Handbook of International Migration: The American Experience*, ed. C. Hirschman et al. (New York: Russell Sage, 1999).

46. Foner, "The Immigrant Family"; Gans, "Toward a Reconciliation"; Rumbaut, "Assimilation and Its Discontents."

47. Zhou, "Growing up American."

48. Ibid.

49. Foner, "The Immigrant Family."

50. Portes, "Immigration Theory for a New Century."

51. Foner, "The Immigrant Family."

52. Meri Nana-Ama Danquah, *Becoming American: Personal Essays by First Generation Immigrant Women*, (New York: Hyperion, 2000). p. xiii.

53. Rumbaut, "Assimilation and Its Discontents."

54. Thomas Wheeler, *The Immigrant Experience: The Anguish of Becoming American* (New York: Dial Press, 1971), p. 2.

PART ONE

Hyphenated Americans

ONE

Edeline Decossard

HAITIAN-AMERICAN

To understand Edeline, one needs to remember that Haiti is the poorest country in the Western Hemisphere. Roman Catholicism is the predominant religion, but African Nature gods are still worshipped and voodoo rites are practiced. In 1957 François "Papa Doc" Duvalier was elected president by using voodoo as an instrument of control over the masses to instill fear with his paramilitary secret police. They were called "Tonton Macoutes" (Uncle Bogeymen) to reinforce their connection to evil spirits.

Papa Doc, a physician by training, was part of a multinational organization that gave every man, woman, and child in the island nation an injection of penicillin to eradicate diseases. To the illiterate population, the disappearance of long-endured disease symptoms made Duvalier seem godlike, creating the cult of the "peekees" (the inoculating needle) among the peasants. After these miraculous cures, Duvalier was elected president by an overwhelming margin. Later on, he declared himself President for Life. Papa Doc tried to keep his connection to voodoo alive by posing for official photographs in dark glasses and a high hat so that he resembled the much-feared voodoo god Baron Samedi. Under his rule, thousands were executed. Tourism ceased. Outside manufacturing fled. The population turned a rusty brown from severe protein malnutrition. Fifty percent of the children died before the age of five. Haitians singled out on any pretext by the Tonton Macoutes were tortured and executed.

Many Haitians tried to flee in overcrowded, rickety boats with patchwork sails. However, Edeline's family took a different route to escape Papa Doc's notorious rule.

For a year she rode the subway, doing her homework and sleeping. Traditionally we think of homelessness as being the end of a misdirected life, but with this young woman it was the starting place for her upward mobility. Although Edeline had money, no one would rent to her because she did not have the proper papers or pay slips. The stubbornness and pridefulness that she so resented in her father was the very trait that kept her going. Ironically, the plucky young woman's choice of a husband was a person who worked at the Housing Preservation Office.

A pivotal point that made the migration possible for six families was when her father "found a hundred thousand dollars in a bag." The quotation marks are mine. "Finding the money in a bag" was the family's whispered myth. Perhaps it is the equivalent of our euphemism that "it fell off a truck."

Physically, Edeline is small, dark, and compact — characteristics that identify her with the peasant class in a country where class standing and social prestige has its basis in height and light skin color. She wears her hair and nails clipped short in an inner urban surrounding where elaborate hairstyles and airbrushed pattern-painted nails abound. Her nose has perhaps a touch of Arawak Indian in it even though history books state that the Indians were decimated during the time of Columbus. Her expressions and voice appear wise. A serious, articulate young woman, she does not smile often, but when she does her whole face rejoices.

Finding One Hundred Thousand Dollars in a Bag

My parents had eight children, and I'm the second child, the first daughter, so I had it really bad. I had it bad because my parents still tried to raise us Haitian. I didn't learn how to speak English until I got into school because everything was Creole at home. You speak Creole when you go to school, you come home and you speak Creole, and that's it. I find it amazing that my parents still can't speak English that well.

Both my parents were peasants in the north of Haiti. When my father was twelve, his mother passed away and he had to stop school. Then my father left to go to the Bahamas because in Haiti under Papa Doc they were killing his family. At that time the Bahamians mistreated Haitians— beating them up for no reason, reporting them, arresting them, and sending them to jail. My father changed his name to an English name so that he could fit in, and he was able to work and save money because for seven years he was working at a Holiday Inn in the Bahamas. Then he went back to get my mother, and in 1969 they got married.

My father and my grandmother told me that my father found money in the hotel before he moved to Miami. He found one hundred thousand dollars cash in a bag. I don't think it was in the hotel. It was probably somewhere around the hotel or something, and he just took it and quickly left and went to Miami and bought a house; he bought three houses to be exact. Then he brought four more families and housed them there in his houses. My father was really the one who brought practically all my family to the United States. Both his parents had died by the time he was twenty, you know, and my mother, my [maternal] grandmother, everyone came and lived in that house. I remember growing up with twenty people in the house.

My parents came here because my father's parents had eight children, and some of them were killed under Papa Doc.

We moved to where all the immigrants were living in Miami. It is called Little Haiti. It's a very concentrated population down there. When you go down there, it's just like Port au Prince.

Visiting the Witch Doctor

When I was four I was sent to Haiti with my grandmother. In my earliest memory, I was looking at the horizon. I saw a band playing the "rah, rah music." They were playing and playing, and I was watching them. Then all of a sudden they disappeared, and then I was looking for them, and then all of a sudden after they reappeared, I got sick. I got very sick, and my grandmother took me in the house. I told her I wanted to go back home to Miami.

She said, "Well, we have two more weeks." And I was very, very ill. My grandmother thought I was going to die.

I asked her two years ago, "What happened?" She said that they were trying to kill me. It was sorcerers. Sorcerers were trying to take my soul. She said she heard things flapping up in the ceiling, so she took the broomstick and hit the ceiling.

My grandmother took me to a *hogan* [witch doctor] to make my fever go down, and the *hogan* told her about the sorcery. He gave my grandmother some herbs. He told her to gather more herbs out in the bush and make it up for me in a tea. Then I got well. But it's amazing that that was the only thing I remember when I was four. I really don't know, but I believe sorcery exists.

I believe that Americans tend to mix voodoo with sorcery, and it's wrong because when you look at voodoo, there's three different meanings. Voodoo as a relation, voodoo as a way of a life, and voodoo as sorcery. People are always looking at the negative aspect, and then they say that voodoo is bad, but it's not true. And I think that was something done on purpose by American writers to undermine Haiti and its people. I grew up in a religious Baptist background where my parents denied voodoo, and I came to New York, and I met my husband. He and I were talking about the church. I didn't want to preach to him, but I was telling him about church and stuff, and he started denouncing the Bible. I'm like, "Oh my God, I'm dating a Satanist here." It wasn't until after, when I finally learned about the history of religion—and I had copies of journals of missionaries in the 1800s when they went to the Caribbean islands to preach to the slaves— that I just stopped going and believing in the church.

Naming the Whip

Even in the States my father raised us Haitian style. The four families my father brought over lived in a two-block radius. We were around each other, and everyone worked. *Everyone worked.* The children went to school. They made sure we went to school, and I remember one day I had a C in conduct in elementary school, and I got the whipping of my life. Yeah, I got the whipping of my life. After that I just kept quiet in class. My parents were firm believers that that is the way to correct you. I got to realize that the way the government treats its people is the same way that the parents tend to treat their child.

My father was a dictator. My parents were dictators, and most of my family—I mean more teenagers were coming into the family—my father beat them all. He didn't care whose child it was. If they misbehaved, he would beat them. So some of the kids, some of the guys, got immune to the belt, so he sent for a bullwhip. The guys were saying, "It was a bull's penis," but it was a bull's whip from Haiti. When the whip arrived, everyone was sitting in the living room because my father called us for a family talk.

He said, "Everybody, this is 'Sans-s'amie.'" "Sans-s'amie" means "no friend" in Creole. He was whipping the thing in the air, and we're like saying, "Ohhh." He told us, "This whip has just come from Haiti," and he said, "Everybody say hi to Sans-s'amie."

All the older kids just kept quiet, but the little kids were saying, "Hi, Sans-s'amie."

My father kept on talking, "If you misbehave, it's Sans-s'amie. If you do this, Sans-s'amie. If you do that, Sans-s'amie."

Everyone's looking at each other, and we're like thinking, "How are we going to plot to kill this man?" That was our attitude.

My father was very strict. I played the piano, and he had to hear me playing the piano every day for two hours straight—no bathroom, no break. I had to go to the bathroom first and then go on in and play. He would lock me into the living room because the living room had iron gates. It was a prison inside. He had the iron gates so that the children wouldn't go in the living room and touch anything. Every day he had to hear a new song. If he heard it a second day, he'd tell me, "Listen, I heard it yesterday. I don't want to hear it again! You know, you should have mastered it."

One day I wasn't feeling good so I didn't play the piano, and he came with Sans-s'amie and whipped my behind, and I had big welts. I was bleeding, so I looked at that whip, and I said, "Never again. That's the last time he'll ever whip me." I felt it, because my brothers had been getting whippings for a long time, and I made sure I got good grades and everything. But they got whippings every day, and it's like they never learned. So I thought that I was immune to it because I was a good girl. And when I had a chance to taste that whip, I said, "Never again."

One day he went out, and I went into my father's room. He locked his room, but my bedroom was connected to his bedroom. There was a wall between us, but inside my closet there was a hole on top, and so I went through into his room, and then I was frantically looking for the whip. I looked around, and looked into everything and finally found Sans-s'amie. I fixed everything in the room back the way it was. No one saw me because if I told the kids, they would have squealed on me to save their own lives. All of them would have, and so I left and went outside in the back yard. There was a house in the back where the grass was so high because no one was living there. That gave me the idea, so I threw it over into the high weeds.

When my father came back, my brother did something, and my father wanted to whip him. He went looking for Sans-s'amie, but Sans-s'amie wasn't there! He went around asking, "Where's Sans-s'amie? Where's Sans-s'amie?" And he comes out and asks the kids, "Did any one of you take Sans-s'amie? Who took Sans-s'amie?" He says, "If anyone took Sans-s'amie, everybody gets a beating." No one tells, everyone gets a beating. And we're crying, and I knew I did it.

I started crying, "No, no, no."

All the kids are like pushing me. "Where is it? Where is it? You were the last kid that got whipped, you know."

I said, "I don't know. I don't know." So I'm crying, and I said I was looking for it, and all the kids were looking for it and crying, and we were just looking up under the mattresses and couches and everywhere, everywhere, and my father just forgot about it. He just found something else to beat us with.

One-Way Ticket

My father—I never, never cared for him until I moved here because he was so mean. We never had a chance to sit down and talk like friends. It wasn't like that. I was suffocating. I couldn't breathe. I couldn't move. I was twenty-one. When I was eighteen, I told my father that I was moving, that I wanted to go away for college because I scored a 1200 on my SAT, and I was given a four-year scholarship from Georgetown. My parents didn't want me to take it. They told me to stay at home.

Even the pastor would preach against sending your children away. The church was really against that—and then whose child went away first? Of course, it was the pastor's. I realized that all he wanted us to do—stay and keep us back. Then I thought about religion in that way, as an oppressor, and I still believe that the church acts as an oppressor. That made me decide to go. My father begged me to stay for three more years. He said, "Wait until you're twenty-one." I said I would wait until I was twenty-one, and so for three years I planned.

I planned it. I worked eighty hours a week. I was working at the post office in Miami and Orlando, and I just worked overtime and saved the money. I didn't spend the money. Buy clothes? I didn't do that. I saved enough, I saved over twenty thousand dollars, and I came here. My parents felt that they failed as parents because I left home. Now it's a little different with the upper-class Haitians, but I'm talking about the peasants. My parents grew up as peasants, and their children do not leave home until they're married. And that's it. If they go to a college, there are local colleges. Why allow them to go away?

My birthday came, and that day I bought a one-way ticket to New York. I had dreams. I dreamt that I was successful in New York, and the dream kept coming over and over again, and then it was like I was on the cover of *Ebony* magazine, so I said, "My calling is in New York."

And my mother was like, "You don't have any family there."

I said, "I don't care. I'll make a family."

Handcuff and a Machete under the Seat

And when I first came here, it was crazy. In Florida you're very friendly and you trust people. So I met this guy traveling from Miami on the plane, and we arrived together. I ended up in Newark at the airport, and I was trying to get to Manhattan, and the guy said, "Oh, I have a car, so I'll take you there. It's just right there."

I said, "Okay, fine," so I got into the car with him. He had this black car, and it had very dark, tinted windows. You couldn't see anywhere, and it was very black. And I got in the car, you know; I was very innocent. And he's speeding. He's *really* speeding down the expressway, and cops stopped him. The cops asked him questions, and looked at his license, and found that his license was suspended.

They took him out of the car and asked him some more questions. "How did I get in the car? How did he meet me?"

He said some lie that he drove his car to New York because the car had a Florida license plate. He drove to New York and blah, blah, blah, and as for me, he met me in Florida.

The cop asked me how I got there. And I said, "We flew to New York on the plane together." So he's telling them that he drove to New York, and I'm saying we flew, so they didn't know what or who to believe.

I had my plane ticket, and I showed them the proof. The police told us to get out of the car. There were two cops, an Italian guy and I don't remember the other guy. They were checking the inside of the car and in between the seats. There was a set of handcuffs, there was a machete, and there was a knife. When they pulled this stuff out and showed it to me, I freaked out. I started crying and weeping.

They were two white cops. One cop didn't care much for me, but the other, an Italian cop, felt sorry for me. The good cop was trying to convince the other—"Let's drive her to the Port Authority Bus Station, please."

The other cop said, "No."

They called a tow truck, and they told the tow-truck driver to drop me off at the Port Authority Bus Station in New York.

I was just crying and crying and crying. I could have been killed. I could have lost my life looking for life. I never told anyone about it except my husband. I didn't want to tell my parents.

Plunking the Baby on Me

So I came here, and I stayed at the Port Authority. Even with all the money I had, it was hard for me to get an apartment because I wasn't working. No one would rent to me because I didn't have a paycheck to show that I had a job.

I ended up staying at the YMCA for awhile, and then I called my parents, and my mother said, "Well, I have friends in New York. Why don't you just go over there?"

I called the friends and they came and picked me up from the hotel. I went to their house, and I told them, "Look, I'm paying rent. I don't want to live for free."

I felt that I wanted that kind of responsibility. Knowing Haitian people as well as I do, I realize now that they're not people to live with when you're a Haitian because they really mistreat you. I was truly mistreated.

It tends to be different if you're someone other than Haitian. Then they respect you, but if you're one of their own, then they treat you without respect because they were taught not to respect themselves. I was trying to find a school, and they didn't want to show me anything. They didn't want me to know subways. I didn't know anything, so one day I said to myself, "Look, I'm going to go out there and look for a school. I don't care what school. I'm just going to go." And I started going to school.

I have a confession to make. I was out-of-state, and I didn't want to pay out-of-state fees, so I went on public assistance so that I could automatically become a New York resident. When I went on public assistance, I was able to go to college. The food stamps that I received, I sent to my grandmother in Miami. I just mailed them all to her and told her to buy whatever to feed herself and the kids. I had the money, so I didn't need them. I just wanted to have that status so that I could get into school. That's why I don't think that welfare should be done away with. It depends on whether you want to go to school or not, because you're bettering yourself to become a productive citizen. I could understand those who sit on welfare and don't do anything.

I could have paid, but the problem was that I didn't have the status, and I didn't want to pay the extra money as a nonresident, so when I finally got the status, I got off welfare. I stayed on welfare for six months or so, and then I got right off, and I started paying for my school.

I had to leave the Haitian family because they didn't want me to use the electricity to study. I was studying, and they would turn off the lights on me. The woman where I was staying, she had a child. Her husband died probably a month before, so she needed help with the child. He died in September, so I started school in February. I stayed home and helped her with the children and cleaned house, even though I was paying rent, because she grew up with my mother.

She had a hard life because she didn't get to go to school because she was born out of wedlock, and her father was killed through sorcery while he was working in the Bahamas. He had a shoe store, and he was doing well and sending money back home to his grandmother. The grandmother would keep the money for herself and take the children to go in the market to sell produce instead of sending them to school like she was supposed to do.

The woman grew up angry. She was angry with her family, angry with people who could have intervened. At times, she was a nice person, but when it came to me going to school, she had a problem with that. I would try to study, and she would plop the child on me—the child was a newborn. She would say, "I can't take it anymore. I can't take it." And I'd say, "I'm studying." I told her, "I can't stay at home. I have to go to school."

She just kept plunking the baby on me. She didn't care whether the books were spread out on the floor where I was studying. She put the baby on the books, and I told her, "Look, I have to study. I didn't come here to babysit a child." At night she would say, "Turn off the lights. I'm paying all this electricity," and I said, "I'm paying rent," you know. She'd reply, "Well, it's not enough."

I was paying three hundred dollars a month, and it was a very small room.

Becoming Homeless

That's when I started staying in the school until eleven at night, when the security guards would tell me to go home, that they're closing up. One night, I came home and found a chain on the door. I rang the bell, and the woman never answered. I knocked on the door; I knocked on the bedroom window. She never answered. She locked the door! I ended up staying outside until the next day. It was cold, and I had to huddle all night outside on the porch.

In the morning when my mother's friend opened the door, she said, "If you don't come home at nine that's it. I'm locking up."

I told her, "I'm leaving," so I packed my bag. She was asking me where I was going and saying don't go. I said, "No, you don't respect my education, and I can't take it," so I left. I had no place to go. When I went to school, I gave away my clothes because I couldn't carry everything. I had five dresses, five clothes to change, and that was it because I couldn't carry anything else because it would be too heavy on my back.

I had my books and my clothes, and that was it. And I went around looking for a place to stay, and everywhere I was refused because I had no proof of a pay stub and other papers landlords look for, so I ended up sleeping in the subway.

I would stay in the school until eleven, and then I'd go up and down the subway until the next day and go to the gym in the school and take a shower there. I would sleep in the subway car. No one bothered me. I usually picked the car where the conductor would be, and then I would change because I didn't want the conductor to know that I was homeless. The A-Train was a pretty long ride on the subway system.

Living on the A-Train

The A-Train took me to 277th Street in Manhattan, and then to Far Rockaway. The ride would take over two hours, and then I would go back again. The back-and-forth trip would take about five hours. At seven in the morning, I would be at the college. In the subway car I mainly sat up. Once in a while I lay down, but I mostly sat up. I slept, and I did my studies on the A-Train.

My first semester I ended up doing well. I had all As and one B. That was when I left the Haitian woman's house. When you do well in the beginning, you tend to do well throughout. The professors got to know me because I always participated in class.

In summer, I went to school again, and I went to a retreat with a friend. The student government went to a resort in the Catskill Mountains, and they talked student government stuff. Because I was a student, they allowed me to come, and I was really interested in doing things in the community and stuff like that. They ended up asking me whether I wanted to run for office, and I said, "Yeah, for senator."

So I ran for office and won. I got an office at the college where I was able to live. I called home almost every day because I also got free phone calls.

The guards never knew I was there. They would only check the front door to see whether it was locked or not, and then after that, they don't go around checking the doors. I think now they do.

There wasn't a bathroom I could use at night. I took a two-liter bottle and cut the top off, and then used that. If I had to go do the other thing, I had to wait until the next morning. The lights could stay on, so I was able to study, but I was really devastated at that time.

As a result I did badly in school the second semester because it was horrible. I felt I couldn't concentrate. I thought I had myself together, but subconsciously, I wasn't there, so I didn't do well. Then my third semester, I didn't do well either. This is my fourth semester, and I was able to take enough classes each semester to be able to graduate in the summer on schedule.

Meeting My Boyfriend

Last semester, I did well. I had all As in my classes because I was with my husband. I met my husband in the summer of 1995. I was homeless at that time, and I didn't want him to know. He would ask me for my number, and I'd give him my office number. He probably thought I was playing hard to get. Again and again, he'd asked for my number. Eventually I gave him my office number, and he would call me and say, "What are you still doing there so late in the evening?"

I'd answer, "Oh well, we have twenty-four-hour access to the office." I didn't want him to know that I was homeless. We started dating. He wanted me to move in with him because he saw that I was distracted and always felt ill.

I was always tired. I was bothered because there were mice in that office. There were a lot of mice, so I was very paranoid. Even with the lights on, I was really paranoid, and I couldn't sleep, and I couldn't do anything. I used to buy food from Food Emporium—from that really nice store near the college. I had to sneak my groceries in around ten. I was going through a rough time.

I Didn't Want to Move in with My Boyfriend Because I Was Desperate

But it wasn't until one of my friends, who was the vice president of student government, came and slept over in her office, and I told her, "Yeah, I'm sleeping over, too, you know," and then she kept sleeping over, and then she kept asking about me. She didn't want to go home late at night on the subway, and she wanted to finish her work. She asked me why I was always there. I told her, "Well, I have work to do just like you," and excuses like that.

But life is funny because I met another girl at the college, and she said she had an apartment with an extra room for $250 a month in the Bronx.

At the time, my boyfriend kept calling me, saying, "You can move in with me. Why don't you move in with me?"

And I said to my boyfriend, "Oh, I found another apartment." I didn't want to move in with him because I *had to,* because I was desperate, because I was homeless. If I lived with him, it was going to be only because I wanted to be with him, and not for a place to stay.

It's funny, I spent only four days with this crazy girl because the house was nasty. It was very dirty, and she had a daughter with asthma. The time I was there, I spent the whole weekend cleaning the house. I scrubbed the walls and cleaned the whole place. When I opened the cabinet where the plates were, there were roaches, and the apartment was in a horrible condition, and so I really scrubbed. I spent days scrubbing the walls, cleaning the cabinets, washing all the dishes, cleaning inside the cabinet. I cleaned everything, and I bought a fancy bed so that after a year I could finally sleep in a canopy bed with a good mattress. But this crazy girl kept coming in my room without knocking.

And she became so obsessed with me because she was telling me to leave my boyfriend because all he's going to do is "use you, use you, use you." I never listened to her, and my boyfriend did not want me to deal with her because he's a very spiritual guy, you know. He feels people's vibes, and he didn't feel the vibes were good ones, and he said she had this demeanor about her that he did not like. Yes, he told me to stay away from her, but I didn't listen to him because I wanted to have independence.

I moved to the Bronx during Kwanzaa Week, and at festivities at the college we were talking about our lives, and we played this kind of game that had questions. I think it was more like an African-American game kind of thing, asking questions, maybe to start conversations, so we started talking about ourselves.

This girl I just moved in with started using the word *nigger*, and my friend, the vice president of the student government, and I were very uncomfortable about that. Both my friend and I said, "Since this is Kwanzaa, and we're talking about sisterhood and brotherhood, can we refrain from using that word?"

"Yeah, like 'my nigger.'" She was talking like that, and everything was nigger, nigger, nigger, nigger. And then I said again, "Can we refrain from saying that word?"

And she was like, "Oh, what's wrong with it?"

I said, "Everything is wrong with it, you know. That's a derogatory word," and then she said, "Oh, there's nothing wrong with the word. It's giving love to my people." I said, "Oh really." I said, "Let's get the dictionary," and she asks, "But who wrote the dictionary, a white man?" And I said, "But isn't every word that comes out of your mouth defined by what the dictionary is about, about what the dictionary writes." I told her something like that. "Isn't every context from what the dictionary says it is?"

We convinced her to refrain from saying that word around me because I'm really uncomfortable with that word.

You Get AIDS from the Food

During that Kwanzaa meeting at the college we started talking about the contraction of AIDS and stuff like that, and my apartment mate said, "You can get AIDS from the food you eat."

I said, "Where did you get that from?"

She answered, "That's what happened to some dean that died in the college from AIDS." We were trying to tell her that you can not get it from food. There's no possible way. I told her, "So you mean that we've been eating food, so we must all have AIDS."

She said, "No, that means you're an asshole," and I was like, "Oh no, she did not say that."

I confronted her because she called me an asshole in front of the group. She asked why I didn't take it to the side about the transmission of AIDS. I said, "Wait a minute. You publicly humiliated me, and you expect a private conference?" I was like, "What are you talking about?" And she got upset, and we had an argument, and she was just cursing. I mean the whole night just ended horribly. I decided right then and there that I couldn't live with someone who wouldn't respect me. The next day I packed everything that I had and moved out. My lovely new bed, I had to leave it there. I paid for that month, but the whole month I stayed away.

She kept calling me, asking me, "Are you coming back?"

I said, "Yeah, I'm coming back." I had to appease her.

It wasn't until I finally decided to move in with my boyfriend that anyone found out that I was homeless. At the time, my boyfriend was getting suspicious. I moved over to that crazy girl's place in the Bronx, not because I wanted a place to stay as much as I didn't want my boyfriend to know. "Oh, yeah," I'd tell him, "I'm moving out of my apartment because I'm in the process of renting a place in the Bronx." He was getting really suspicious. I wouldn't allow him to walk me home. I wouldn't allow him to do anything, but when I ended up telling him what happened, he was shocked.

When I started living in the office, I had a place. I was able to buy new clothes and shoes and stuff, so when we went out dating, I always looked nice, and I had my makeup and everything, and my hair was permed. My hair wasn't natural then.

I'm Stubborn Like My Father

Every time I called my mother, she would say, "Are you coming back? Are you coming back? Come back. Your room is still the way you left it. You know, you can always come back."

I said, "No." The woman who I lived with in Brooklyn had called my mother and told her what had happened.

My parents knew, and they kept asking me to come back. I was very stubborn. I'm more like my father, very spiteful, you know. When I'm going through something, I don't give up. I don't give up. Life is a struggle, and you take the good things and you take the bad things.

Now I'm planning how I'm going to get my bed because I'm not going to let her have that bed, even if I throw it away. She told me, "You can't come in the apartment because my cousin is here, and you know, you can't come and take anything."

I was pregnant and I had moved in with my boyfriend on January 29, the last day of the month, because February would be another rent. I had lost my baby the twenty-eighth. Last month was our second miscarriage. While I was in the hospital, I was planning—calling movers—to get the bed out of the apartment. The movers were not available until ten o'clock in the evening. I waited outside in the cold. I was hemorrhaging. It was horrible. Yes, it was worth it, because I was determined. I said I'm going to get that bed even if I end up throwing it in the garbage. It was a beautiful bed, a real nice canopy bed. Very beautiful, yeah.

I called up friends, asking, "Do you want a bed? Do you want a bed? Do you want a bed?" I called every friend that I had.

One woman said, "Yeah," because she was sleeping on a cot.

I said, "I have a bed, and you can have it for free. I'll pay the moving cost." I called the cops, "Look, I want to get my stuff out of the apartment, and she won't let me because her cousins are staying there."

She was shocked because I called the cops. "Oh, there's no reason that you should come."

I said, "You disrespect me one time, so I do not want to deal with you."

I'm such a prideful person that if a friend hurts my feelings, I do not want to have any affiliation with them ever again. I told her, "You're not a friend. You don't know what it is to be a friend." She was twenty-nine at the time, and I told her that I left my home because it was such a negative environment, and here you are giving me another negative environment. I said I'd rather leave.

She said, "I found you," because she knew I didn't have a place. "I found you in the streets." She said she was going to tell people.

I said, "You know what? I don't care where you found me because I know where I'm going."

The movers put up the bed at my other friend's house. We put a sheet on it, and I fell asleep.

My husband, actually he was my boyfriend at that time, called, very worried. He was very afraid that he was going to lose me because he knew I came from the hospital, and here I am very weak, but I'm doing these things.

He was telling me, "Forget about the bed, please, forget about the bed." I was answering, "Look, I don't care, I'm not letting her have the bed. I don't care. I'll be back, I'll be back." I said, "I just want to sleep. I'm very tired now. I just want to sleep." The next day, I went over to my boyfriend's, and that was it.

Can I Get a Witness, Please?

We got married. It was so funny. I married him in the morning and had an exam that night. We got married down at City Hall. It was really quick, except for the fact that he lost the ring because we didn't have a witness.

The clerk said we had to have a witness. "Can I get a witness? Can I get a witness?" The person who agreed to be our witness then had to leave, so we're like, "Oh God." My husband went around again chanting, "Can I get a witness? Can I get a witness?" We finally met this West Indian couple that was getting married, and they didn't have a witness, so after we got married we were their witness.

When we couldn't find the ring, I emptied my bag all over the place, and he opened his pockets. Then I said, "Go back to where you were sitting and ask." A woman had the ring in her bag. She told us she had the ring in the bag because she wanted to wait until the person came to her and asked.

He had asked her, "Did you find a ring there in a heart-shaped box?" She was like, "Yeah, here it is." We bought the ring that day. It was a last-minute thing, boom, and so we kissed goodbye, and he went back to work because he worked at the Housing Preservation Office downtown. I stayed to be a witness for that couple, and then I went to school and had an exam that day. I did well. And ever since then, we've been together in Brooklyn.

We Tend Not to Appreciate Where We Live

There's a mansion I love on McDonald Street. It's beautiful. See, the thing is, and I don't want to talk down about my race, and I don't want to generalize, but we tend not to appreciate where we live. We throw garbage on the floor, and we don't value where we live. That's a problem because if you really look at the area, it's beautiful. Look at Park Slope. Our area could be like Park Slope. It could be nice. People litter. That's the problem. I don't think garbage pickup is the problem, because we would have two garbage pickups a day. The problem is that we don't care, and that's why people run away when we move in. The property values are going to go down.

It is troubling. It bothers both my husband and me because we really enjoy living in the West Indian neighborhood because you hear familiar voices, and you have foods you like. My husband and several friends are working on building a Caribbean museum, so once that is established, we can write letters to businesses to try to fix up their property. Then people will be attracted to the neighborhood. We're trying to work on those things. Also, we're trying to have a center for children to learn about the history of the Caribbean islands because a lot of our children don't know that history. We're trying to bring self-pride and a sense of appreciation of our life and our environment. I'm even getting Papa Jube to play Haitian music at the college along with some good dancers.

All These Positive Activities Make Me Feel Good about My Life

We have a not-for-profit organization, and we're trying to learn about the history of Haiti and the different types of music—like the Copa from the early 1960s and the Racine music from the Gonave area in Haiti has the best carnival. We're trying to replicate it here on the Grand Parkway in Brooklyn. It's all very exciting, and my life is very full. All these positive activities make me feel good. My new feelings can only be compared to the music of my land—intricate, insistent, and joyous.

TWO Azra Hodzic

BOSNIAN-AMERICAN

Azra is willowy like a fashion model. She works for an international company in Manhattan that designs and markets leatherwear. Her glossy hair is cut in the latest Eurogeometric sharp-edge shape. Sometimes her teeth are slightly stained with nicotine and coffee, hinting at the connections she maintains with her Eastern European past.

Azra, a Muslim, does not like to think or talk about the war years. I gained her trust when I brought her an article and told her, "This will make you mad." In "If the Walls Could Speak, Serb Epic Would Unfold," reporter Chris Hedges related how the Christian church took an active, revengeful role against the Muslims (New York Times International, Nov. 10, 1997). "Look at Radovan Karadzic," the abbot of a Serbian monastery said of the former Bosnian-Serb president, who has been indicted on war crimes charges. "He is a decent and good man, a believer. I would bless his presence here." The article ended with the song "O beautiful Turkish daughter, our monks will soon baptize you."

After reading the article, Azra told me she wanted to talk with me. At the end of each interview, as if in a therapy session, she would reveal something painful, such as her father getting wounded.

People tend to think of war in grand terms, but Azra tells of being denied the simple, private pleasures of life — having a cigarette over a cup of strong coffee while reading the weekend newspaper. We have often heard people second-guessing historical moments: "If I had been in Germany, I would have gotten out before the Nazis gained control. . . ." Azra had more foresight than most Bosnians and convinced her family to flee from Sarajevo to Turkey in 1991. After six months nothing more seemed to be happening so her family made the mistake of returning home just as full-fledged fighting broke out.

It was interesting that even during the war, learned, polite cultural responses were still in effect — such as when the Bosnian Muslims were sitting hip to hip with the Christian Serbs in the bomb shelters.

As with many immigrants, Azra's sojourn in the United States was supposed to be temporary, but as she put it, "Recently we found an incredible deal and bought a co-op in Forest Hills. It is a very safe neighborhood. In one way I would like to go back, but meanwhile we bought a car. In other words, we made a life here."

It's Not Going to be Good

Three and a half years ago, I came from Bosnia to the United States. It is only me and my husband here. I grew up as a Muslim in Sarajevo, but I was studying in Zagreb when the war started. I saw what was going on and realized that I had to flee and get back to my parents in Bosnia. When I arrived at Sarajevo, I said to my family, "Well, you know, it's not going to be good. I think we should leave."

I couldn't convince my parents. They said, "Oh, you think you know. Don't be silly. Nothing's going to happen."

It probably was hard to believe. This was August of 1991, so I said,

"Fine, you don't have to go. I'm going." Then I went to where they sell plane tickets, and I said, "Where is the next flight going? I want to go to Italy."

They said, "We have Istanbul, Turkey."

I said, "Good, give me one." I bought a ticket. I ran back home, and said, "I'm leaving tomorrow."

My parents said, "How are you going to go by yourself?" Then my mother went and bought more tickets, so we all went there.

In Turkey we rented an apartment. I studied Turkish and worked. It was very nice. I love Turkey. I didn't like some parts of the city where the people are really poor and the streets are dirty, but everywhere else, the city is a shiny thing. I love the food and people. We had a beautiful apartment on the coast by the sea. It was truly lovely.

The war didn't start for another six months. We stayed on in Istanbul, but then my father went back to Bosnia because he had a company. He couldn't leave the business for this long, when nothing was happening. There were just little kinds of disturbances, but nothing of any major significance. He went back, and then in March the first barricades were erected. It turned out that was the time when everyone left Sarajevo, and we were coming back because my father was there, and he didn't want to leave. And that's how we got back just when the war was starting. There were whole bunches of people at the airport trying to leave. On the roads, we saw everyone was heading to the airport.

Going Back Three Hundred Years

When we went back, we basically stepped right into the troubles. We came back on the April 4, 1992. At first, like every new situation, you don't know really what's going on. It was a totally new environment. When the first restrictions with electricity started, we had to get used to not having electricity all day. First they would have it partially turned off, just for a couple of days. Then it was the water. Actually, the water was cut off first.

This was planned because it so happened that the Serbs were holding the place where water was, but you could go to a spring and take water. It was like you're going back three hundred years. You would go to the spring outlet, and it would be open all day and all night, and people would line up.

Then the electricity went. They would cut it off for a month or two. In one respect, it was a very good time because I got so much sleep. You go to bed early, but you could make up little things for candles. You would take a little bottle; you would fill it up with either diesel or cooking oil. Cooking oil worked very well. Any oil would burn well. But there was basically nothing to do. You would go to bed, or you'd wake up. It was really like going back three millions years to being cave people.

I was a college student, but I didn't attend classes. Later I tried to attend off and on, but then two years passed, and at that point it wasn't worth continuing. You were supposed to go to school on a regular basis, but either there was shooting or some other disturbance that would interfere, and that might be the time that you had your exams scheduled. It was too weird to go. One time I went, and it was a beautiful day. Over there you have written examinations, but you also have oral examinations, and there I was taking an oral exam; I was talking to my professor about laws of marketing, and it was as if all of sudden everything happened; the shooting started, and he said, "Let's move." When we got to the hallway he said, "Well, go on, continue."

I said, "Just forget it," and so that was that.

There were lines for everything. They say it was like Russia or perhaps Germany, but I don't know what Germany was like during the war. Usually my father would stand in line because you have to wake up early, so he was the one. You have money, but you have nothing to buy. The first couple of months, nothing was coming in.

And then there was the cigarette problem. That was the worst thing. Everybody's a smoker there.

Everyone smokes. It's unbelievable. I think American health officials would commit suicide over there, because people were trading food for cigarettes. It was that bad, because they don't find satisfaction in eating, but they find satisfaction in smoking and having coffee. Those were the two most precious articles in Sarajevo—coffee and cigarettes. You could buy a pack of cigarettes for twenty deutsche marks, which is about twelve U.S. dollars, and there were times when you had to pay about thirty dollars for a pack, depending on supply and demand.

The Doctor

We would kind of start connecting with people to whom we usually only would say, "Good morning." We would start to meet and get to know more about them, to help our neighbors out if they needed help. But also it was a great opportunity to see people's vices, because it was a survival thing, too. People do a lot of things they wouldn't usually do, or they would, but you wouldn't know because you would never be around to see it.

It was not unusual vices. It was just normal vices, but in situations like that, it becomes heightened. An example is greed. People would have food sometimes, but wouldn't share. Let's put it this way: We had a neighbor that was living right next door to me, and he was alone. His wife fled Sarajevo, and he's a Serb. He was an older doctor. He was a cardiologist, and so we were receiving this humanitarian aid, and then the municipalities divided it, and then it was subdivided again by the person who headed each apartment building. They would come into the lobby of the building. They would bring whatever they had for that time, and during the worst period they would divide this stuff into very small amounts. It would be only twenty grams of this per person, so there has to be a person who divides and measures.

This doctor from our floor would come and get this little bit of oil. You would almost feel sorry for him, although I didn't feel sorry for the Serbs, ever since the war started, no matter what. I really hated them. This old doctor's brother died. His brother got killed on the other side because Sarajevo was divided. It was divided very close. I guess a sniper from our side killed his brother on the other side. Somehow this news got into the city, and he was a well-known doctor, and as a matter of fact, my primary school had the name of his brother who died in the World War II as a hero of the revolution, whatever. We found out about it, and so people were telling him, "My condolences."

He said, "Why?"

They said, "Isn't your brother dead?"

And he said, "No." For some reason he would never admit his brother died.

Then one day he said that he's getting out of Sarajevo, but he was coming back. I think he could do it because he was the chief of clinical cardiology at the time. As I mentioned, there was no coffee, no nothing, so whenever someone was going out, somehow, you would give your money so the person could bring you stuff back in. He collected fifty deutsche marks, which is like thirty dollars from fifteen people to bring them coffee, but he never came back.

I think he ran away. Since there were a lot of refugees in Sarajevo, people were looking for apartments. Whenever someone fled, refugees would find out, and they would move into the apartment of that person. Police came into the apartment after the doctor didn't show up, and then the police started bringing out all this food. The war had been going on a year at that time, so it wasn't just at the beginning of the war. We saw all this food that I would call exotic at that time because it was not like something that was normally available. He had all these luxurious foods, and he was the one person who would be waiting right there first in line in the lobby when they divided up the little portions. He had all these gourmet foods and detergents and soaps, all this stuff that you don't usually consider luxury, but this was during the war. And his garage was filled with gasoline, which was very expensive on the black market. I could not believe all the items he had, and every week he would come down and get his tiny, little nothing. I was shocked.

Some refugees moved into the doctor's apartment. They had fled from another part of the country. We would start finding stuff on the street from his apartment, and that was interesting because people—you would call them peasants, because mostly they were forced to leave the small villages—they would come into these apartments of these rich people. These peasants would move in, and you could find all these beautiful paintings in the garbage.

They should have taken the paintings to the museum, where someone would take care of them. I guess people just didn't know, and then the peasants would take clothes of those rich people and wear them one on top of the other, which I found funny, but also I thought it was absolutely okay. There were many funny situations. People would cut legs from pianos and burn them, which is okay. It's winter, it's cold, and you have to burn something, right?

There were a lot of very nice dogs whose masters fled and couldn't take them. They just left them in the street. You would see this really beautiful Italian mastiff running around the garbage looking for food, and people are adopting all these pedigree dogs. I saw that a dog could get used to eating anything.

In my immediate family it was my mother, father, brother, and I.

My brother is ten years younger. He was a baby, I mean, a baby of ten years, so he didn't have to fight. At the beginning of the war, my classmates and everyone volunteered. It was the time when people were idealistic about how war is supposed to be won, and they would not realize that they would have all these missiles aimed at them. People would not know what goes on in a war. How could someone of eighteen years of age know, right? So there were all these idealistic feelings. They're going to win, and everyone joined voluntarily. And then later, maybe in the second or third year, the draft started, but not before that.

Goddamn It! It's My Own Kind Shooting at Me

We had some Serb neighbors like that doctor on our floor and nothing happened to them. Many of the Serbs fled because they couldn't stand either the shooting or the cold; many others remained there. The local people didn't take it out against them or anything like that. That's what I couldn't understand. I guess people are too nice for that. Seriously, I was always the rebel in my building. I would not say hello to them. I would do all kinds of mean things to them only because I knew that they didn't let a single Bosnian person on their territory. They either kill them or move them out, and they live perfectly normally when they are with us. No one touches them.

No one did anything to them, and that's okay, but the Serbs would never say they were sorry, like if you would sit in the basement with them. Sometimes there was really hard shooting going on, so you went to the basement, and none of the people would say something against the people who were shooting so as not to offend the Serbs among us. It is not like they don't know who is shooting. There were people, Serbs, who would ask, "What's going on?" They knew what's going on, and they knew who's shooting, and they knew whose fault it is. The big majority of them would never say something like, "Goddamn it," you know, "it's my own kind shooting at me."

A lot of them lost their family members from their own people, and they would never say the Serbs did it. Instead they would say, "I wish I knew who shot them." Of course, they knew. And so that's what was said to protect their feelings. We all knew, we let them live there, they're there, and I didn't know what they would do to me if Serbs ever came to occupy this area. So how can I like them if they're not able to say openly what they think?

I don't think they were uncomfortable with us. No, I think we were more uncomfortable with them. It's like, you know how you have certain words you can't say if it's a black person, and so you would feel uncomfortable to make the other person comfortable. The same thing happened there. You know that these people are killing you, but you're too polite, even though someone close to you died yesterday. You would not say, "I'm going to kill you," or anything bad to them just because you're very nice and it's your close neighbor.

Bad French Wine

In May 1993, I started working for the United Nations, and I was out a lot. I was a driver/interpreter. I had one close call when I was with my father in the car. A missile hit the building by us and missed us by just a little bit, and so that was really scary. Other times, it would just hit a building or get someone really close to us, but I did not consider those close calls anymore.

Then I got married. I met my husband at our friend's house in Bosnia.

One night we were playing cards. He just came to see his old friend, who was my new friend, because he was from the neighborhood. We tended to visit people that lived close to us, and so we didn't have to go all the way to the city to see somebody. So we met, and at that time he was working for the United Nations. I called him once to take some letters for me to Croatia. We started dating, and after a month, we got married. And then I started working for the United Nations.

We had a very small wedding—a very nice, family-oriented wedding. Then seven days later, we had a party for friends, and that was fun. People were growing all these vegetables on their balconies, so we had friends over, and we had some French wine. It was a present from the French Legion for our wedding, and it was some really terrible French wine, and our friend drank a lot of it. And at some point it was about three in the morning, so he became really sick. Our friend vomited over the balcony onto another person's tomatoes that were growing in containers. It just burned the tomatoes from the stomach acid.

My downstairs neighbor said, "You know, if you did anything else to me that would be fine, but you destroyed my precious tomatoes." That was funny. We had to wash her balcony the next day, and we had to fetch a lot of water from the spring. It took a lot of water to wash up the mess, and, of course, we didn't have running water. He was so apologetic, but you know, it happens.

Fleeing the War

Once we got married, we decided to leave. Our parents, both his and mine, thought that we should go, and we didn't really know where to go. Where should we go? We're already packed. People liked Turkey; I didn't like Turkey that much to go live there on our own. It wouldn't be the same as when I went with my family. At the time I was there I had money. I was with my parents; I had a beautiful job and a car, and I lived by the sea. If I would go now, I would go in the worst part of the city, have no money, and it would take me time to contact people that I knew to help me find a job. It wouldn't be the same thing as before, and I know how it is to be poor in Turkey. It's not fun at all. All the Serbian countries would not let you in, because they were all up to here with Bosnian people.

We got out to Croatia. We would just go like it was for a business trip, and then we just didn't come back. That was it. And a good thing in that is when you work for the United Nations, you can get on a military plane for a business trip or a medical emergency, and then you would come back. So I did go out a couple of times and come back.

I didn't plan, no. I hated like the idea of leaving my family. I was really reluctant about the whole thing, and plus I would go out to either Croatia or Italy, and go to a normal life where you had electricity and water, and everything was normal, and I would buy stuff. Then I would come back.

My husband left for his vacation, and he stayed. I just said, "I'm going to go." I just went with my boss for a business trip. I told my boss, "I'm not coming back."

We went to Croatia. We were there for three months, and it was a very bad time in Croatia because there were these conflicts with Bosnia. It was almost like I landed in the middle of Belgrade. It was the same thing. We had very good friends there—Croatian. We heard about the program that the U.S. government was organizing for refugees from Bosnia, so we applied to go to the United States, and the first time we were rejected.

The reason that they gave was that the person who we were going to use to sponsor us in the United States was not my real uncle, but he's my mother's uncle. The official said it's not my immediate family; he's not my uncle, he's my mother's uncle. And since my mother was in Sarajevo and not in the United States, then no one will go.

It was necessary to have someone send an affidavit of your relationship. He sent us that, but he was my mother's uncle. This guy said, "That's not immediate family," so he rejected it. The girl that worked there saw that we were really sad, and we had nowhere to go. We couldn't go back to Bosnia. We were not working for the United Nations, so we can't get on a plane anymore, and we can't get in by land because eventually someone will arrest us or kill us.

Come Back, He's in a Good Mood

In the meantime, we got visas for Germany. Our friend helped us get that. And so we said, "Let's go to Germany."

Then this girl called from this organization, and she said, "Come back today. The guy in charge is in a good mood." We went back, and, sure enough, it was just such a relief. It was the States that really gave you a chance with your life. Germany will take you in, but they'll keep you there only while the war is going on, but then they will deport you. Let's say you stay five years in Germany, you build a life of some kind, right? You have to go back, and you don't probably have a house there anymore, nothing, so the States will just say, "Okay, you come in and you get your papers, and that's that." Right? It's not like, "Okay, the war's done, now go back." That's the reason we decided to come to the United States, in case we do come in and make something for ourselves in five years, it won't be a lost life. That was the main thing.

Those Creepy Jobs

Once we were here, we worked hard. We've tried to regain what we had in Bosnia. It's working out fine. I guess everyone has to go through the same thing when you just come here. That's when you find these creepy jobs that pay zero.

My husband is a mechanical engineer. He has very good job now. He had a creepy job in the beginning. They invited him to an interview at this same company. The organization that brought us to the States found him a job. They told us, "You go for an interview." You have to imagine how it is for us. Everything for us is new, so whatever someone tells you, basically you think it is true. When you come into the States, the organization gives you this small book that tells you how to do certain things. There were some things that were really basic stuff that everyone knows.

They have a job-searching section, sections on the subways and the bus and how to shop and do the laundry. In the job-searching section, they tell you that when you go to an interview, you have to look good, to get dressed up, and so he did. It was his first interview, and so he got dressed really nicely, a suit and everything. He went there and it was a factory that made lamps. He was supposed to spray some metal plates and then scrub them really hard. He took the job. At that time, we would not reject a job. I had to find old, old clothes for my husband to wear to work. He was there for almost a year, and eventually he moved up to the engineering department, and I think he's very—I don't know the word, when you want to do something and you're trying all the time to do it. I know the word: He is *persistent,* yes.

At the time I didn't work, so I was looking for jobs. I found a great job for my husband and called for him to get an interview at the company where he's working now. I called up, and I said, "I'm faxing you my résumé," and his boss thought that he was a woman since I made the call.

He went there and he got a great job. He's doing some programming and 3-D drawing.

Translating Madonna Songs

We learn in school how to speak English. It's very important that you speak at least one other language. I had German and English, but I pursued English more. And then you watch movies, and you listen to the music, and you try to translate everything. I translated old Madonna songs. That helps a lot. I find a job, and it was through the same company that actually helped us come to the United States. It was a company that sells and makes jewelry, and I was an assistant in the design development. When I came there the first day, I didn't even understand what those people were talking about to each other. That was so frustrating and so hard. I knew English, and I would have really liked to respond. Recently I have been promoted, and I am director of domestic sales in a leather company. I have even designed my new business card. The company originated in New York, but they sell overseas to Asia and the Pacific Rim. It's not a big company, but the products they sell are nice. My boss is very smart, and she is easy to work with. In fact, she's great. It's a mother and daughter who own the company. The mother is seventy years old, and she is so physically great, and mentally she is unbelievable. I wish I looked like her, because it's unbelievable how great she is. She has more energy and enthusiasm than I do. She's just amazing.

Nothing in the States Amazes Me Except the Smoking Laws

Nothing in the States really amazes me. The thing that concerned me is why they wouldn't let people smoke where they want. I couldn't understand where this campaign is coming from. In Bosnia, everyone smoked, but you would never see anyone smoke on the street. They would smoke in restaurants and bars. Here you have to smoke outside. Women wouldn't smoke on the street. It's so cheap.

It is considered very cheap. That's what I did last summer. I went back to Sarajevo, and I lit cigarettes while walking as part of my new American attitude. It's hard to quit. All our friends smoke.

And I don't really want to quit because I too much like that sensation of coffee and cigarettes; you know, Turkish coffee, not American coffee. It is really relaxing, and I don't smoke much, but on Saturday morning, you make this coffee and you sit and smoke for hours and drink coffee until you're sick, but that's just fun.

Religion Spiced the War

I'm not going to say the war was religious, but the war was definitely spiced with that, too. And they had Muslim Bosnians, and there were Catholics. Our community was mainly Muslim, then Russian Orthodox, then Catholics. My family is Muslim. Serbs were Orthodox. But it's not until the war that I personally could recognize you by name. Now I could say that you were not from my religion by name, but I didn't know which one you were. Now I know, but when I was twenty, I really wouldn't be able to say. And then this war started, and it just erupted so hard with these divisions, and you would not believe that there was so much hatred. They were saying about the wars that this hatred couldn't happen in two days—that these feelings must have been accumulating over years and years. To me it was absolutely surprising.

We lived in the Old City which is mainly Muslim. The middle of the city is the heart. There is a wonderful book I have here that shows how it used to look. You had a Jewish temple. The mosques were concentrated in the Old City; that's what was left from the Turkish empire. Then there were a couple of churches of different kinds, Catholic or Orthodox in the Old City, but I would say they were everywhere.

In one mile, you would find all four different religions. Russia thought they wiped out all religion, but everyone was practicing in their home. There were some people who really believed in this atheism with no God, but I know people who were Communist yet they would go home and celebrate Christmas. This war now shows that everyone knows everything about his or her religion. Young people were taught everything about their religion, so where was Communism? I don't know.

Marriages Splitting Up

My husband is a Muslim. But it's not that I wouldn't marry another religion. Maybe if I got married before the war it might have been different, but since the war I saw what was happening with mixed marriages. In Sarajevo, fathers would go and join the other army and show up against his children and wife. That doesn't sound normal to me.

It happened in many marriages. One son would go with the father; the other one would stay with the mother. Unbelievable things were happening in so many families. There were so many divorced marriages because of different religions, and I would never marry another religion because I don't know what can happen tomorrow. Maybe this person's religion becomes more of a factor over the years, and their life together becomes miserable. I saw what happened. People were just split apart after thirty years of marriage and raising up kids—one was Serbian, the other was Croatian, or one was Muslim, the other was Serb, and it was just terrible, terrible. It didn't happen to all of them, but I saw what happened to many families.

Dumb Newcomer Mistakes

We didn't have the concept of going out and doing the wash with so many people. I didn't feel good about it at first, but everyone was doing it. Back home everyone has their washing machine in the bathroom. We used very hot water, so our whites are really whites; here nothing is over thirty degrees Celsius.

Communicating topics are a bit different here. There was a woman at my first job who was overweight. I felt sorry for her, so I went out and searched for a good diet. When I presented it to her, she was offended. In Bosnia, if you showed concern, it would not have been offensive. Another difference is that here people don't talk about how much they make. Back there, people are more laid-back about money.

All my friends my age had a very easy transition. Maybe it was because they were more educated. We are able to find better jobs and communicate better. Going to the community college was very helpful to me.

We made some dumb newcomer mistakes. There were stupid things like, "Where is the thirteenth floor in the elevator?"

Initially we would meet people in the immigrant center, and they would say, "We live in Queens."

"We live in Queens, too. Let's get together." We would say, "There is a school on the corner where we live."

They would say, "Oh, there is a school where we live, too."

And we would be fifteen miles apart. When we would go to visit them, instead of going directly, we would go to Manhattan back to Queens. We would travel three hours on the subway. We could have been there in five minutes.

I didn't know when you bought something that there was tax on it. I would say, "I'm sorry. You made a mistake." We didn't have the concept of tipping. At first we didn't have money so it was not an issue. I didn't tip cab drivers. I always bought the wrong yogurt. It was always the wrong flavor. We did buy a telephone on the street, and when we came home the box was completely empty. Then we discovered the Ninety-Nine Cent Store. It was the greatest discovery. We came here and didn't even have a spoon. We lived off the Ninety-Nine Cent Store. It was both fun and hard.

Our Perception of My Father's Loss of Legs Was Much Worse Than the Situation Turned Out to Be

I was incredibly worried about my family while the war was still going on. To get phone calls in and out at first was difficult. We couldn't get through from the States, but others could from Canada. They had connections, so we did some conference calling from New York to Canada to Sweden to Bosnia and managed to talk to them. I had friends at home in Canada. He said, "Let me see if the lines are open."

"My God, if you dial this, you can talk to your family." It didn't work from here. That's how I learned it could only be done from Canada. I spent an enormous amount of money on these phone calls. My father had been wounded on one of those last bomb shellings. Of course, it was much worse for me then, but since that terrible time, he had prosthetic limbs made, and he's walking. We didn't think this was going to happen. Our perception of my father's loss of legs was much worse than the situation turned out to be. It was difficult because I couldn't even go there. Everything ended five days later. That bomb was the cause of NATO intervention. A year later everything was over, and he was able to go to a hospital in Italy where they specialize in lost limbs. My father spent time there, and they taught him to walk. It was a new skill he had to learn. It was both legs. The good thing was it was under the knees. Now the prosthetics are sophisticated. He is fine, so now we don't pay attention to it. He is working. He is walking. It was a difficult episode, and we have healed mentally and physically.

In Other Words, We Made a Life Here

I went back this year, and it was really good. I almost stayed there. My husband was saying, "Your school's starting, get back." I think he was afraid I wasn't going to return. But it's really good there. It's great, all these things happening, all these companies are investing money and building up, and it's like you would think nothing had happened there unless you came across some of the buildings that are not fixed up. It was so hard here in the beginning without my family and when my father was injured with that bomb. We all survived it.

Recently we found an incredible deal and bought a co-op in Forest Hills. It is a very safe neighborhood and quite a lovely apartment compared to what we had before. In one way I would like to go back, but meanwhile we also bought a car. In other words, to say it simply, we made a life here.

THREE

Tommy (Yang Hang Gil) DeLuise

KOREAN-AMERICAN

When I met Tommy, I was immediately taken by his exceptional good looks. This eighteen-year-old Eurasian is over six feet tall with teeth that an orthodontist would love, a straight nose, and clear, tawny skin. The only thing that was a little off-putting was his vivid blue eyes that seemed to float until I deduced that they were tinted contact lenses that covered a more subtle hue.

I realized that there was a whole category of recent immigrants that I had not considered — immigrants by adoption, which might include transracial, transcultural placement. According to the Immigration and Naturalization Service, in 1997 more than twelve thousand children were adopted from other countries, with the bulk, 6,483, coming from Asian countries. Great proportions of these Asian children are going to non-Asian families. These strangers in a new land did not elect to be in the United States, or to give up the foods they liked and the language they were fluent in, only to be immersed in new families that physically did not resemble them.

Tommy had lived with his so-called mother near an army base, and his physical appearance showed a mixed heritage, possibly Caucasian and Asian. Tommy was a "child of the dust," an outsider of society. In Korea, I do not think Tommy thought at all of his future. All that the child wanted was to have his abusive mother take him back after she had given him up to the orphanage. Looking back with the "worldly perspective" of an eighteen-year-old, Tommy states matter-of-factly that he would have been dead in his early teen years had he remained in his native land.

Whenever he mentioned his American mom, his face and voice softened, and when he mentioned the Korean woman, he always put a legal disclaimer on her as "the woman I assumed was my mom."

It must not have been easy for parents with three biological children to raise their new son. Tommy had been on his own in Korea, staying out all night since he was three. He was intelligent, but all the cues and skills that he had mastered to survive were of no use in an upscale suburb. He had to mimic the social skills until some were absorbed. The fact that the fork goes on the left and the spoon goes on the right probably would not mean much to a person who had to grab food from a stranger's table to survive. He was smart, but there was no avenue for transference. Tommy discloses that he had difficulties sitting still and concentrating, and after only a few months, he had dropped out of college and seemed to be floundering without any career plans. He was working nights, stocking shelves in a supermarket. If he had arrived a century earlier he could have "headed West to make his fortune" in a rough and tumble world. Now most upwardly mobile careers require a person to be deskbound and professionally educated.

Tommy is now working in construction. It has taken him his whole young life to surpass the anguish of a mother figure who burned and beat him and a culture that devalued him as a "child of the dust" to become "typical New Jersey." One can not help but wonder — At what pain, at what cost?

The Woman Who Was Supposedly My Mother

I was eight when I came from Korea to be adopted, but I can't spell the town where I came from. My name over there was Yang Hang Gil. I lived in one room that was in a compound of other one-room houses. I shared the room with the woman who was supposedly my mother. I always thought she was my birth mother, but I really don't know the story. Once she gave me a picture of a lady and said, "That's your mother." But I found out later that that woman wasn't my mother either, so I really don't know who my true mother was.

Back in Korea, the woman—who I thought was my mother and who took care of me—was not kind at all. I don't know why she took care of me. That is one of life's mysteries that I still have to find out. She had long black curly hair and was about forty-six, and I think she might have been a prostitute. She worked at a bar and came home real late. I stayed home by myself. As far as I remember, she never brought guys back with her to our room.

One night when I was sleeping, I heard some guy coming after her, and one of my neighbors went out to beat him away. My American mother here said, "She might have been a prostitute and some guy was trying to take her money." I don't remember what she wore or how she dressed to go out because I was out doing my own thing.

I went to school for a little bit, but then I left because it was too hard for me, and the kids made fun of me because I was half-Korean and half-American. I didn't fit in well because I was taller than everyone and stood out. Once I came into school and the teacher thought I walked funny so she beat me. I walked back to my desk and she said, "Come back." She hit me again. I walked back and she hit me again. It was weird, but actually I liked the teacher who hit me. I thought she was nice. I would like to know now what happened, what I did wrong. School was different over there. At lunchtime, everyone went into a large field and did sit-ups and jumping jacks. I always came in second for running. The prize was a book. That was fun. I went to the next grade, and it was too hard. The work entirely changed. My mom, the lady, had no problem with me dropping out of school because you had to pay.

I had some good friends that lived around me. These kids were half-American, too. We played tag and manhunt together. From the golf course brook at the nearby American base, we use to collect golf balls and used them to play marbles. We used to also go to the base to go to this church thing, and we'd go on retreats with them. They would take us to the city to meet other half-Koreans and have something to eat.

The woman who was supposedly my mother didn't give me any restrictions. She would come home and make my dinner and that was that. I'd walk outside until four in the morning. I felt lucky being part of a bunch of kids out having fun. I found out later that we were living in a dirty place. The agency lady said, "It was filthy, worse than Harlem."

I hung out with two kids especially: one kid who was really dirty and almost homeless, and a girl who was black. At five and six, I hung out all night. When I came here, my mom thought I was a little baby. You can't even cross the street here. At six I did everything by myself. I took the bus to the city—to the big city. I did a lot of things. Once I took somebody's bike to learn to ride it. When I was returning the bike, the security guy at the place had acted really nice and said, "Come here." So I went. Then he took me behind the building and started pounding me and said, "Never come back." I never returned.

When the Train Door Opened, I'd Run In

The woman who I thought was my mother took me to another city, to a lady with kids who were going to America. She said, "This lady is your mother. You're going with her."

I ran away from that woman. Then she put me in the orphanage. I ran away, and again I tried to live with the woman I thought was my mother, but she put me back in the orphanage. When I ran away from the orphanage, I used to take the train back to the woman who used to take care of me. Imagine a seven-year-old sneaking onto a train, jumping over fences, and walking dozens of miles. She wanted to get rid of me.

I asked my mom here, "Why?"

She said, "In Korea if you have a child and were not married, you can't get married again. Guys wouldn't want you."

But sometimes the woman was kind to me. When I was sick she bought me toys. But I used to steal from her a lot, and she would beat me with shoes and sticks, whatever she could find. There are a lot of stories. I was talking with my mom, and she was crying. She had just gotten off the phone with the agency. She found out that I used to get tied and dragged around town naked, and people laughed at me, and I was poked with hot pokers. There are scars on my upper arms. I blocked a lot of that out.

She wasn't nice, but I preferred her because I didn't know anybody else. I didn't understand. I thought, "Why is she trying to get rid of me? She is my mother." She must have been my mother because I have pictures of her when I was a couple of months old. She is holding me. So it was confusing. I remember the beatings. Where I live, there were a lot of markets, so I would buy cookies and stuff with the money I took from her purse.

She got rid of me without warning. I was taken to the orphanage. In front of the building there was a gate. Inside there was one big huge room for the girls and one for the guys. We kids would sleep on the dirty floor. They would get us up at seven in the morning, and we would all go out into the neighborhood. At a certain time we would come home for the meal and to go to bed. They taught you English in hopes that you were going to America. If you got in trouble, the priest would beat you. I would sit on the floor with my legs going back in an "m" position. They wanted me to sit yoga style, so the father said, "Sit in the Indian position."

I said, "I can't."

The father took a belt and started beating me. That was pretty bad. Sometimes you got beat for no reason. The other kids sympathized with you. Another punishment was that you had to put your forehead on the ground and bend your back in an arch. You had to hold that position for an hour. Another position for punishment was a half-down squat that you had to hold for over an hour. They were pretty bad punishments, worse than beatings.

I did run away all the time. I ran back to the lady, and she would give me money to go back by train to the orphanage. It was a two-hour train ride with a lot of stops. I had a very good memory, so I walked to the train station, which was a couple of miles. Then I hid behind a pillar, and when the door opened, I ran in and sat until my stop. When the train stopped, I just jumped off when no one was looking, and I climbed over a huge fence. I was seven years old. I want to go back now and see how long the trip was.

He Left Us to Die

There was a bad kid from the orphanage. He used to me beat me up and stuff like that. He was a rebel. So he, this other kid, and me ran away somewhere. We broke in some guy's taxi and got all this change, and we took the train somewhere. He wanted to see his mom, and we started searching for her, but we couldn't find her. We slept in this abandoned dirty building on this filthy mattress. At four in the morning with rocks we cracked open these vendors' places and ate the food, and we just walked around. At one point we saw some people sitting around a table. They went inside, so we grabbed their food. We also hunted for food in the garbage to survive. This guy just disappeared and left this other kid and me, and I had no idea where I was. It was his area. He left us to die.

One night we were walking around, and we got arrested. They took us to the police station, and we told them what happened. They called the orphanage, and they came and picked us up. That was the worst time. It was freezing cold there, and we had no jacket. I was about seven, but I never cried at all. I was a tough kid. I'm not afraid to cry anymore. Actually when I was a baby I cried all the time when the woman beat me, but she didn't care. Then after a point I never cried at all. But the funny thing was that I always ran away to go to her. She was all I knew.

Don't Pick Him

My mom always wanted a Korean child when she was growing up. It was a feeling she said she had. They sent pictures out to people who wanted to adopt. She saw my picture and said, "This kid looks really, really depressed." She said she wanted to put a smile on my face, so she adopted me. I didn't know I was being adopted, so I kept running away, so that put long delays on the process.

The agency lady kept saying, "Don't pick him. He's a bad kid." But my mom still picked me.

The first orphanage that I had been in was with the fathers, and it was a dirty place. The second was in a building with one big room where you played around and another room with beds. When I was at the second orphanage, they sent me a picture of my new American family, which I only got to see for a second before they whipped them away. Right before I left for the States, they sent me to this huge orphanage, which was the best place. There was a swimming pool; there were movies that you can relax in front of. It was such a change; maybe it was so you tell the people in the States that the orphanages were nice. The first night there, they gave me a bowl of soup and a bed, but the beds were really small. I stood out because I was so tall; my feet were sticking out. The boys were saying when I fell asleep, "This kid is huge!"

No one messed with me though. Some kids were twelve, and I was much bigger than them. I stayed at the nice orphanage for a couple of weeks.

My New Mom and Dad Grabbed at Me

On the plane there were a whole bunch of kids and babies that were being adopted. It was a twenty-hour trip. I wasn't nervous at all because it was happening too fast, so I just went with the flow.

When we finally landed, I was looking at the huge buildings. I saw my mom and pop who were adopting me. The agency lady said, "They are your parents."

I just stood there. My new mom and dad grabbed at me and gave me a doll and some food. They even let me pick my name. I actually have three names. My first name is Yang Hang Gil, and when I went to the orphanage, I met this black kid. I really like him. He was nice to me. He said his name was Tony.

So I said, "My name is Tony, too."

He said, "That's cool."

On the paper when I was getting adopted it said "Tony Yang," but that was a big mistake.

My mom said I should pick a name. First she was going on with names like "Trevor" and "Trevis" that had a meaning like traveler, but then I heard "Tommy" and I said, "That's good."

It was a good pick. I fell asleep on the way from the airport to New Jersey. I wasn't shocked; I wasn't scared, I was neutral—"Whatever." The first time I saw my brother Larry, I thought he was a girl. He had long curly hair and looked weird. I saw [my older sister] Tracey just a little bit.

She would go to Florida with her friends. She would be in and out. The other sister was away in college. First I shared a room with Larry, then I got my own room. It was fine.

What amazed me the most when I got here was seeing my mom drive. In Korea I never saw a woman drive. I saw her and started laughing.

"Why are you laughing so?" she had asked me.

"You're driving."

In the beginning, I watched *The Jeffersons* on TV. I had no idea what it was about, but every time there was laughing, I started laughing. I knew some English, a few little things like "tree" and "outside." I learned English from my brother. He used to watch HBO. At that time they had a lot of swear words. So every word out of my mouth was a swear word, so my mother disconnected the TV.

I didn't start school for a couple of months. I'd wake up, have breakfast, and watch cartoons and *Sesame Street*. I picked up English very, very fast. I have lost my Korean.

Everything just stopped here. I didn't run around like I used to, but actually I did go with my bike to the interstate and go to the nearby town of Ramsey when I lived in Allendale. This man told my dad, "I think I saw your son in Ramsey."

"It can't be him. He doesn't know where he is. He just got here about a day ago."

Then they found out I was just riding around, and they were amazed that I didn't get lost. I didn't hang out with my brother Larry that much, but when I went to school I met a kid who was Korean and whose name was also Tom. We became friends. I met another kid whose mom was American and dad was Korean. I became a friend with him, too. I used to play video games all the time, so my mom said, "There is a kid I would like you to meet."

The first thing I asked, "Does he have video games?" She said yes, so I went over there and we played all the time. He was Polish.

I liked the food in America, but I miss the Korean food a lot. That was one thing my mom always wanted me to do—to go to Korean restaurants. My mom finally found one place that sold Korean food, so she bought Asian cabbage, and it stunk up the whole house.

My dad started yelling, "This food is disgusting. It stinks!"

The Hardest Part of School Was Paying Attention

My first difficulty was the language. I didn't want to be made fun of because of my accent. But eventually I lost my accent. Nobody teased me in school. Everyone was very friendly. The hardest part of school was paying attention. They did everything fast, and I couldn't understand the language that well. I was going to be in third grade, but they put me in second. In third grade, they had ESL. Currently, I just dropped out of college and I'm working.

It's Not You

My parents split up when I was twelve, but it didn't affect me at all. Every time my mom says something like, "We're getting divorced, but it means we still love you. It is not like we are separating because of you or anything." She kept saying, "It's not you. It's not you."

I said, "I understand. You don't have to keep telling me. You guys are getting divorced. It's not a big deal."

I don't have as close a relationship with my father as I used to. Now that I'm getting old, he nags and nags me about getting a job and stuff. But I finally got a job at the supermarket to get him off my back.

My mother works at a day care. She is too overly protective. I couldn't play manhunt [hide-and-seek] when I got here. I tried to explain I ran around since I was three years old. We used to have a big family thing, but everyone got old, so it's just her and me in the apartment. My mother wakes up at seven in the morning and goes to work. I'm still sleeping. I go out and come home at ten and see her for a few minutes. I work from eleven to seven, so I never see her until the weekend. She gives me money for food, but she doesn't cook or do the family thing anymore.

I was going to go back to Korea for my high-school graduation present. My dad told me this about a week ago, "You could have gone to Korea after your graduation." But we never had a real discussion about it. I'm just waiting for that day to come when my dad gets real serious. I would love to go back. I told my friends the stories, and they fell in love with the place. I would like to go with my family first, then go with my friends later. I'd go tomorrow, as soon as possible. It has been eleven years, so probably a lot has changed. Where I lived was probably cleaned up.

I was resentful that I was adopted for the first couple of months, but now I love it. They say that I wouldn't have lasted in Korea, probably only until age fifteen. Then I would be dead because I didn't fit in, and I would have been by myself.

I Don't See Myself with a Family of My Own

I haven't figured out my future. Maybe I want to do something with animals or creating video games. I went to study computer programming, but it was too hard, and it didn't have anything to do with video games. Recently, I tried to work with animals. I volunteered for the pound, but as soon as I walked in I started sneezing and my eyes turned red, but maybe I could work with just a few animals without having a reaction. I don't see myself with a family of my own, but I want to move back to Allendale, New Jersey. I got fond of that place when we lived there as a family. It is a quiet, nice town where a person could be happy. I'm not interested in joining a Korean cultural society or anything like that. I am pure New Jersey American.

FOUR Sarah Lee

KOREAN-AMERICAN

It is interesting to compare two people from the same country with entirely different perceptions and experiences. The idiosyncratic details that make a person unique are evident in the narration of these two young Korean immigrants, Tommy and Sarah. Their differences start early in their respective childhoods. Sarah had Korean parents who were devoted to her, unlike Tommy's natural mother who abused him and tried to rid herself of him. Sarah's parents were educated and had to "come down in life" in order to immigrate to America so that their children could have "a better chance." When Sarah had run-ins with the neighborhood toughies, the only way her parents knew how to address the problem was by moving, even though it might have meant personal upheaval, a new job, or a longer commute. They did not know from their own experience how to deal with physical street confrontations, but they would do anything it took to keep their children safe. Hypothetically, Tommy would have been able to fight his way into acceptance by the street gangs from the very start if he had lived in that same rough neighborhood, but he had been sent to an affluent suburb where he didn't know the local cultural cues. Sarah's mother and father worked long, hard hours in jobs that were beneath their educational levels and prior experiences in Korea. They changed their addresses again and again, always to advance their children's well-being and education. They were willing to suffer in the short-term in order for their children to have the chance to become whatever they wanted, moving beyond the constraints of money, class, and gender.

At first glance, Sarah seems like a street-wise person who is always in a rush. Fast talking, even her sentences run into each other, as if in a hurry themselves. Hints of the tough neighborhoods she has lived in show in her inflection and body language as she angles her shoulder in a subtle exhibit of strength. Sometimes her short curly hair has a purple or red streak in it. Unlike a lot of her more timid countrymen, she seems at home with punks, campy gays, and artistic types who wear dog collars instead of gold chains.

Although she tries to project a mellow persona and a loose lifestyle, the reality is that she is also a true child of immigrant parents. She is always in a bind to complete her assignments and to obtain good grades — in opposition to the laid-back, native-born students at her university. She might have the ripped jeans of a slacker from Generation X, but she is firmly, if covertly, striving for success.

Love and All That Blah, Blah Stuff

My parents met in Korea. My father had been working as a director for a movie company. At that period of time, he was doing a lot of B movies. My mom took some acting classes, and my dad saw her and fell in love and all that blah, blah stuff. She was just taking some lessons because somebody said that she was really pretty.

Since the age of seven I knew that I was going to move to America.

I also moved around a lot as well. Mostly I lived where my relatives lived, because they watched me while my mom worked. At times in Korea, my parents were separated both geographically as well as marriage-wise. Sometimes I would stay with my grandmother, but usually I would live with my aunt because she was home all the time. And she was located in a part of Korea called Inchon, which you would consider the equivalent of New Jersey, but I was born in Seoul, which is considered like New York.

My dad was an artistic man. He couldn't become the painter he wanted to be because when he was going to school, his father and grandfather wanted him to go to trade school, and they didn't think painting was something a man should do to support a family. Art has always been his passion. It still is, but he has never pursued it, career-wise.

He made movies because he knew people. While he was doing his painting, he made connections in the film industry. I didn't really know him that well when I was young because at that time I was living with my mom, but I know what he told me. At first, he was just an assistant to the director, and then he coproduced some B movie that you never heard of, a long time ago, so to this day he still knows a few prominent directors. If I mention him to other people who are his age, they probably know him.

Finding My Half-Brother and a Decent Apartment in Queens

It took two years for my father to settle down so I could live in America. He had been looking for apartments near a good school, so I didn't have to commute too far. When my father finally found a decent apartment in a very good neighborhood in Queens and a good school, I finally got my visa cleared, and I came. But my mom had to stay back because her visa was taking a lot longer than we expected.

My parents got back together. In Korea, the fathers get the custody of the child automatically because they are pretty much the partner who has the jobs. When I came to America with my dad, I missed my mom, since I had lived with her. They knew that it wouldn't be natural for me to be away from my mom, so my mom came back, and now we're a family again.

I have a half-brother six years older than me, but he doesn't live with us anymore. He did for awhile, when we first came to America, but then he had a disagreement with my father and was forced to leave and be on his own. He has a different mother. His birth mother remained in Korea.

The thing that I remember the most about my brother is that at an early age, he was very, very tall.

The Guy with the Third Most Votes Won

I had two years of schooling before I came to America. When I was in the first grade in Korea there were two sections of classes. There was a first grade honors class and the first grade regular class, and I never went to kindergarten. I just kind of took a test and skipped over to first grade. In first grade, I had a female teacher, and each class voted for a president and a vice president. In the first grade, I was voted the president. The president's job is to erase the blackboard and stand up and have all the students greet the teacher in unison at the beginning of the day.

When I moved to the second grade, I had a male teacher. Again I had the most votes, but he didn't believe in female presidents, so he gave it to the guy who had the third most votes. And I remember crying at my desk, and my mom coming to talk to my teacher, but I still wasn't president. He just didn't believe in it.

I had more friends in my neighborhood than I had at school. At school, you have friends, but it's such a huge school that everyone comes from all different parts of the place, so they might live in a different neighborhood. Little kids didn't really go to another neighborhood to hang out with their friends, so I pretty much hung out with the people that were in my area.

We played house, of course—the normal games. We played a lot of school, and we played supermarket a lot. We took things from our parents' houses and sold them.

They have department stores, but to go buy food, you went to a big, huge flea market. It's sort of like a Chinatown, but it's more compact, where there are food courts on one huge lot, and people just walk down the aisles and there are different sorts of food. Each kiosk is stacked right next to the other, and once you go there, you just smell all these different aromas of the food, and they give you little pieces of things to taste, and nobody feels any qualms about picking things off and tasting them before buying them. I used to do that with my grandmother a lot because she was the one that I always went shopping with. When I came home from school, she would take me grocery shopping, and we walked around and picked up every little food that I could get my hands on.

Meanwhile my mother worked for a small boutique where she was a seamstress and did tailoring. But while I was in Korea, I never knew my brother. I had seen pictures of him, but I never knew him. The first time I met him was actually the week before we were coming to America. He came with my father and me.

No Tall Blondes or Pools

I was shocked when we moved to Queens, because in Korea, all my friends were so jealous because the stories you hear of America are always about clean and beautiful houses, and every house has a pool in the backyard. All the people are tall blondes, with beautiful skin and beautiful blue eyes. And my first sight was the subway, and I was petrified by it. It took my dad a few months to finally get me used to the subway. I was afraid of it, all the graffiti, and I thought it was so dirty. Everywhere I went it was dirty and smelled, and I was in total shock.

Where I lived was predominantly Greeks and Italians, and I didn't see that many blondes. I also saw a lot of Hispanic people, which I didn't even know they had in America. That also came as a big culture shock.

I never even saw a white person in Korea, much less a black. I mean, I know that there were some blacks, but we didn't have them except for one of our celebrities. She is still around giving concerts. This singer came from a black father and a Korean mother. She didn't speak any English. She was Korean in most respects. Her parents were divorced, so she lived with her Korean mom. But I remember thinking, she's really dark, and she has kinky hair, and so I never really thought much of it except that everyone knew that she was half-black and half-Asian. A lot of people used to say, "It's a good thing her parents got divorced, and she's living with her mother."

If she was living with her father, they thought that she was a stereotype—"the darker the skin, the poorer the person." In Korea the farmers are very dark skinned, and they are considered poor, and they are considered laborers, noneducated, and that is how they picture blacks and Hispanics who are dark as well.

My Dad Thought of Every Little Detail

In the United States, my brother and I were pretty much latchkey kids. My dad had to work, and because of that, I belonged to a lot of after-school programs my dad enrolled me into. And so that helped me learn English really fast, and I made friends easier that way, instead of coming straight home from school. I took piano lessons. I went to dance classes.

Most of the classes were in the school. The dance class was only a block away from where I lived. My dad thought of every little detail, so I didn't have to get on the subway, and I didn't have to get on the bus.

My dad also made breakfast and dinner. I bought lunch at school. My father was actually a very good cook, and he was into making everything pretty.

My dad had many jobs. When he first came to America, he taught English. He tutored language when he was in Korea, but compared to the standards in America, where he had to communicate with American people, it was really hard for him. He could write and read better than he could actually understand the fast pace of English speaking.

He got by, though. The first job he had was working in a hospital as a maintenance man. From then on he had a lot of hard-labor jobs, and then he moved up to working for an art distributor where he made sure that everything was framed correctly, and it was packaged well to be shipped out to galleries. From that point, he made many connections, so he opened up his own art gallery. But that went bankrupt after a year. Right now he's working in translating at the *Korea Times*.

Our Only Solution Was to Move

I really didn't start liking being in America until I got to college because I didn't speak English well enough. Because I took the adult English course in Korea, I understood little bits and pieces, so I knew if somebody was talking to me, maybe I didn't understand every single word, but I got the gist of what was being said.

In public school, when you go to the bathroom, you have to take a friend with you and a pass. I had to go to the bathroom once, and the teacher sent me with a girl that I didn't like and who didn't like me. In fact, she had never talked to me. I had wanted to go with one of my friends, but the teacher didn't want buddies to go to the bathroom together. The teacher sent me with this girl who never liked me because I was an Asian. In the bathroom, I ran into this black girl who had been harassing me since the first day of school, and she told this girl, "Leave Sarah here. I want to talk to her."

And I remember being very scared because I was able to understand what was being said, and I was praying that my escort wouldn't just leave me. Fortunately, she didn't abandon me, but instead grabbed my hand, and we ran as fast as we could out of the bathroom.

Ever since then, I was truly scared to go to school, but I didn't want to tell my dad. Instead I told my cousin, and my cousin picked me up after school and walked me to school, and he told me, "If you have to go to the bathroom, try to hold it in." During lunchtime, I would sit with just a small group of friends. I felt fearful for a long time. Eventually I finally told my father that I was afraid. When I told my dad, he didn't know what to do about it either, and the only thing he could think of was to move to another place.

That is why we moved around a lot, according to my dad's job and according to certain places where it was just really racist, and I couldn't deal with it because I couldn't communicate well enough to fight against it. Our only solution was to find a new place to live.

They Threw Rocks and Pennies at Me

I got into a big fight in junior high school. There were these twins who were Puerto Rican. They were really big, and they looked exactly alike. And they used to harass me and one other Chinese girl who wasn't really good friends with me, but I knew her friends. Sometimes they would see us together and just assume that we were sisters or something.

One time walking home, the Puerto Rican twins and their sister were following us throwing rocks and pennies and telling us, "Pick up the pennies. Why don't you take the money and go back to where you came from?" They were yelling things like that. And I was holding a Coca Cola bottle that I was drinking from, and I just broke it against the fence, and I held it up against one of them, and that made them kind of stop, so we ran.

A few weeks later, one of them pulled my hair. This encounter developed into a major fist fight. She was only able to land one blow to my face, but I had been able to throw in a lot of punches. One of my friend's brothers just dragged me out of the whole thing. All I remember thinking as I was pulled away was the realization that because I fought back during the original rock throwing episodes, our battles have now escalated into a higher level of animosity and violence.

Everyone talked about the fight for two weeks.

New Jersey Was Another Culture Shock

I think my parents knew about the violent encounters. They didn't say anything, but they found out. About a month later, they asked me if I wanted to move to New Jersey. To me New Jersey was out of it. By now I was used to being in the city. I had heard of this New Jersey suburb where you couldn't get anywhere without a car. So I was really unhappy about that but also kind of glad because I really was afraid of living where I was living, because it was getting worse and worse. We started getting metal detectors at school, and it was a place where I wasn't feeling safe walking home from school even though I had become a tougher individual.

Living in New Jersey was another culture shock because all my life, my parents moved me around places where there were no Asians, so that way I could learn English and adapt to the American lifestyle. Then we came to a New Jersey suburb, where it was predominately Korean. It was a mix of Jewish-Americans and Korean-Americans.

It was a huge shock to me because I never knew how to relate to Asian people. I have always been friends of Hispanics and black people because that's who I grew up with, and then I come here and I'm dealing with another sort of population where they thought that I didn't fit into either sector. Because the Korean-Americans there were very wealthy, and so were the Jewish-Americans. It was a very wealthy neighborhood. Celebrities lived there. It was a very prestigious neighborhood, and I was living in an apartment kind of away from the prominent houses.

New Jersey is the place where I experienced prejudice stemming from social and monetary backgrounds. I think that is where I grew up a lot. I really didn't like living there because I felt pressures in many different ways. In high school, it can be a lot crueler than the overt hostility of younger kids. Because I was older, I was able to understand these different forms of cruelty, and it just made me feel that if I can take a punch in the face, I can deal with these new kinds of prejudice. In truth, it taught me a lot about myself and what I can do without.

I couldn't hang out the way the Korean-Americans hung out, because whatever they did cost a lot of money. Maybe they would go to the mall, but they wouldn't just go to the mall. They would probably go to a place like the Donna Karan store or something equally expensive, and I couldn't compete with that. And they thought I was strange because I spoke Korean fluently, and none of them could speak a word of Korean, so they were kind of like, "Well, you're not a complete Korean-American because you speak Korean." Sometimes I translate for new international students who just came to this country.

I used to think that maybe it was sort of jealousy because their parents would say, "Oh, but look at Sarah; she speaks Korean and English." It stemmed from that, but the international students really didn't like me either because I liked to hang out. Therefore, I became friends with the non-Asians. That caused backlashes from all the different races.

But by the time I was a senior in high school, I had managed to find a group of Korean-American friends. They were all born in America, but they lived the same lifestyle where they weren't constantly around a lot of Asians. So those were the people I really connected with, but still to this day, most of my friends are non-Asians.

He Looks White

I have a Colombian boyfriend. I knew that this was going to be a big deal, but I just figured, once my family got to know him, they would really see the goodness in him. But it was never at a point where they wanted to get to know Carlos. They remain at the level where they just have this stereotype of a Spanish person in mind. They think that he will never amount to anything, because my parents believe all Spanish people are womanizers and uneducated. My parents also believe that they're rude and they're dirty, so even though I showed my mom the picture of my boyfriend, the first thing she said was, "He looks white." And he does. He doesn't look like the typical Spanish person she was used to seeing on the street.

My mother knew a lot of Hispanics because when she first came to America, she worked in a sweatshop. She thought all Spanish people were like those girls who were fourteen, high school dropouts, pregnant, and working in a sweatshop because that was the only way they know how to make money. To this day, my dad told me that if I marry Carlos, I'm going to be disowned.

My boyfriend once came to our house. My dad didn't like that, so, he said, "I can't stop you from dating him because you're going to do it anyway behind my back, but I don't want him in my house."

I go to his parents' house. His family has embraced me since the very beginning, but I can't do the same thing for my boyfriend. It was really hard in the early stages when I felt like I had to make this huge choice between my boyfriend and my family who has raised me all my life. It took me until early this year before I started to realize that I have to live for myself. I'm not in Asia anymore where the culture forces the parents to break every bone in their body to help you get an education. Once you graduate from college, you live with your parents until you get married, and once you get married, you help out your family by marrying into a nice family. But the fact is that I'm moving out when I graduate. That will already break tradition.

I'm Such a Bad Daughter

I live with my parents now. They moved back to Queens when I was a senior in high school so I could be a New York resident in order that I can qualify for a TAP [Tuition Assistance Program] award. For me, they have made a lot of sacrifices, so you know that is one of the reasons why I felt I was being such a bad daughter by dating somebody they didn't like, and by moving out, and doing all the things that a traditional Korean daughter shouldn't do. Once I graduate I'll find me a place.

My boyfriend works for a communications company doing accounting. He had a lot of jobs while he was in school. He wasn't like me, where right after high school he went straight to college. He didn't have that kind of opportunity. His family was poor, so everything he had to do he had to do on his own, and my parents don't think that he has a responsible family.

My parents think that a responsible family should put their children through college right away, even if a parent has to get six jobs. So they don't understand that in America, people are independent as soon as they're eighteen. Sometimes parents kick their kids out, not because they don't love them anymore, but because it's actually good for them. They don't understand that. They don't understand when I tell them my friends are paying for their own schooling. They think automatically that they have bad parents. "Why be friends with them?"

My parents point out another difference between our cultures. After high school my boyfriend didn't have money to attend college, so he went into the navy. He knew that once he got out of the military, they would pay for his schooling, or at least they would pay most of it. In Korea, there is a stigma about people who go into the military; they go because they can't get into college.

Also while he was in college, he attended for a year, and then took six months off, so it took him awhile to finish school. And he doesn't have a B.A. He has an A.A. He wants to eventually go back to school to get his B.A., and my parents think that is ridiculous. He is twenty-five, and he doesn't have a B.A., yet it doesn't matter to them that he is making more money than I earn with a B.A., and that Carlos lives on his own in an apartment. But to them, there is a procedure that everyone should follow, and that's the only right way to do things.

We do not discuss my boyfriend situation anymore. I'd rather not talk about it with my parents because every time we do talk about it, it just causes another fight. They're stubborn; I'm stubborn, and there is no way I'm going to convince them of anything because this is how they are. They're almost sixty. For me to be able to change a sixty-year-old's mind I think is impossible. The only thing I can hope for is if Carlos and I ever stay together and we get married, and we live really well, then they'll realize then that their daughter has made the right choice. That is the only hope that I have.

There Is Personal, Verbal, and Mental Space That You Can Not Violate

My brother doesn't exist in my dad's life anymore because my father disowned him because he did something that my dad had forbidden him to do. And I don't know what that is, but all I know is he's completely cut off. So I know my dad's capable of doing that to me.

My father is very, very stubborn. It's his way or the highway. And I've always told him the reason I can't picture myself with a Korean man is because every single person in my family is dysfunctional. When my uncle cheated on my aunt, everybody blamed my aunt. The women blamed my aunt. Her own mother blamed her—because it's your place to keep your man happy. If he strays, then it is your fault. You're not doing something right. And that is the kind of thing that I can not live with. I can not tolerate it. I have always thought that the reason why they moved me to the United States was because they wanted to take me away from the stigma of a woman living in Korea. And yet they want me to be successful, but in my mom's own words, "I want you to be really successful, but I want you to be able to not work and still have money to do what you would be doing if you were making your own money."

She has basically told me, "You should marry someone who will let you stay home instead of working."

That to me is bullshit because my mom is one of those people that cannot *not* work, and I am also one of those people who has to work because I don't like taking money from other people. I like having my own money, and she has taught me to be like that.

As I got older, things that they said when I was younger and they're saying now are contradicting each other. When I was young, I guess they wanted me to be ambitious and have goals, and now that part has come where I have achieved my goals, now it is about marriage, and it is about having a family and being dependent on your man.

My brother's name never really comes up in the family. Everything that is unpleasant is not talked about. If you want to talk about family secrets, then you're stepping on a lot of glass. Also there is never really anything clear that comes out of any discussion. As I get older, I have learned little bits of family secrets here and there, tidbits about so-and-so, about my aunt and my cousin, little bits and pieces that maybe they over-heard and then I overheard somebody else talking.

Korean families are like that. Whatever is said behind these walls stays in these walls, and no one is allowed to know that we have a dysfunc-tional family. To everyone, we have a normal, perfect family, but it's not that way at all. But the fact is that I tell my friends things. When I tell my parents, "Oh, my friends know that you guys were separated a long time ago," they get irate.

"That is nobody else's business. You don't tell people that!" And I'm thinking that is normal here. People get divorced left and right here. People have mistresses, and people are open about it. They also do it, but to them it is still a very private matter.

I go to my boyfriend's family, and I love being at their home. It is so refreshing, but at the beginning I was thinking, "Why are they telling me these things? They only know me a little while," but they are so open about things, and they're very affectionate, too. In Korea it is not that way. You're not very affectionate. You don't even give an adult eye con-tact. Personal space is a very private thing, and verbal space, mental space—everything has a certain amount of space that is already set by tradition, and you can't cross over that. If you cross over the proscribed limit, you're being disrespectful, or you're being rude, or you're being one of the street kids that doesn't care about anything.

That is why I think I can't really see myself with a traditional or even a nontraditional Korean man. I have had Korean-American friends who still have some carryover of this mentality of the Asian male ego and the male's position in the household as opposed to the woman's.

Spanish men have that, too, to a degree but I guess my boyfriend's family is not like that. At least I have not noticed it from them, but I've heard about other people whose family was very much like that, where the woman stayed home. I don't want to be identified as Korean or American or even Spanish. That is why I see myself in the future living abroad in Europe as part of an international community. I don't want to get stuck with one tradition, one culture, or one type of life. I have seen where that can lead you. My parents want me to be a good Korean and a loyal American, but I have not even voted. Since I am getting my degree in fashion, I think I will be able to achieve my goal of living anywhere and not being stuck with one country or one culture. Styles come out of Milan, Paris, London, and the Far East and I hope to be part of that transient international community. In that way I will be able to sample the best of all nations and have choices that would be unimaginable to my parents. Then I would be free from ethnic expectations and be my own person.

FIVE

Dianne Barker

BARBADIAN-AMERICAN

A thin Brancusi sculpture of a woman in her early forties, Dianne Barker always appears immaculate and professionally attired. She attends night school after a full day at her job at a bank. Her schoolwork is always perfectly typed. Last winter she developed breast cancer, yet she never missed a class. She had surgery and radiation, yet she still was in the plastic seat, front right, night after night, her work neatly typed and on time.

I told her, "You don't have to come if you are ill."

She answered, "I like coming to school. It takes my mind off my problems. Besides I get to laugh here."

When she feels safe, Dianne has a wicked sense of humor. She can do a great imitation of her Americanized son holding a television remote, and she privately makes acute assessments of the people with whom she comes in contact.

Vacation brochures state that Barbados is one of the Caribbean's most popular escapes. "Barbados is wildly tropical and captivating in its beauty. It also has another side that warmly embraces a British heritage." The United Nations core document on Barbados introduces a few less bucolic facts. Although there is 99 percent adult literacy, unemployment was at 27 percent until 1998, when it fell to 14 percent. At that time many homesick labor immigrants in England and the United States returned to Barbados.

Dianne found her new life difficult when she had employers and a brother-in-law who took advantage of her. The famous "nanny case" was in the news when I first interviewed her. In that incident, the caregiver was accused of killing a child. Like the British nanny of tabloid fame, Dianne worked for husband-and-wife doctors, but her scenario was completely different. The woman was addicted to drugs, and Dianne was the kindly mainstay of the troubled family.

Although her family could only afford to eat meat once a week, she states that she had a good life, came from a good family and felt as if she were exiled from the Garden of the Tropical Eden to a place of cold. It is like the famous line, "I didn't know I was poor, until society told me so." Even if she only ate one meal a day, she felt protected by her mother's love.

My Sister's Kids' Father Wanted to Have Intercourse with Me

When I was twenty-five I came from Barbados without a visa. I was here alone, and my brother-in-law tried to take advantage of me both financially and sexually. There is no way that my sister's kids' father was going to be having sexual intercourse with me. No way. I didn't want to tell my sister about her husband, because the kind of temperament that she has she probably would have tried to hurt him. I didn't say anything to her—in fact, I didn't mention it to anyone. I decided to leave, cut all ties that I had. I just left.

I Can Not Stay: I'm Too Skinny Already

The first job I got in this country was as a sleep-in housekeeper for a family with two kids. It lasted one week. They would lock the door and take the key. I was a virtual prisoner for seven days. They didn't give any explanation for this. That's why I quit. It was very scary.

Doing sleep-in work is not easy. There were many nights that I prayed that I would be helped. Their dogs were treated better than I was. In my next position I was put in the basement in this small room, a prison cell: no window, just a door. I can laugh now. At the time, many nights I cried, and I said to myself, "Why did I come here? I am not accustomed to this. I am being subjected to do things I would normally never do in my country." It was very humiliating for me. In Barbados, I had a very good home: a father and mother. My sister went to London, and she sent me to one of the top high schools in my country. So this was very new to me. I never had to clean a house. Then at my jobs, I had to eat whenever everyone had finished eating, whatever was left. It's not easy. In the second house, that whole week I had nothing to eat. I had to wait until they came in to have something to eat. Then it was whatever. The food was so kosher. It was so new to me. I never really ate the whole week. Then I met a friend; she worked across the street from where I was working, and she slipped me some of her food.

The live-in across the way cooked her own meals because she was diabetic. During the day she slipped me some of her food. That sustained me during that week. But I had to leave my employer's house before the sun went down. That Friday I said to my new friend, "Vashtine, I can't stay here. I'm too skinny already. Not to eat. I'm going to die. And to let my parents say that I came here and I'm starving and it's supposed to be a place with a lot of resources where you can get a lot of food."

She said, "Don't quit."

I said, "Vashtine, I can't endure this."

That position lasted about three months. Somehow the kids couldn't take to having a black live-in maid. And the little one refused to take water from me. He was six. I felt very uncomfortable, so I told my employer that I didn't feel very comfortable, and I was going to leave. I was sorry that it didn't work. She said she understood. So I left there.

The Shoe under the Couch Lady

There was one lady I worked for who was a nutcase. One day I cleaned the house where the kids were pushing their shoes under the sofa. Every day I had to clean the house. When she came home, I think it was from a mah-jongg game, she was looking for something and was very upset. The woman was slamming the cupboards. I hate that, because I thought that I had done something wrong.

I said, "Are you okay?" She snapped at me. I said, "Okay." So I went downstairs to the room that was given to me. Then after about fifteen minutes I heard her calling for me at the top of her voice. Frightened, I ran upstairs. I thought something was wrong with her.

She said, "I thought you cleaned in here."

Apparently she had pulled out the sofa, and the little boy had put his shoes under there. I said to her, "Mrs. Weisberg, I did clean in here. But Sean came in and pushed his shoes under the sofa. When I cleaned and vacuumed, those shoes weren't under there."

She said, "So why didn't you move them?"

I answered, "I couldn't move them if I didn't know they were there." So I think that threw me off a little after that incident. She had started doing my immigration papers for me. Somehow she started holding back on the papers. Then she wouldn't sign the papers. Every day I would say to her, "My lawyer will call. He is still waiting on the papers." I would ask the lawyer, "Did Mrs. Weisberg send them back to you?"

He said, "No. Why do you think I am calling you?" Up to that point I had spent eighteen months there. I left a few weeks after she wouldn't sign the immigration papers. I kept having these setbacks.

Mrs. Weisberg was a Jew, and she had different silvers for different occasions. You couldn't mix poultry with dairy and it was very difficult for me. Every day she came home and did a white-glove inspection. It was very stressful. That was on Long Island. When I left there, I went to another job.

The Doctor Was Addicted to Morphine

Then I went and worked for two doctors. They had two sweet girls. One was five and Sara was, I think, seven. They were very nice people. I was employed there for four or five years. The woman doctor had a lot of problems taking medication. Many days I sat upstairs with her because she was going through muscle spasms. The first time I experienced this I went upstairs and saw her shaking. Saliva was coming from her mouth.

I got scared, so I called her husband. He said, "Let her lie on her stomach so that her tongue would not fall back in her throat."

At first she also gave me problems with my papers. I remember this incident. I gave her the papers. She took my papers off the dining room table and up to her bedroom. The next morning I went up to clean her bedroom. There were the papers on her dresser unsigned. So I took them and carried them back downstairs. At night when she came home from work, I gave them to her and asked her to sign them. It was like a ritual that went on for a whole week. It so happened that she was going to Puerto Vallarta on a vacation, and she wanted me to stay over the weekend with the children. I threatened that if she didn't sign my papers I wasn't going to stay. She immediately signed the papers.

Working with her was hard. I know that in the summer, especially in the summer, when the kids wanted to go to the park and the pool, I couldn't take them because I was really babysitting the mother and not the kids.

One time she called me upstairs and said, "Can you wash my hair for me?"

I said, "Sure." I had to stop in the middle, and I had to towel-dry her hair with the shampoo still in because she was having muscle spasms.

She kept hitting her head against the faucet. At one point she hit her head and I saw blood. I was so afraid. I towel-dried her hair. I said I thought she ought to go into bed immediately. She had muscle spasms so bad that she urinated on herself. In truth, she was such a nice person, but it was an awful situation.

The wife was addicted to morphine and Demerol. It was so funny because she was driving the car the whole time when she was in that condition. She had this custom-made curtain that formed a type of pouch where the material folded in on itself. That's where she hid her drugs. I knew they were in there. I couldn't point it out to the husband because it would be like telling on her. After I called the husband during one episode and told him that she had passed out, he came home and started frantically searching all over, but he couldn't find the drugs.

I said to myself, "My God, Dianne, tell him." But I just couldn't. He took away her car keys. She would write prescriptions for herself and sign his name, since he was a doctor also. She would go to the pharmacy and fill the prescriptions. When he went back to work, she went to the neighbor's to get their car and got the Demerol. The neighbors knew she was on drugs and wouldn't let their kids drive with her.

One night her receptionist called and said, "Listen out for the car." It's a wonder she drove and never got into an accident. Many times she would be just sitting at the table, and she was just like hanging her head, nodding off.

I remember the year we all went to Martha's Vineyard. The husband decided to stay back. While we were at the Vineyard, she started going through withdrawal symptoms. That night she was vomiting and sweating, and I said, "My God. I am here alone with this woman. I don't know what to do." I called the husband for her. He came up the next day.

That night before he arrived, she nearly killed us all. She drove her car into someone's boat. Even talking about it I get kind of shaky. It was a very bad experience, a very bad experience.

It was funny because she hid the medication everywhere she went. Downstairs in the den, she hid it under the cushions. Being the careful person I am I would just pick up the cushion before I would do anything. And many days I would find the needles all over. I love watching *The Honeymooners*. This night it was about eleven, and I was watching *The Honeymooners*, when I heard the telephone ring once. So I knew she usually picks up because her patients would call. Then I heard this loud bang. I said, "Something is not right." Then I heard this labored breathing.

When I opened the door, because my room was next to the kitchen, I saw her on the floor. The phone was off the hook; the syringe was by my bedroom door. I went and called her husband, and he said it was funny because she tried to call him on his line, but he was in the bathroom. We called the ambulance for her. I tried to gather the needles and stuff off the floor because the cops usually come first. I got it off the floor and the cops came in and the cops said to me, "Did you see anything else?"

I said, "No I just heard a bang and that was it." I gave her husband whatever I picked up off the floor. She spent two days in the hospital and she signed herself out.

But I did like them because they were very kind people. I remember when I came here and my papers were in the process of being done. I had no social security number, so I couldn't pay taxes. My lawyer said that at the end of the procedure I would have to pay all of the back taxes. I had no money to pay those back taxes. She paid them for me. She was a very nice lady, but suicidal, I guess. I still keep in touch with the children. They are fine, well brought-up kids.

One night she overdosed herself. She died in front of me—with her two kids standing next to me trying to give her mouth-to-mouth resuscitation! It was very traumatic for me.

She was an endocrinologist. She was thirty-eight years old at the time of her death. For months I just kept seeing her face in front of me. It was a very awful experience. I worked there for one year more. I went to Barbados and got my permanent visa. Then I came back, and I spent six months more with that family. Then I got a job at a bank. I still keep in touch with them. They were very nice people. Before I left, the husband was dating. When I saw them last he did get married again. Her mother still doesn't accept it.

The Three-Hundred-Pound Man

While I was away doing sleep-in work I called this lady. She died recently. She was like a mentor to me; she was like a savior to me. She got me a small room in Brooklyn. I spent one year there, but it was not fit for humans to live in. It was in a basement; it was very cold and damp. The walls were all mildewed. I had to share the bathroom and the kitchen with a man. If it were a woman, I wouldn't have minded. But being a woman living downstairs alone with a strange man, I said, "No, I can't." I spent most weekends in Harlem with a friend I met. I never gave that man a chance to get me.

I only ran into him a couple of times. He was about six feet, three hundred pounds. Soon I joined a social organization so I could have some friends.

Six Golden Rings in Each Ear

There were many days when I was working for that [first] couple, I did not want to go to work because whenever I heard the INS was out sweeping I refused to leave my house, afraid that I would be picked up. I had no papers to show that I was here legally. Once I got my papers, I worked at Chase. Right now I'm a supervisor in the tellers' area at Chase. I hope to move on from there.

I always thought that this country was paved with gold because people came here and they came home all bedecked with jewelry, a ring on each finger, six earrings in one ear, six chains around their neck, and they always gave us that gold impression, but it's not. It's not easy coming here.

I said to my sister a few weeks ago, reflecting on my life here, "Whatever I got here, I paid for in sweat and tears, I really did." It's just amazing that the last family I worked for those things had to turn out that way. I guess that was meant to be.

This Country Has Not Lived Up to Expectations

Then I started school. I decided that I didn't want to keep on doing sleep-in work and working in a bank. I needed a profession, so I started school at Kingsborough. That's in Brooklyn. I went there for one year. Then I moved from Brooklyn to New Jersey. I transferred from Kingsborough over to Manhattan because it was closer for me to commute over here from work, and so here I am. Life is still tough.

I really cannot predict how my life would be different if I stayed in Barbados. Judging from the way I was scoring on the entrance exam, I would have joined the police force there. I probably would be a sergeant in the police force there. The pay is very good. Judging the way that it was going over there, I would have been okay.

Some things are the same in both countries. The same holidays that are celebrated here with the exception of Thanksgiving and probably Columbus Day are celebrated in Barbados. But Christmas and Easter are celebrated. Religious artifacts and stuff in my country, you may find some people with it, but culturally we don't go into that stuff.

Now I am living in a townhouse in New Jersey with my husband and son. The City of Bayonne is a very nice, mixed area. It's very quiet. I haven't really met many friends over there. Been living there six years. I'm not really a person to go from house to house. In comparison to Brooklyn it's heaven. It's heaven.

When I first came to the States, I joined a social organization. I am the secretary of that organization, and we meet monthly. I go just to have friends, socializing. The meetings are held in Brooklyn.

I Find It Very Remiss

From work, I wouldn't really call them friends. They're my coworkers. I try to be separate. Being a supervisor you have to have that separation; otherwise, they will believe you are friends with them, and the others will say I have favorites. I try not to do that.

I would gladly go back to Barbados. That has been on my mind recently. I'm finishing my education here. I cannot take the cold. If it's not Barbados, it's going to be someplace that's warm.

This country has not lived up to the expectations people have laid on it, where I'm concerned. When I looked around and saw people eating out of garbage cans, I was shocked. I never saw this in my country, as poor as my country is. When I see kids hungry and they are spending billions of dollars to go to the moon or sending people into space, I find it very remiss. I don't know.

Keep Walking

I didn't know anything about racism. In my country there is a class struggle. If you are light-skinned, then you are believed to be more important than a person who is dark-skinned like myself. But coming to this country I experienced racism, I mean to the *max*.

I was walking down the street in Bayonne one day, and this lady she passed by me and all of a sudden, she just ran into a doorway and held onto her bag.

I said, "Are you okay?"

She started screaming.

I said, "My God! What did I do?"

This guy came by and said, "I would advise you to continue to walk because this is kind of a hick town and the cops over here are kind of crazy, and I would advise you to keep walking and don't say anything to the lady." That was shocking to me. This was in New Jersey.

I was robbed of my paycheck one day. I was going to the bank to make a deposit. This elderly man, he could have been sixty, he approached me and he said, "Do you know where this hospital is at?" Being the nice person that I am, I stopped because he said his aunt was in the hospital and she called and she was dying and he couldn't find it and could I give him directions. While I was giving him directions, the other guy who was with him snatched my bag. So I experienced that, and it was not nice. For weeks, I refused to leave my house alone. When I would leave to go to work, there was this guy who worked at the bank with me, and he would call my house and I would meet him outside my door. It was devastating.

My Husband

Then one day when we were driving, my husband and myself, we were parking the car. And this guy had stolen something and he was running and he pulled my door open and tried to drag me out of the car.

My husband said, "You're so naive. I told you to lock the door." I guess that could happen anywhere.

My husband is also from Barbados. But he has been living here thirty years. I met him at my social organization. Well, he's a very nice guy. At least I can say that when I met him he was very shy. I was the one who did all the talking. Now the tables are reversed. He does all the talking and I just listen. I am very fortunate to have met him because being alone in this country, having no family, having no one it can drive someone crazy. You can lose your mental facilities. He has been there for me. If I want anything, he will never let me ask anyone for anything. I am fortunate that he came along.

Just as an example, last night as a matter of fact he met me to take me back to New Jersey.

He said, "You know there's nothing home to eat."

And I replied, "Yes, I left something in the fridge that I can eat.

"I ate it," he answered.

So I said, "What am I going to eat?"

He said, "I'll take you by Kentucky."

And I said, "I have no money." We went to Kentucky Fried Chicken and he gave me five dollars. I said, "What can this buy?"

He said, "A couple of pieces of chicken."

I told him "Forget it. Take me home." So I was feeling mad with him and got up this morning still feeling mad at him.

About 2:30 my telephone at work rang, and he said, "Are you still mad at me?" He's a very nice guy.

He works for Lucent Technologies. He was affiliated with AT&T, and after the spin-off he chose to go with Lucent, which takes him out of the state. He's always away on business. I've been married thirteen years.

I think he might also go back to Barbados because the cold is getting to him, too. I think he is planning it, too.

Kevin-Ma-I-Want

I have one boy who is twenty. He is not from my husband. I had him when I was seventeen. Right now he is going to New Jersey State College. Very lazy child. Oh, my God, very lazy. Very lazy. He hates to clean the sink. He won't put the garbage out. He's always saying, "Ma I want." So I call him, "Kevin-Ma-I-Want," because he always wants.

He lives with me and takes the bus to college. Recently I've been giving him some driving lessons. But that's a mistake, because I think I'll have to sell him my car. He has become so Americanized that he is— what do you call it—enculturated. He doesn't have plans of going back to Barbados. When I say, "I am going back," he says "You can go by yourself."

"Kevin-Ma-I Want" is Americanized because he likes to eat a lot of junk food. Also he plays the video games at night until one, two o'clock in the morning. And this MTV madness! I call it madness because there's no sense to the music he listens to. Also he is laid back. He's very lazy. I have to keep motivating him. I told him that he's emancipated. He should be on his own. He's not fifteen or sixteen now. When he was that age, there were many times when he just would not go to school. He would wait until he thought I was out of the house and figured I was gone to work and he would sneak back home.

It was so funny: One day my husband didn't go to work. He went back home. When he got there, he went into the bathroom to wash his hands. He looked in the bathtub and saw shoes sticking out from behind the shower curtain, and he said, "Huh!" He walked out. He thought the house was being burglarized. Then Kevin came in. The point was that it was Kevin's friend who was also playing hooky and who got frightened when the door opened.

Kevin wants to go into designing. He draws very well. He wants to go into fashion designing. So I don't know if he's going to pursue it. Everything is just a phase with him. He wants to do one thing today, and tomorrow it's something else.

I started working in Barbados when I was seventeen because you know you finish high school at sixteen there. You have high school, you have middle school. . . . We start school at five years old and continue in one school until age twelve. Then at that age, there's a common examination you take. You go from there into high school. You finish there at sixteen. You can't afford to go to college there. There's one university, and it's very expensive. When I left there I had one certificate in typing and one in English. But I could not afford to go to the university.

We Ate Meat Only on Sundays

My mum died in November last year. My father is still alive, but I don't see him. After I was twelve, he just decided not to help my mom with us, so I have this resentment towards him. He wasn't there for me. He was there for the others. My sisters and brothers he was there for. When I became twelve, he just disappeared. So my mother actually raised me personally, but the others had my father there. Somehow I never had that closeness with my father.

My mum worked very hard. She was a maid. She did a lot of odd jobs to feed us. Although we had a nice home, food was very hard to come by some days; she struggled with all of us. Then my sister immigrated to London and became like a mother to us. At least we had income coming in. Then my oldest brother was working for a bakery chain in Barbados, so that helped out with food.

We usually had a tiny something in the morning, but not a real full breakfast. Yet we could always be sure that by the time we got home at least we had a meal. If it was only one meal, we had that meal at night. We never really went to bed hungry.

It's funny. It was only once a week that we ate meat and that was on

Sundays. And I guess that's why we tend to live long; my aunt, she died when she was ninety-two. My grandmother is ninety-nine, and she's still alive. Even though we were poor, it was a healthy diet because we ate meat only on Sundays.

It was devastating when my mother died because she was like a mother and father to me. I remember I was in class, and when I got home I got the message. When I got back to school the next night, I told the professor, "I just want to let you know that I can't stay for the class," and the next two days I flew down to Barbados. It was tragic.

Of the six children, one brother still remains in my old house. Everyone else has moved out, gone on his or her own. I have the one brother, a good-for-nothing brother who is still in the house. He's an alcoholic. He just squanders all his money on alcohol. I don't think anybody really bothers about him. *I* don't.

Children Eat Their Parents

I am basically here alone. I have a niece here; but I hardly really talk to her because somehow she has a very nasty attitude. She thinks that the whole world owes her something. I told her, "I don't owe you anything; so don't take that attitude with me. If I have anything you want, I'll give it to you. But don't come and say that I have to give it to you."

I rarely ever see her. I talk to her once every few weeks. Originally I didn't even know she was here in this country. Her mum came here and spent her vacation with me. She said, "Do you know that my daughter, your niece, is here?"

I was shocked, but I said, "Really?"

She said, "Yes."

I said, "That's nice." Her mother was here for three weeks staying with me and didn't even get to see her daughter, although she did call. That girl always has that attitude that you did her a great injustice.

Then my sister went back to Barbados. Her parting words were, "Kids can eat their parents, but parents cannot eat their kids."

Sometimes My Husband Is a Little Racist

I'm majoring in liberal arts, but I'm hoping to get a teacher's certification and teach. I wanted to be a nurse; that was my second love. But what with all the AIDS, I have changed my mind. I am hoping one day to open a nursery, so that is my goal right now. My banking job is just a means to an end. Right now they pay my tuition. So I am taking advantage of that. This country has not been all bad to me. I know that the things that happened to me, like being mugged, that can happen anywhere. But the mere fact that I came here looking for trees that had gold hanging there like apples—in reality it's not so.

Reflecting within myself I know that I have come a very long way. I know I have a long way to go, but I don't think it is as long as I've come before. Also, I am satisfied that I'm a nice person. The encounter I had with that woman didn't change me. My mother brought me up to be a loving person and I always say that to people. Sometimes I think my husband is a little racist. I say to him. "Just think for a second that you cannot see. Could you tell what color a person is? No you can't. So just pretend you can't see."

My sister met this white guy. My husband wouldn't let me live it down. He's always talking about my sister and her boyfriend. "Just let it go. What is it?" I said. My mom didn't bring us up that way. She taught us to love everyone regardless of what color they are. He's a very nice guy, my sister's boyfriend.

I have a lovely townhouse in New Jersey. It's two levels, two bedrooms, a kitchen, a living room, a dining room, one and a half baths. It's nice, compared to the place I was living in Brooklyn.

Sometimes I Don't Know If I Am in Communist China or Communist Cuba

Lately my bank job has become so tedious. A job that was so simple has become so stressful, so tedious. At night I go home, and I am grouchy. I have a manager, and her manager is of the opinion that she does everything in there.

She calls me "Princess Di."

I said, "You know what? You're so right. My mum baptized me Dianne. So Princess Di is so right. So thank you." And somehow I think she hates me. I treat people with the utmost respect, and I expect the same in return. If you have to speak to a person, you speak *to* that person, you don't speak *at* that person. I said to her, "I know there's a joke that we came here on a banana boat—which I did—but you're an immigrant just like I am who came here for the same goals. Why do you want to treat me that way?" She doesn't like when I say that to her.

She's from Cuba, and her boss is from China. I said, "Sometimes I don't know if I am in Communist China or Communist Cuba." She is very rigid, and she has that Castro mentality. I said, "You know what? I am not a slave. Probably my poor parents were slaves. But I didn't come up with slavery. I just read about it. I do not want to go back to slavery because what I read is not very nice," and I said, "History is not going to be repeated. Slavery was not nice, and you're not going to push me back into slavery. All you need is a whip, and you would be a good master."

I Still Can't Stand the Cold

In the future, I see myself probably having my own business, a nursery school. It may be in Barbados. I am a U.S. citizen; that is one thing I prided myself in when I came here. I was told that when I had my green card for five years, I could apply for citizenship. So that year when it became my fifth year I went to apply for citizenship because reading history I knew we had a struggle in getting the vote, and the only way you can be heard is to exercise your rights. I became an American citizen. So I have that leverage, that I can go and come without having to report to the government no matter how long I stay. I see myself five years from now in Barbados. Maybe not all the time, maybe just for the winter because I can't stand the cold. I dress in six layers of clothes in the winter and a coat, and I'm still cold. Maybe if I spent the cold months there to thaw out my bones, I could return to America with renewed fondness and forgiveness.

SIX Navid Daee

IRANIAN-AMERICAN

Wiry and energetic, Navid spills ideas and emotions. He has thought a lot about his life and can smile affectionately at himself and his misadventures. Navid laughs easily and often — and mostly at himself. A slight man in his mid-thirties, he wears a short beard and wire-rimmed glasses. His appearance can transport him easily to the coffee shops in Berkeley or to the all-male cafés in Tehran. His language expressions are mostly American, but he has a tinge of romantic Persia with an occasional lush verbal image. As a filmmaker, he thinks deeply about the split in his consciousness, about being the perpetual voyeur, the outsider focusing in for close-ups, the framer of life retold.

Nostalgia a Lot of Times Is Like a Mirage:
You Go to It and It's Not There, But for Me It Was There

My memories were really split in two parts; one is when my father was alive, and the second part is after he died. I grew up in a small town near

Shiraz. My father was the principal of the high school, and my mom was the principal of an all girls' elementary school.

We had the first brick house. It was situated in a developing area on the way to the cemetery; everything else around it was desert.

I remember a lot of funerals. We just sat in front of our home and watched people passing by. Ironically, my father died, and then we had to move from that place where my father was buried. The cemetery was very flat, because they place the stones horizontally. The cemetery is right by the mountain. There's sort of a holy figure buried on top of the mountain, so everybody goes there. He's called Khajeh. Khajeh was not noted for any miracles, but he is an excuse to climb the mountain, do a bit of praying, and have a picnic.

There were four of us: my parents and me and my brother. My brother is seven years older. I'm the youngest. It was good because my mom likes me better than my brother, so I was pretty spoiled.

The Happy Daees

Before my father died life was very good because we had high status. My parents were educated, so we were pretty well off. We were known as "the happy Daees." Of course, always there are family problems, but as a kid, I sort of accepted them.

My dad drank a lot, and he would stay out gambling and not spend enough time at home, and my mom did not like that, so they would get into fights. But other than that, he was really cool. I had a really good relationship with my father. One thing that he did with me, which I don't know if it's good or bad, but it is one of my memories: My dad had just bought a car a year before he died. My dad used to buy three bottles of beer and then just him and me—I was seven and he was thirty-nine—we would go out of town and watch the sun set and drink beer together. I would drink one, and he would drink two. That was really cool.

I don't know if people would approve or not, but it's a nice image, a seven-year-old boy and the sunset in the car.

He totally communicated with me, because he studied psychology and philosophy and stuff like that, so he was really good in dealing with me. Even though I don't have a lot of memories of him, but certain things stay.

It Was Like Old Persia

One place that always stayed as a nostalgic source for me was a garden and a garden house we had outside of town. It was a huge family. Maybe thirty people including the kids would just walk with big pots and with lots of dishes, rice, meat, this and that, and dirty clothes, lots of dirty clothes. We would go to the garden. I have a really good memory of this picture.

Right away the women would start cutting the meat. My dad was in charge of making barbecue, and so I would go help out and get the meat, and my mom would cut it, and the bees were all around, trying to sting us, and then we would eat lunch. After that, the kids would have a great time, climbing the trees and swimming in the water. And then my grandma and my mom and the other women would go and wash the clothes by this stream of water, and then they had special stones right next to the stream, which was made for washing clothes. And they had a beater, and they would go on the wet clothes—bam, bam, bam! We loved that. And then my grandma used to take off all of her clothes and swim in hiding. My brother and I would go and sneak a look. That was a great one!

At that time, like in my small town, our family culture was very westernized. All my aunts were fully educated; they were all teachers.

My grandpa was the first educated person in our town. He started the school. He was an intellectual guy, into music and poetry. So our family is unique and strange; we were totally open minded, but still my mother would be too shy to not wear a chador—a long, black body veil worn over hair and cloth—so everybody wore them. If they didn't, the townspeople would talk behind their back, basically. But then once we got to the garden, they felt free.

Then my grandfather, sitting on the carpets under the tree, would play a stringed instrument. We'd just sit around while he'd play. My dad would drink with his buddies and play cards. It was total leisure, very peaceful. We would make mud houses and, of course, always get into trouble. One time my brother got stuck in a really high tree. He went way up and then he couldn't come back down; he was screaming.

It was bucolic, like the old Persia. We would play swords, with a piece of a branch. And then the sword would become a horse.

It Didn't Last Long Before I Figured It Out

My father died when I was eight and he was forty. It was one of the nights that he promised my mom he'd be good from now on, and he was going to come home soon, and he actually came home. He felt uncomfortable. I was asleep; my brother was still awake. My father felt pains in the chest. It happened overnight. I have only one memory. I remember waking up, and I ran automatically, half asleep and opened this door, and the only vision that I have is that whole bunches of people were sitting around and some white thing was in the middle. As soon as they saw me, they grabbed me and took me out. That's the only memory I have.

The funeral was in our home. The first couple days I didn't know what had happened and they didn't tell me, but it didn't last long. I figured it out.

The way I found out is they had told my school to request that the kids not tell me, so everybody was all of a sudden nice to me. It was a very strange thing for a second grader. I would beat up the other kids, and nobody would beat me up, so it's like, "Oh, what's going on?" Then we were walking down the street almost at the end of the school year, sometime in June. It's a small town, so everybody knows everybody, so some woman saw me and she said, "Oh, are you the son of Daee?"

I said, "Yeah."

And she started crying. So then I kind of think, "What was that all about?" So I come home and then I asked my mom, "Is my father dead?"

My mother started crying. Then I knew.

After he died, they took all the memories out of our lives. All the pictures were banished; nobody would mention my dad's name.

That was my family's approach. Nobody wanted to talk about it. It was a big tragedy, for he was the only son of my grandparents, and he was only forty when he died. My mom was thirty-three. The family was in shock for a long time. So the only way they dealt with it was to not deal with it.

Our life changed. We moved into this older neighborhood, and we lived with my aunt who was much older. It was her home. Her husband had died, and she didn't have any kids. She was living with and taking care of my grandmother who was about seventy-five at that time. When we moved, the whole neighborhood changed. That was weird for me. The types of people around were lower class. I would play with them, and then my mom would say, "Don't play with them." It was all this duality.

My old friends came to the same school with me. But then we weren't that close anymore, because I started playing with my neighborhood kids. My mother didn't approve of them. These kids and I became really good friends. One year, my mom decided I should part with them and not talk with my new friends. So I went outside and told them, "I'm not talking."

"Why?" they asked.

"I don't know why," I answered. But I obeyed my mother and we didn't talk anymore. I lost my relationships. Their parents were selling hardware or had little shops, and one kid's father was a janitor. Our family was class conscious. The way they dressed wasn't the way that I dressed. When we played soccer, they sometimes played in pajamas, and I had team shirts. The language that they used was street talk.

But I totally, totally enjoyed hanging out with them. They were good kids to play around with.

The Protection Was Gone

My brother, he hated the small town and wanted to go to Tehran. He desperately wanted to get out of that town. So when he was in the twelfth grade, which was two years after my father's death, he went to Tehran and lived with my aunt, and then he got accepted to the university. Everybody wants to live in Tehran, so it took three or four years for my mother to get approved to move. There was a lot of talk as to whether it was good for me. Finally we decided to move, and by then I was in the eighth grade, which meant six years after my father's death. In Tehran, nobody knew, so the protection was gone and I had to deal with reality. My grades dropped. I had a village accent. I had to learn how to speak Tehranian, which is fast and filled with slang. Tehrani kids were very tough. After a year, I became one of them.

The first year, we rented a place, and we lived with my cousin, who was older, around thirty. She had gotten accepted to the university. She had a five-year-old kid; the husband was working, so he would just come once in a while to visit. The apartment we shared was in a nice area opposite an uncle. My brother was in the dorm of the university, so he didn't live with us.

There were six of us with six different last names. My brother changed his last name when he became eighteen because our last name "Daee" means "uncle." We hated our name when we were growing up. Everybody called to us, "Aunt this or that." When you are eighteen, legally you can go change your last name, so he did that. Mine is my dad's last name; I didn't change it. My mom's is different from us, as she never changed her last name when she married. Then the servant had a different last name, and my aunt's kid had the husband's last name.

Although my mother was only thirty-three when my father died, she didn't see other men. For one thing there is repression. There's shame involved, so she just devoted her life to raising us. And she was really beautiful, too.

We Were Totally, Totally on the Revolutionary Side

I don't know how going to America came about. It all happened so quickly. There was no master plan.

I was sixteen. My high school was opposite to Tehran University at the center of town, and most of the trouble was coming from the university at that time. My brother was in Tehran University, so I somehow indirectly got interested in politics and banned books and banned Russian movies. It was trouble, and there was this man who later became a big figure of the revolution. We would go to see what's going on. My mom saw that my brother was already into politics.

In 1978, we were totally, totally on the revolutionary side. These are people who are against the shah or they weren't political. Pro-shah people never did anything. They just enjoyed life. There were a lot of different factions, and my brother belonged to a party that was different from what I believed. We had a lot of fights at home. We threw things at each other. It was a very uncomfortable situation outside and inside. There was really no peace at home. My mom was worried about me and didn't know what to do about it. A couple of years before, it was the rage to send kids to the United States. Everybody was doing that. We could afford it. The price of oil had gone up to thirty-five dollars per barrel. The economy of Iran had just moved up. Middle-class people were doing well.

At that time my mom invited all the elders of the family, plus another guy whose thoughts everyone respected. There was a big gathering, and then my mom brought up the issue, "Should I send him to the U.S.?" That guy's son was in the United States. They asked me questions. I never even sat in an airplane before so the whole concept of another place was very abstract. But my friends were going.

My mom said, "Why don't you go and see if you can get a passport and visa."

In three weeks I had my passport, my visa, and a ticket to go. I did it all by myself.

We had a good-bye party, and a lot of my relatives came. They were nice, and then the next day I just left. For me it wasn't a big deal, but for my mom it must have been hard. I sat in the plane with some guy who knew English, and he sort of took care of me.

At school I had learned grammar and a few words, but nothing that really helped me out. I had some writing on a piece of paper on how to make a collect call. You need an invitation, and I had one from my cousins who lived in Louisiana and who I had never met. She was three years older than me, and she had just got there three months before. I looked at the map and said, "Oh this is Louisiana and this is California," and "Oh, wow, there are two Washingtons."

Wow! Money All Over

I had one big piece of luggage; that was it. In 1979, I was seventeen, but I looked like I was twelve or thirteen. I went from San Francisco on a little airplane that flew low. It flew above misty, redwood trees. I never thought America would be like that. I always thought "high-rises." I had a dream about America before I came, and the dream was totally a western movie, and that's what we envisioned. Later I went to Universal Studios, and I realized my images. California was shocking and strange.

The first thing that was shocking when I got off the plane was that the airport was very small. I always thought America had no villages, that everywhere is New York. My cousin was living with a woman whose husband was a truck driver, and she was really skinny and kind of a nice-looking woman, very sexy, but she was driving a Ford pickup truck. She lifted up my luggage with one hand and bam! She dropped it into the truck, opened the door, and sat there as if it was nothing. That was the first shocking thing, to see a woman driving a truck and lifting up luggage just like that. Then she told me she had nine dogs and six cats, and that was another shocking thing because in Iran cats and dogs don't go together. A dog sees a cat and they run after it. So it's like how could that be, wow!

I wake up the next morning and see a lot of pennies scattered all over the place. "Wow! Money all over!" The place was really dirty with a lot of junk around, and they needed to vacuum that place. They had the TV on twenty-four hours, and that was very strange because in Iran you just have a few hours at night.

The woman had a kid. I totally connected with the kid, more than anybody else. He could somehow communicate; he was eight years old. We rode bikes together. He was teaching me a few words. I didn't stay there long, only a week; then I moved into an apartment by myself.

It was at the college, but this was the summer and the town was dead, so I had the place to myself. Then I had a roommate, Rodney. He was black and a basketball player, and he smoked pot. Rodney also had a girl-friend, so he was my first encounter with an American guy.

I'd never seen a black person in my life, so it's like wow! He was so tall and had big hands for a basketball player, and I was small for my age.

Sometimes I would go to his room, and he was smoking pot and offering some to me, but I would say, "No." I didn't know what it was, but it was kind of scary to me to hang out with somebody who did drugs. He listened to loud music. I was interested in the music because I really didn't know anything at all. I lived there three months. Then I found an American family, and I lived with them for a year.

The Family Was Totally into Multiculturalism

The family was very interesting and very difficult. I was culturally growing aware of codes and how things are supposed to be done.

The first time I went there, they must have thought I was really strange somehow. They were very nice. They had four kids: one daughter, who was in second grade, a son who was six years old, an older son who was thirteen, and the oldest son was fifteen, and I was seventeen. I shared a room with the older two, and they didn't like the idea. The woman went to Berkeley, and she was a sociology major, but she was also a housewife, and she was into the family; they had been in the Peace Corps. The husband had a Ph.D. The first day I had asked for some water, and it was strange for me that they didn't have cold water in the fridge. She just poured some water from the faucet and gave it to me. So it's like, "Can I have some ice? Ice?" So she has to go to the trouble, but she didn't want to do that. That's not normal. And then there were a couple of flies flying about. and I'm asking, "Do you have a fly swatter?" And then I'm running after the flies.

One time, my mom sent a gift. The family I stayed with didn't charge me for anything. They wanted to experience multiculturalism. To thank them, my mom sent me a little card with a gift, and I gave it to them. In Iran the custom is to say stuff like, "Oh it's not good, it's not good enough for you. You deserve more," so of course that's the only way I know to interact. She puts this carpet on a wall and she's all excited and says come see it. So I look at it and she asks, "Is this nice?"

I said, "No."

And she was freaking out. I kept saying, "No, this is not good." It was a beautiful carpet.

The boys were not really happy with the whole situation with me staying there. But after I left, we stayed in touch. The mother really loved me, and I loved them. They were my parents here. It was a very strange but enriching experience. I learned a lot about American culture.

I love the food. But that was another thing. In Iran they put a lot of rice on the plate; that's normal. The amount of rice that Americans eat here is just one portion of the plate. In Iran I could never finish all that rice. My mom always forced me to eat, and I was famous for not eating, and everybody was giving me a hard time. Here, I would finish the rice and then would go for some more and then she would say, "Oh yeah, he eats so much."

I remember before I moved in with this American family, I went on a camping trip with my cousin and some friends. We went camping in Canada. Later I realized I didn't understand the beauty, or I couldn't know how to enjoy it. I was very paralyzed. There is a mountain, and everybody was somehow connecting with it or with the wood or with the jungle or with the bear. But for me it was like walking in a vacuum in some way. For a long time, and it still somewhat continues, I have the problem of not making connections.

One thing I hated was the experience of high school.

I went in two different places. In the morning I would go to ESL [English as a Second Language], and that was great because there were people of all ages, all foreigners, and we connected. I had Japanese friends and Mexican friends and people from Laos and Vietnam. I got to know the world through that place. But then in the afternoon it was a different story because it was regular high school, and the other kids thought I was weird. They weren't used to foreigners. I wouldn't talk because they would make fun of my accent, or I was afraid that they would. It was very unpleasant. I was really passive and scared. But in the morning part I was very involved; it was like having split personalities.

I would walk home, and that was good. That's how I learned English. I started thinking in English. I would talk articulate English in my mind. But then nobody would understand me when I spoke because my accent was just so heavy, and I mispronounced things. I would buy a Snickers or something from the market, eat that before I get home. That was a problem, the whole eating thing. I didn't feel comfortable to just go and eat by myself. I never really felt at home, because I thought they were doing me a favor. I was not paying any money. The relationship wasn't well understood by both sides. I hated cats; they had nine cats. And I didn't have enough freedom. I liked to stay up late, but I couldn't. And I didn't listen to them. They wanted me to study harder or to do this and do that, and I felt, "Who are you to tell me?" So it was a strange relationship. But they really cared for me, especially the mom. She was into it. The other people, even the husband, really wasn't into having me there, but he had to go along with it. It was a very strange relationship.

A lot of times I wanted to get out and just be by myself, but then my mom would say, "No, stay, it's good for you."

Then the revolution happened in 1979 while I was with the American family. I remember I burned the shah's picture. They were like totally pro-shah, so I burned shah's picture in the fireplace. They got really pissed off at me. I hated the shah, and they'd say, "Oh, he is our friend." So politically they knew I was leftist, and they were really religious. One time she asked me, "Are you a communist?"

I said, "No."

She said, "Well because if you are, you have no place in our home, because we believe in God." They would go to church all the time, especially the mom. She had the power in the house; the guy had to go along with it.

I Got Shitty Grades and Blamed It on the Revolution

I was in Eureka with the American family, but then I went back to Arcata, and I went to college. I got my own place again, one of these apartments set up with two other roommates, but I had my own room. By then two of my cousins were living there also. So that was kind of fun and interesting, but I was supposed to study engineering; that's what they programmed me from Iran. I didn't have a good concept of what college was all about; nobody gave me good guidance. I was totally lost. My English still wasn't that good, so I took algebra, physics, and chemistry in the first quarter, and I failed miserably. My background wasn't that strong. A lot of Iranians would come here and do well in sciences. They didn't even need to know English. I never studied in high school either. So I wasn't one of them, and I failed badly. I got really shitty grades.

The first year that I was going to college, we would get money from home. Things that happened politically didn't really affect me, even when they took the American hostages. Arcata was a cool city. Everybody was smoking pot and there were teepees the students built; nobody cared. I never got a hard time.

I used that as an excuse when I had to take a test that I wasn't ready for. I would say, "Oh, it's the Iran revolution." It was total bullshit, but it worked.

They would say, "Okay, come and take the test again."

I would never go to my classes. I got lots of incompletes.

The first year was like that. But then I met some other Iranian friends, and I had an older friend who was thirty years old. I was nineteen, and I connected with him. We became very good friends. He was into photography and art. And that kind of opened the door. I became fascinated. I would paint a lot and draw a lot, and then I got fascinated with photography. By then I was always doing art. I never took art classes, but I knew the art department better than the engineering department, I hated the engineering department. So then I quit school in 1981 because the money got cut out and because of my grades. My family couldn't send me money. That started a new life. I lost my status. I became illegal. I had to work, and that was the hard thing because I'd never worked in my life, and I didn't know what to do. I worked in a gas station in Eureka for three months. And then I went back and lived with my American family, totally panicked.

My mom was panicking, so I cut all my relationships with them. I said, "This is the direction I'm going. Leave me alone."

I had tons of letters saying, "Oh, this is no good." I had to argue why I like art. Those big guys who sent me to the United States now were writing letters, "Art is not good. It's not going to make a life for you. Go study engineering."

I wrote them back giving them this logic that Van Gogh fascinated me. I made a tape and sent it to my mom. That must have been hard for her, because I just said, "You know I don't want to have anything to do with you guys. Don't even call me." I didn't leave any trace of myself for some time.

Then there was an incident with this Iranian photographer. It changed my thinking. This photographer and I were very close. Then his American girlfriend had gone and slept with somebody else so he told me, "Let's go. I'm gonna find this guy and talk to him," and stuff like that. I was really nonviolent, but then he goes and beats the shit out of the guy.

The cops come. They catch us and we are very proud, "Yes we did it." We confessed everything and they threw us in prison. The courts assigned me to a great lawyer who became my friend. The judge said at my hearing that I was not a bad kid, just stupid.

There Were All These Iranians and They Weren't Intellectuals

I couldn't get a job or anything. By then I felt shame concerning my mom, so I said, "Okay, I failed. I'll listen to whatever you say now." I had lost my confidence totally because my projects failed.

She said, "Go to your cousins in Louisiana. Get a job there and go to the school there, which is exceptionally easy."

A degree is so important in our culture. A lot of people were doing just that, basically buying degrees, and then they would go back and get jobs. Nobody has to know. "It's all paperwork anyway," was the idea. For my family, education is a big deal, education and a degree. "Okay since you couldn't do it properly," you know and blah blah, "just go there and get a degree and we will help you." So I went with that idea of being a failure. And then I didn't last more than six months in Louisiana. I hated it. It was miserable.

Louisiana was dead, and there were all these Iranians, and they were not intellectuals. There were no books around; there was no bookstore where we were in Louisiana. I was into reading Kierkegaard with my Japanese friend. In Louisiana, they just had malls, and they had one dinky bookstore with a little philosophy section of tiny books of Plato and Socrates. And so I asked, "Do you have Kierkegaard?"

They said, "Who?"

So, I'm like what, is this America also? So that was another face of America that I wouldn't know if I hadn't gone.

I believed that America was California. Living in Louisiana gave me a totally different exposure. I got a job driving for a caterer. They had offshore oilrigs, where people lived. I had to get the food at two o'clock in the morning, put it into the van with dry ice, and take it to these offshore places by different beaches in Texas and Louisiana. That was a good excuse for me to do a lot of driving. I saw a lot of different places in Louisiana and parts of Texas. It was amazing how life is different: life, culture, people, and especially the black and white issues.

I had black friends there. One time I went out with one of them to buy beer, and then the guy wouldn't sell any beer to us. And we didn't understand why. But apparently they didn't like it when white folks hang out with black folks, so the black guy was just saying, "Let's just leave."

I was aggressive, "No, why aren't you selling it to us?" I was going to pick a fight.

But then the guy just pulled me off and said, "Don't worry about it." But I wasn't getting it. Then later he said, "Yeah, we leave it like that or we'll get beat up." I had a couple of friends who got beat up because they had a white girlfriend.

I hated that school; there was no campus. It wasn't a *real* school. I said, "I'm not going to do it." I forged some documents in order to get money from Iran. My mom sent me two thousand dollars. That kind of saved me, because then I had money to leave Louisiana.

I Got Jobs at Two Gas Stations

While I was in California I would visit Berkeley and had lots of friends there. I really loved Berkeley, totally loved it. Still with my one large piece of luggage, I went to live with my cousin, who was the sister of the cousin who was in Arcata. I had one week to find a place on my own. Everyday I would look. I got lucky, and I got this small room in an old building where the landlord lived downstairs on College Avenue. It was a beautiful house, and I got one room upstairs: there were three rooms on the left, three rooms on the right, and each section had a kitchen and bathroom. That was the start of a new life for me. I was paying $120 rent a month, no deposit. The landlord gave me a bed and a little old carpet. It was cool. This is it! I opened my luggage and that was it.

By now I knew how to buy cheap things. Previously, I had accompanied my cousin—who was just there three months—to buy plates and some other needed things. She took me to Safeway and ended up spending $350 in the supermarket. By now, I knew better. So I went to the Salvation Army and bought some used dishes and set myself up.

I needed a job. I would walk different streets every day and go to every store. It didn't matter what. I would just go and ask for a job. I didn't care what it was, and I went into some really weird places. I went to a massage parlor; I went to a whorehouse. Within a week I got a job in a Round Table Pizza on University Avenue, and I stayed in that job for two years.

Then I started my life. I went to college, studying film and photography at San Francisco City College. I finished the program in photography and started studying film. Meanwhile, I changed my job. I was working in another Iranian-owned A&P minimarket, which was also a gas station. Then I started teaching art in a nursery school. Sometimes I worked seventy hours a week. I was working in two gas stations and the nursery. The wages were low so you had to put a lot of hours in. For a couple of years I did that and saved some money to buy the equipment that I needed. With the first paycheck I got myself a good camera, a Nikon. I still have it. I put together a darkroom in the closet; then my clothes were hanging from the ceiling. I had a light table and everything. The outside portion of my room was like a lab and further inside was the darkroom. I had a futon that I would pull out and sleep on at night. I was happy. And then I bought a new car. My mom came in 1985.

She didn't like my lifestyle. It was, "What are you doing with your life?" As soon as she arrived from the airport it is, "Okay let's think about what you are doing now. What is this?" So she brainwashed me to go and study engineering. Again I went to San Francisco City College and took calculus.

After she left I wrote a letter. I said, "I can't, you know. I tried. I really can't. I don't want to go in this direction, but I'll be fine, don't worry. I know what I'm doing." I finally went to college, got my bachelors in fine arts in 1991 from San Francisco State.

Immigration and Criminal Justice Weren't Hooked Up

Meanwhile I became involved with a big Iranian community. And I was totally a part of it. We did a lot of cultural activities.

Eventually I got my green card, and that solved a lot of problems. In 1988 they passed this law that whoever has been illegal for seven years can now come and get a green card. Because of that I could go to the university again and became functional. Before the green card, it was very difficult to move or get jobs as an illegal. That whole notion of being illegal makes you invisible in a society, so we just belonged to our own Iranian community.

At that time, immigration and criminal justice weren't hooked up to each other, so they didn't care about my court record.

I met somebody in 1991. For the first time I had a real relationship. She was an American. We moved in together.

I just got my bachelors in fine arts. "What am I gonna do now?" Then a friend of mine said that he had a cab in Seattle, and I should go drive his cab and make some fast money. He said, "You can make a lot of money, one hundred dollars a day, tax free."

I said, "That sounds good." I would work for six months to save up some money for grad school. So my girlfriend and I moved to Seattle and that was a disastrous project because my friend was bullshitting. The business wasn't good. I ended up not getting anything. He didn't even show up to give me his cab; we were both out of jobs, out of money, and I had to sell my car to have enough money for a month.

My girlfriend got some horrible job that she hated. I finally got a cab and started driving in a city that I don't know, and I'm horrible with directions. So that was another story; six months I worked there. But it worked out somehow. I made enough money to make it happen. My girlfriend moved to San Francisco to study in grad school. She got a place to stay, and I sent her money in August. After that I was just living in my cab, basically working twenty-four hours a day. And I made a lot of money that way. That was a great experience. And I shot some video that I'm working on right now, a documentary on Iranian cab drivers. Then I went to Iran for the first time after seventeen years.

Time Started Running and Catching Up

I said, "Okay now it's time to go back," and it basically took two years to catch up with Iran. In a way, time had stopped for me when I left. I felt like I was still sixteen. I wouldn't take myself seriously like an older, thirty-year-old guy, but I was acting like a kid and acting toward the people that I knew like a kid. There were kids who were five, six years old when I left, and now they were married, they had children who were in college, and they had pensions. So I had to grow up really fast. I also got bored really fast. Time started running and catching up. My brother had a wife and two kids that I hadn't seen. But it was amazing how fast this all happened; it takes two days to catch up on seventeen years.

In Iran, I did a lot of different work. We had a company with a couple of my friends who were in the same boat who graduated from San Francisco State. Those are the people I connected with, and we could trust and understand each other. We had an advertising company that in the end became disastrous because one of the guys, the Iranian-based partner, cheated us and took our money. But we made some television commercials.

My girlfriend wasn't happy about me going back to Iran, and we sort of broke up because she would ask, "Are you coming back in six months?"

I said, "No, how can I put time on these things?" In Iran I taught at the university. I taught in the philosophy department—art theory and art philosophy. I translated some articles and published some articles here and there; I got hooked up with Iranian intellectuals who wrote the first Iranian postmodern-oriented journal. It was a heavy-duty journal, and I was right there, knowing the people, being involved.

There I Got to Do What White Americans Can Do Here

This is the never-ending story because in Iran I did all this, but I was very frustrated with the society because it is not efficient. Here it's not efficient either, but the thing is that over there I got to do the things that the white Americans do here. Here I was always on the margin. I wasn't anybody. But over there I was accomplishing things, but I thought, "Oh, in America everything works good, everything is systematic, people don't lie to each other, people don't cheat each other."

So with that concept in my mind I hated it in Iran. After coming back and getting involved with the university, I understood what was going on underneath the film business. It's the same. Everybody is a backstabber; everybody's trying to get ahead somehow.

I came back here, my girlfriend picked me up from the airport, and I said, "I want to go back to Iran—right away!"

Not even after one hour. I was going crazy, crazy. After seventeen years, when I left America, I had no problem. I didn't have any emotional attachments to this place. Nothing whatsoever. Two years there, when I returned to America, I felt exactly the same way the first time. It's like a chunk of you is left behind. I used to walk on the streets here and have that distance, that feeling of not belonging. It was just so obvious. In Iran you walk and you feel this is part of you. It's in your fabric; you're part of this culture; they taught you Persian. They know and understand you. You see this guy with three kids and his wife, on his motorcycle driving in the wrong direction, but in a way, in a very strange way you have some kind of understanding about that. It doesn't shock you.

But here you see everybody walking, and I say, "Who are these people?" I don't have anything, so there's no connection. Stores, so beautiful, so nice, but I'm always distant from it; there is no attachment. But over there, I smell something from a store, bang! I see some visual thing.

I smell pee on the street, and it's "wow," that takes me back twenty years ago when I was a kid and I smelled the same things. That was very fulfilling. I went back to the same house when I was doing photography.

My teachers always said that I was a failure in photography, nobody would like my pictures because they were always gray and there was this distance all the time. And I always had in my mind to go and photograph that old house that I lived in because that was one of my nostalgic sources. When I went home, on the first night, I went to that garden and that was very good. I took pictures there; it was like, "Yes!" Nostalgia a lot of times is like a mirage. You go to it, and it's not there. But for me it was there. It worked in my heart. When I clicked something happened that had never happened here, and the pictures, when they came out, they happened. It satisfied me. It was something that I was longing for, and I felt right.

My Heart Is Split Culturally

It is impossible to know where I want to remain. In Iran, in a way it is much nicer because I had my station there, it was my home there, I was relaxed, and I had money to spend. I see the street, and I know everything. Iran is the same as it was twenty years ago. It's not like here, always constant change. It is impossible to answer where I want to remain. My heart is split culturally. Certain things here are extremely satisfying. One thing that frustrated me in Iran was that I wasn't learning. I felt like what you might call "sitting water." I was sitting because nobody challenges you. I was like the source of information for so many people, and that's sad. If I am the source of information, it's not because I'm good; it's because you guys are just so out of it. Some people enjoy that position—to be powerful in terms of status—but it really didn't satisfy me. I'm not after that. I realize that I need to learn: therefore, yet again I returned to America with my split heart to rejoin the quest for the unattainable.

SEVEN

Thuc Nguyen

VIETNAMESE-AMERICAN

In his thirties, Thuc Nguyen is small, darting, and worried—a wren. He acts as if he is trying to avoid harm. Dressed warmly in a plaid wool buttoned-up jacket and a brown wool cap with earflaps, he continues to wear the protective clothing even when indoors, as if wearing camouflage or prepared to flee. When spoken to, he answers shyly—sometimes writing his response to be better understood. I have known him for two years, but any time I ask him a question or try to be friendly, I feel that I cause him more anguish by being too loud, too nosy, and too American. Although his agitation shows when he runs out to smoke, I also sense that he appreciates that someone takes an interest in him.

Even though he is studying building construction, the only time he relaxes and loses his guarded look is when the subject of music is mentioned. Suddenly his face opens up, and he becomes assured. Music is an area that Thuc can address without personal embarrassment or personal pain. Music has saved him in Vietnam, rescued him in the refugee camps of Thailand, and provided succor for him in the United States. He is the choir leader of his church; the members are his New World family.

Music sustains him more than rice. The scores and notes are not the inscrutable tenses of the English language, but true "Esperanto" coming from the Almighty and returning back to him in bursting hymns of praise. For Thuc, when all the choirs of the different languages and cultures join together for Easter, he is truly part of the family of humanity, and he knows a home on earth. Even in the most desolate places and times, as in the internment camps, music has offered him hope and allowed him to dream and soar and to forget his daily embarrassments as a shy person in an inscrutable society.

That Was Not My Full Life

Before I went into hiding, I lived with my aunt in the country in the south. We lived on a farm that grew crops of wheat. I lived with my aunt for a few years, but that was not my full life. When both my parents died in 1972, my aunt took in my brother and me. An Australian army truck killed my father when soldiers accidentally ran over him. My mother died from a sickness that also killed one of my two brothers. At the time everyone died, I was only eight years old.

When my brother and I were older teens, this aunt helped us flee, although she did not want us to leave Vietnam, but we had to. It was very terrible there. Once before, I tried to leave the country, and for that I was put in jail for one year. I had tried to escape from prison several times.

Eventually, I made my last escape.

The Forest Has Many Trees

In jail, we are kept in a group of twelve people, and the police watched us all the time. If you go just about five minutes in the jungle, there is no way they can find you, no way to search. Our job was to trample the trees. And I tried to look at whether the police were unaware of us, then I ran.

After ten minutes, they knew I was not there, and they opened fire, and I ducked. But in ten minutes, there was no way they could arrest me.

The forest has many trees. When anyone escapes, they report the person's name to the city, which is about two hundred miles away. They reported my escape to the city of Saigon, but I lived very far from there, so the information never got back to where I was hiding.

My brother at that time was at home. He also had run away from jail.

Leaving the Motherland

Like every young man who has reached the age of eighteen, I had to take a physical exam and enroll in the army. The government required this law. Anyone who did not follow the law or refused to register was put in jail. I would have been caught if I refused the draft registration. I swear I'd rather be a prisoner than become a draftsman under the Vietnamese Communist regime.

By that time, 1982, I was forced to leave my family and move to a farm for temporary hiding. While I was staying at the farm with a country family, my brother had found the sole way to save me: to escape the country by a boat. Once the time had been scheduled, I left my homeland without hesitation.

On the way to the harbor, we encountered too much difficulty. We had to cross in the muddy fields and slippery banks. Some of us even slipped in the mud. After an hour, we reached the harbor. However, the boat had not shown up. We had to wait for it by moving back to the forest nearby the river. We moved because most police were patrolling the riverside. In the forest, we were miserable from mosquitoes. We had endured the cold and rain. The night was dark and full of fear. We waited until two in the morning.

One man with a black uniform appeared in front of us. "Let's go. Follow me," he said to us in a serious, whispered voice. We were all rushing after him. About fifteen minutes later, we all stood in a flimsy boat. This boat was about fourteen meters long and five meters wide. We were eighty-four people in the boat. We did not feel comfortable in the small boat. We could only sit where we were and could not move a bit.

The captain came up to the cabin and opened the cover of the hole. "Don't talk while we're traveling on the river," he said, then checked the cover. He did this because the police might be patrolling.

After five hours we reached the sea. Crazy waves began splashing onto the boat. We all fell to one side of the boat. For thirty minutes, the boat moved up and down violently. Most of us began feeling dizzy and seasick and started to vomit. After twelve hours, we could only see the tiny shape of the homeland. For three days on the ocean, we only saw the sky and the water. We went on for five more days.

I don't think we slept on the boat. Maybe we slept when we were so tired, just one hour or two hours, but we had to wake again because on the ocean no one can have good sleep. We just sat and did not move. For meals, we had dried food. Most people were fleeing the country for political reasons, but some of them wanted to make a better livelihood elsewhere.

Our boat had only enough fuel for one more day. The captain was busy checking a map to find our destination. Water and food were running out. The heavy wind sometimes pushed our boat the wrong direction. The boat might have sunk into the Pacific Ocean if it ran out of fuel.

Again the heavy wind came. Everybody was in a panic and screaming riotously. "Stop, stop screaming. The boat will sink if you go on yelling," the captain shouted, "Don't be afraid, people."

My heart was speeding faster and faster. I thought we would sink in just a few minutes because there was a terrible hurricane. It made us so afraid that nobody could feel hungry or thirsty. But fortunately, the hurricane calmed down an hour later. Everyone thanked God it was over.

The engine was stopping gradually because it was overheated. The captain stopped the boat temporarily to cool off the engine. We took a rest for two hours and then continued our journey.

Many people were worried and scared about how many more days the journey would take. Our lives would be in danger. I felt sorry and feared for us. Looking at the ocean, I imagined that the sea was a monster. It opened its mouth and waited to take our lives.

Surprisingly, we saw a tiny smoke line on the horizon.

"Oil driller. We've got it," the captain cried out. He assured us of this because he had experienced it in the navy. He steered the wheel straight to the destination. Everybody in the boat felt happy. The pressure of fear had blown out of their minds. Finally, it took six more hours to reach the oil driller.

The Malaysian navy saved us all. They brought us to the Pulau Bidong Island refugee camp just a few hours later. Thank God, we all survived. Our journey took six days in the ocean.

The Fish That Fly Were Wondrous to Me

On our trip, I can remember something good. I just looked out in the ocean and saw a great thing. I saw the fish that fly. That was wondrous to me. The people did not know each other before because we came from different parts of the country. But by the time we came to the island, we knew everybody and became friendly.

We had heard many incidents where pirates accosted people. Many of my countrymen were killed. The pirates steal jewelry, watches, and money. Some people have U.S. dollars. They steal it, and of course, they rape women and teenagers, some brutally. When they survive and come up to the island they told us their stories. A woman was raped in front of her husband, and when the husband tried to attack they killed him.

Many of the young women were missing. They would sell those girls into prostitution—terrible! The Thailand government tried to stop it, but it still happened.

There were a lot of people in the camps that had these terrible experiences. We were lucky. Most people who were mad at the pirates were forced to go by land. I'm not perfect with the geography, but they came from central Vietnam, and they tried to go to Malaysia, but before reaching Malaysia or Indonesia, they had to pass through the shore of Thailand. That was where they had to face the pirates.

The Police Were Cruel

Most of the Malaysians at the camp were police. There were no civilians. Most of the police were cruel because the people who lived in the island didn't have enough food for themselves. They wanted to have all the food on the island. If there was a coconut tree, and someone from the camp climbed very high to pick the coconut, the police caught this person. The police would bring him to the taskforce office and cut and beat him. The haircut punishment where they shaved off the hair was not so bad, but the beatings were. They even had a punishment where you had to serve them for one week in the office.

The food we received at camp was sent from many other countries. I was in the camp two and a half years. We had to live very simply. Life on that island was very difficult. Because we had relatives in the United States, we wrote a letter to them, and they helped us by sending money. But for many people they did not have anyone in another country, and they had to suffer terribly.

We had to go to school three days a week to learn English. We also had to do public work. I wanted to work for the church because I knew music. The priest then made a recommendation requesting me at the labor office. Many of the newcomers had to do the sanitation for the long houses. When the United States government accepted us, we moved from the island. My cousin from Connecticut sponsored us.

A Strange and Interesting Time in Connecticut

By the year 1985, I came to the United States with my older brother and lived in the house with my cousin, Ben, in Danbury, Connecticut. It was quiet and as peaceful as the countryside. Its population, of course, was not as crowded as New York. However, everything was strange to me, but it also became the most interesting time I ever had. I remember that fall. Three months after I came to America, I needed to go to school. There was an American nun who was Ben's friend. She helped show me how to apply to school. One morning, she came over to our house to visit. She talked about the process of entering school, which I was going to attend.

The bell rang, and Ben went to the door to greet the sister, who hugged him. They sat in the living room and talked to each other. Sometimes they had a big laugh as they talked. While they were talking, I sat at the table in the kitchen and dared not to move. I was afraid she would ask me something. I could hear them talking, but I understood nothing. I heard my name spoken, and I became nervous. I wanted to go from the kitchen to hide somewhere, but I could not because the kitchen door was facing them. They could see me as I passed.

I felt very embarrassed, and after a moment, Ben called me. "Thuc, are you there? Come up here. Sister wants to meet you."

"I'm coming," I said. My heart beat harder and faster. I did not know why, but I was ashamed anyway. Perhaps I could not even speak with a foreigner. I walked curiously like a girl. Perhaps someone standing by my side could hear my heart rumbling. How poor I was.

"Thuc, this is Sister Teresa," Ben introduced me.

"Hi, Thuc, how's everything?" she asked. I was completely puzzled by what the words meant. In the meantime, Ben smiled and looked at me and translated into my language.

"I'm fine." I answered with a trembling voice.

"Do you want to go to school?"

"Yes," I told her and forced a smile.

"Well, I think you can make an appointment with a doctor and ask him for a general exam first. I'll take care of it. Don't worry."

Two days later, she drove me to a doctor for an examination. I spent half a day to complete all health documents, the X-ray, blood tests, immunizations. The first important thing I had done by that day. She drove me home and stayed for awhile. Before she left, she informed me that the new school term would start the next week on Monday. She said if there was nothing to interrupt her schedule, she would bring me to visit my school that Friday. She was concerned about me because she thought I would have a problem finding the room.

On Thursday after we finished dinner, I thought, "Only four more days until the school would start," and my mind was too much worried.

Ben was busy taking a shower in the bathroom. The telephone rang abruptly. I began to feel nervous. Even though I was eighteen, I had never answered the phone before. I hastened to the bathroom and knocked. "Telephone, telephone, Ben," I said loud and fast.

Ben told me to get it.

"No, no, you do it." My words were tense.

"What the hell. I can't understand. You're as timid as a rabbit. Is it a tiger on the phone? I'll be right there in a minute," he said angrily.

I rushed to the phone. My heart was beating hard like a drum. Taking the receiver, I said in my low and whispered language, "Hello."

"Ben," the sound came from the receiver. I did not hear clearly. I only heard the word "Ben"; I understood that someone wanted Ben.

"You, you, you wait, okay," I said in a silly way. Ben rushed out of the bathroom. His hair was still wet, and even his head had unfinished shampoo. He ran up to me, frowning at me a certain way.

Ben told me that I was holding the receiver upside down.

A few minutes later, Ben came over to me. He said, "Sister Teresa cannot take you to school tomorrow as she promised last Tuesday. She'll be busy. I'll drive you there. She said you must bring the big yellow envelope and show it to Mrs. Brite, your counselor in Room A250, but don't worry, I'll take care of it."

The next day came, and Ben had to call his company to be excused for a sick day off. He drove me to the school and met my counselor at Room A250. We had found it. My cousin opened the yellow envelope and took out some of my documents and gave them to her.

She gave Ben a piece of paper and reminded him, "This is a class schedule. Keep it, follow it, and do all the classes as indicated." She said, "This is your school bus number, 397. The bus will stop at the funeral home on Main Street to pick you up every morning at 7:15. It drives you home. Make sure you come on time or you'll miss the bus."

I Dared Not to Ask Them. How Poor I Was

When I came home, happiness and worry had been mixed up in my mind. I was happy because I was going to school, and I was worried because I could not speak English. I would get lost or late to class. There were so many floors, rooms, and buildings.

I wondered if there were any students who spoke Vietnamese. The next day, Monday, I woke up with so much worry; I could not eat breakfast. I looked at the clock that hung on the wall. It was 6:50. I hurried to take my book bags and left the house. In the fall, early in the morning, the sky was filled up with smog. I felt a little bit chilled.

After ten minutes, I walked and reached the funeral home on Main Street. There was nobody there but me. "Is this the right place?" I asked myself. Taking out a piece of paper from my pocket, I checked it. "Yes, it's right," I thought.

I glanced at my watch. It was seven sharp. Perhaps I came too early. I looked around, and there were two people coming toward me. "They are students, aren't they?" I asked myself.

These two young guys had book bags on their shoulders. They stood in the same place in front of the funeral home. I was sure that they waited for the school bus. I walked around and around. I wanted to ask them to make sure they were going to the same school as mine. I dared not to ask them. How poor I was. This time, I risked myself and came closer to them. "Excuse me. You go to Danbury School," I asked with hesitation and shame.

"What kind of Danbury school, high school or university school?" one of them asked.

"High school," I answered.

"Yes, we do," he said.

Asking them for more, I went on. "What school number do you have?"

"What do you mean by school number?" he asked.

"Oh no, no, school bus number, I mean," embarrassing myself.

"It's 397," he said.

These two young guys were handsome and very kind. They spoke to each other very fast. I couldn't understand it. They asked my name and how long I had lived there and some other questions. Even though I could not understand all the questions they asked, they tried to understand me. They looked nice and friendly.

As we were busy talking, the bus came slowly toward us. We got on the bus. During the way to school, we seemed quiet. I wanted to ask them questions, but I was afraid to ask them something that they could not understand. Therefore, I just sat quietly except when they asked me something.

After about twenty minutes, we reached the school. On the first day of school, there were many students stuck in the hallway. I had seen many of them in the front of the school. I could see their faces appeared happy. They gave hugs and kisses to each other when they met their old friends again.

Time was up. The bell was ringing. Everybody came into the classes. I took out my schedule and looked at it. The first period was ESL3 in Room G412. I began to look for it. I had a problem because I had found the wrong section. Instead of section G, I found section A. "Oh, God, where is it?" In the hallway only a few people remained.

I did not find my classroom. Then the second bell rang. A huge crowd of students rushed out of their classroom.

I wondered if school was finished. But they did not go home yet. They went to class again. They changed to another class. I began to blame myself.

Why I did not ask somebody for help? How clumsy I was. I felt disappointed and hated myself.

What's the Problem, Boy?

There was this lady walking toward me. She looked like a teacher or staff member. "Excuse me, Mrs.," I said in a very soft, low voice, but she did not hear and kept on walking. I tried to walk closer to her. "Excuse me, Mrs.," I said again. This time my voice raised louder, so the lady got it.

She stopped walking and turned to me. "What's the problem, boy?" she asked.

"I can't find my classroom." I showed her the schedule.

"Oh, your second period should be in Room A120. Do you know where it is?"

I shook my head. "Follow me," she led me, and I felt a little bit better. However, after this class, I would not know when the next one happened. Room A120 was full of faces.

"This young man is a freshman student. He can't find his classroom. I helped him find it."

I remained standing at the table. Many students in the classroom stared at me. I became nervous and very embarrassed. Most students were Americans. She marked my presence. "Have a seat in the second row," she said very fast. She did not look at me, but I did not understand what she just said, so I kept standing there. She walked directly to the chair and touched it. "I said you sit here." The students' burst of laughter filled up the room. The teacher continued with the rules of the class. She spoke too fast. I did not understand anything.

About five minutes later, the bell rang again. The class was over. Students went out of the classroom. What the hell, school runs so fast, I can't believe it. "I can't study each subject in fifteen minutes," I said to myself. The classroom was empty except for the teacher, and I remained. I began to ask her why the class was so short.

She said, "Classes are short on the first day of school. Other days should be an hour per each subject." That was one interesting thing I learned on the first day of school.

I Was Nearly Crying and Insisted, "Please Drive Me Home, Sir"

Most of the time, I was late to every classroom the first day of school. The last bell would ring longer to warn the ending of a class. Every student was happy and rushed out of the school. The school bus had been waiting in a long line in front of the schoolyard. Students began searching for the bus.

I did not find mine because I couldn't find the piece of paper with the bus number. I searched all my pockets. I found nothing except a five-dollar bill. I opened my schoolbag and fumbled everything. When I was busy looking for it, many buses had already moved out of the school. "Is it gone? Where is it?" I started to rush to any bus that still remained there, and I searched for the number as if I knew it. How could I guess? There was a bus still waiting there. It was my last chance. The bus was moving out of the school. It passed through many strange streets I had not seen before. "Where in the hell is he going?" I dared not to ask the driver. I just sat still and peered to see if there were some places I knew. The students in the bus got off and off and the bus went up to a curve with a lot of trees growing by the edge of the pavement. A student got off. Now I was the last one on the bus.

The driver asked me, "Where do you live, boy?"

I told him Danbury.

"Well, this is Bethel. It's not Danbury. You should get off here, boy," he said unpleasantly. I felt very confused right then.

I was nearly crying and insisted, "Please drive me home, sir."

"I'm sorry, this is the last stop, so I can't," he said and opened the door to let me out.

I got off the bus and did not know where I was. I just walked and walked on the strange pavement. I had been walking for two hours on the unknown streets. I kept on walking until I reached a cornfield. "Goddamn it, it's a farm."

Again, I walked to the place I got off the bus. In the farm there was little chance to see any cars passing through. I became hungry. My throat was dry, and I was thirsty and tired. Finally, a car ran toward me. The driver came slowly and closer to me. The old man in the car beeped his horn.

He wanted to ask *me* something. "Excuse me, do you know where Harrison Street is?" he asked me.

"No, I have no idea," I told him.

The old man continued to talk, "I've been lost for an hour."

"You, you're lost," I said, and had a big laugh.

The old man spoke unpleasantly. "What's funny?"

"I'm sorry, I'm lost, too."

He seemed to understand my situation. "Oh, Danbury," he went on. "My sister lives there. Come on in. I'll give you a ride."

The First Few Years I Had to Communicate with People in English,
and I Couldn't Speak English

That day was the beginning of my life in an American school. Everything was new and strange to me, but it was the best, most interesting day I ever had in my life. My cousin and my brother worried about me, and they didn't know where I had gone. They just waited for me, and I just entered the house, and they asked me where I had been.

"How come you come home too late?"

I told them that I got lost.

"How come you don't call?"

"But I don't have a phone, that's why."

The first few years, I didn't have any Vietnamese people to contact, but most of the people I came in contact with were Americans or foreign people, and I had to communicate with them in English, and I couldn't speak English.

My cousin, he paints houses. My brother now works in a machine shop that makes metal parts. He lives in Danbury. Right now I live in the Bronx. When I came to the United States, I lived in Connecticut for five months. Then I moved to New York, and I've stayed here. My brother came to New York. One month later he moved back to Connecticut because he got married. I'm working in the Bronx for a small business, delivering material.

The Spanish, the English, and the Vietnamese Choir

When I was sixteen years old, I had a chance to learn music for only three months at this seminary in Vietnam. The director of music asked me to help him with the choir rehearsal. For the first time I rehearsed. A few months later, I left the country, and when I came to Malaysia and the refugee camp, I sang in the choir. I taught myself how to make musical arrangements for the choir. Then I learned the song of the seminary—all that music I learned by myself. Music makes me fortunate.

Now in the Bronx, I study and lead a Vietnamese choir. But we don't have our own place. The church belongs to Spanish and English people, so we are assigned a special, different hour. At Christmas, the whole choir gets to rehearse together. We get to perform at their Christmas and Easter. When we practice and sing together, it is brightness. The Spanish, the English, and the Vietnamese choir unify and we all sing together, our voices swept up into the roof and then the sky.

EIGHT

My Le

VIETNAMESE-AMERICAN

The plastic-fantastic malls of franchised Maryland seemed an unlikely place to find a Buddhist monk leader from a secret sect. This religious order is called Nga Mi Son Phat Gia Queyen. According to My Le, its name could only be whispered out loud for the last three hundred years, but its existence goes back to the first century. I was going to meet a holy leader who had successfully adjusted to the American way of life. I couldn't help comparing his journey with Thuc Nguyen's, a fellow countryman, who found the American transition difficult but paradoxically found his own spiritual succor in religious music.

Off the main highway of Burger Kings, Foot Lockers, and Sleepy Mattresses, there was a parallel universe: a small strip mall that contained a Vietnamese restaurant and a pizza parlor that was also being run by a Vietnamese family. Three glossy-headed children of the owners played in the doorways of the eating *establishments. Next to the two restaurants, sharing the same parking lot, was the Spiritual Mountain Martial Arts Center.*

According to their self-published book:

> *The Buddhist Nga Mi Son Phat Gia Queyen group's training ground in Vietnam was a place of solitude, ferocious animals, and constant changing weather, which could be lethal to humans. The disciples were taught with the external and internal art of surviving, to resist attacks and to protect one self. Since this was taught secretly to disciples who renounced the worldly life, the great concern was that the sect was at risk of becoming extinct with the demise of the master.*

My Le bowed in greeting as he came forward dressed in a red cloak; a wispy moustache adorned his round beaming face and smooth skin. I would guess his age to be in the mid-thirties. He told me he could talk to thousands. He could walk into fire and be protected. He had learned all this, yet he was still willing to take the time to talk to any individual at any time. His mission was to reach the spiritually empty youth in the Baltimore area.

My Le had gained his center in America by working at several fast-food jobs. "All I need is a bowl of rice a day, nothing else." His air-conditioned office was filled with computers and photocopy machines. I gestured to all the electronic items.

"They are for my brothers." His face was illuminated.

Given Away at Five

In my country, according to the essence of a superstition, if you have five sons, you are raising five white demons. That means with so many boys competing there will be bad luck in the future. Mine is a Catholic family, but I was given to my master because he was a monk of a secret Buddhist sect. He came to the village in which my family lived. He just came by my house, and he would talk to my mom for two months about what was best for her boys. You know, a woman always worries about her children's future. A person might have some fears that are not real, but if the possibilities are repeated in her ear, she might take a chance. As it turned out, my mom just gave me to him to make a future in the spiritual world.

I was five years old. At that time, I didn't know anything at all about what was transpiring. Mom told me later about what had happened. I was to follow my master where he would lead me, and in the beginning he would bring me back home for a while, and then I would follow him again.

The Inside Memories of My Mom

I did not really miss my family. In other words, my master was very powerful. He knew how to train me in how to live alone but still be loving toward my family, so leaving really didn't bother me that much. You love your mom, you love your brothers and sister, you remember them, but you don't suffer with your feelings if you stick with someone very powerful. That is why I followed my master for many, many years.

And I really loved my mom. I don't feel that I missed her very much. A couple of years after I left the country, she passed away, and then I started the feelings of missing her. Right after my mom died, then everything just came back to me, and I felt that inside memory of my mom—I really needed her.

The Final Lessons

My master died two years ago. I am really lucky because I knew that he was about to pass away. Therefore, I came back to Vietnam, and I spent his remaining time on earth with him. When he died, he was eighty-seven. He had always treated me like his own son.

My master told me that he had to go, and then he taught me the final lessons: about living, about how to be happy. and how to treat all people right. I don't know if you believe in our spiritual ways or not, but my master taught me there is no death. That death is just a myth that you're born with. We are really, really strong, and we follow him to learn how to offer that gift to all the people, no matter who the person is. No matter how old and what is in the person's past, they can learn to get help and help others.

Mr. Johnson is one of the pupils here. I met him five years ago. I show him; I talk to him. He was hunting for something. I offered him spiritual help as well as martial arts.

The last message that my master said, "You have to take care of young people. I took care of you when you were young, so you have to look down and see that boy as you were and take care of him."

That is the seed my master planted inside my mind. When I came here, I realized that Asian martial arts would be the path to bring young people into contact. In that way, I have a chance to talk to them, to understand them, so I see martial arts in this country as a transportation to link together all the young people and then to have a chance to sit side by side and find out what is happening. There was a young man who met me about a year ago. Now he has stopped the gang violence he was involved in, and now he tries to be a monk like me and have all young people come to join us. Maybe the reason martial arts generally work in pairs is so that you learn to communicate and reach out to the partner.

Ours Is a Secret Sect and the Name Was Not Said out Loud

Thanks to the planning and power of my master, during my exodus from Vietnam I didn't have to suffer the tremendous hardships of many of my countrymen. I did not face Communist soldiers, pirates, or a rough sea. My master knew how to avoid all trouble, so even during all the years we traveled throughout our countryside, we were never captured, so I never have been inside of a prison. Spiritual practices weren't allowed in our country. Mine is a sect that nobody knows. It was only since the last two generations that we were allowed to say its name out loud. Under Communism, religion is forbidden. But nobody really knows about ours because it is a secret sect, and the name is seldom spoken. In our country, if you are a normal person, you have to do the job of serving in the army because you have to protect the country. As a monk, I didn't perform that task, but often the soldiers searched for us to try to capture us. We had to hide ourselves frequently, and my master had to devise plans for escape.

We didn't live in the same village for very long. We moved often. We traveled from village to village; when my master was in trouble, we had to move to an even smaller village. He did not live in a temple. He did not even live in a house. He had to keep traveling. He had keen senses to do his job. He knew whenever a village had needed him, and he would come.

There were other disciples my master trained and turned over to the villages when he departed. Even though there were often children around him, I was the one who always stuck with him and got to go wherever he needed me.

During this time my four brothers and my sister were okay. They were really fine at home because my mom was a businesswoman, and my father was a dentist. I don't know the whole story because my father never talked about it, but in 1975 when our country fell to the Communists, they captured my father. He was in jail for four years. Since my mom was a businesswoman, she was able to take care of the family while my dad was in prison.

The Soldiers Surrounding the Camp Were Good Protection

My master decided that I should come here for freedom. He knew he would miss me, but if I was able to get here and have more freedom, it would be what he really wanted for me, so that is why he decided for me to leave the country.

This was bad for him, but good for me. I know my master; whenever he sees good for someone, he just does it to help him, whether it is bad for him or not. I know when you give your children to someone else—if you're a mom, you miss your child, you want to talk to that child every day, but this is done because the mother wants a future for her child where he will be safe. And that was the way of my master as well as my mom. I came here and then later my three other brothers also came here.

I traveled from Vietnam by boat to Thailand, and I lived there for about a year and a half. I was in a small camp for immigrants. It was really good protection, because all the soldiers were around there. I'd say that millions of people my age have made this escape. I came at age twenty-five without any nightmares or anything. At the camp, they respected me because I was a monk. I am really good at fortune-telling, and I had to read people's palms. All these skills I learned from the master helped me to get along with everyone who surrounded me. The master taught this to all the lads: "People will come to try to kill you; learn how to be with them." I think we are lucky, because we learned tools and skills to survive and be happy under any condition.

When I left the country, I was not just thinking of my master but of my family because I knew that I might never have the chance to see them again. I didn't know what the future would be.

Work, Work, Work

In this country, I was by myself for a few years. But then my three other brothers came; Mom just let them go. I left the country with my master's help. My brothers left the country with Mom's aid. When they came here, I was able to help them find work.

My first job in this country was at a nursing home washing dishes. Once I learned a little English, I went to the floors and helped the patients pick good food from the menu. I have had a total of seventy-five jobs over here during the last seven years. I have worked at Roy Rogers and 7-Eleven. I worked all the time except for the times I was in school. I hold onto my dream. My dream is to try to get several karate schools with temples so I can have all the people around so that I can teach them spirituality. I need the karate schools for a hook for the young people so that they will come and listen. If I just talk, they will ask, "Who is this?" But I want to tell them who I am. The first seven years, I was working, working all the time. After school, I worked eighty hours a week. One of the reasons I labored so much was because I had nothing else to do. I just shared a room with a Vietnamese family.

The Lutheran Church sponsored me here for six months. After that, I left the association, and I took care of myself.

I just kept on doing all kinds of jobs. All the time, I still held on to my dream. I never thought it might not happen. I talk to myself all the time about it. About five years ago this man came to the 7-Eleven store where I was working. I saw that he had a T-shirt that said, "Martial Arts, Kim Studio." I ask him, "Do you know martial arts?"

He said, "Yes. Talk to me sometime."

I said, "Okay." I went over to his office, I introduced myself, I said I knew martial arts. He gave me an hour lesson every week. So since then, I was mainly a student there. I learned how to teach martial arts. I have been teaching this for a long time, but in this culture, the way of educating is different. In our country, in martial arts, if the student doesn't remember something, the instructor might slap him, but here we teach children by really talking to their subconscious. You have to know their behavior, their skills and talents, by seeing the good inside them. I learned this approach from the man in school. I figured these methods out, so now I do all kinds of schooling, but it is easy with American culture. Sometimes I still figure stuff out between Vietnamese culture and education and American education. I see both as good; I have to pick the best things from both sides and put them together.

Too Many Choices

The only part of the American culture that I don't like is that there is too much freedom for children to pick what they want. Sometimes they might go in the wrong way. They have so many choices, but you know children. They don't really have a good mind yet, so maybe they choose the wrong way. Yet freedom is also good for children; it teaches them to be stronger and to build up their skills. Give them the freedom to choose, but still direct them a little bit. I saw a teenage runaway who had too much freedom as a little boy, and as he grew up he wouldn't listen to his parents anymore. That is not good. The parents have to direct them.

In Seven Years: A Beauty Parlor, a House, a Martial Arts Academy, a Book on Spirituality

The only prejudice I personally experienced was when I worked at Roy Rogers. The Spanish people, they tried to separate me. They pushed me to the back, to wash dishes and fry the chicken, and they spoke Spanish all the time, but I did whatever I could to make money. But I knew that I was able to do something else besides washing dishes. I know myself, but they didn't give me a chance. So I worked there for six months, and then I left to get another job, quit that job, and then my brother came over. I worked with him finding jobs. I went to 7-Eleven. Finally, I went to the *Washington Post*, and I delivered the paper every morning. Seven days a week, I got up at two in the morning, rode in the big truck, and then I became the distributor. Then the *Washington Times* had a job, and I applied for it and got it. My brother and I shared the money together, and

I got a studio—my brother got a beauty shop. We accomplished this in seven years.

We bought a house roughly one year ago. I don't know much about money. I'm not supposed to care for money because I am a monk. But I have to take care of my brothers. All four brothers had to move all our finances together to buy a house for forty thousand dollars.

Now we are looking for the second school. I've got this school in my mind, but I let my brother take care of it. I don't have any money. I don't need money, so now my brothers take care of all the financial aspects. Recently my brother told me, "We're okay on the second school."

Personally, I can get by on two hundred dollars a year. I need money only to buy rice. I don't have to wear any kind of clothes. My younger brother, we're the same size, so I just use his. He gets the equipment we need for the school. They made me free now. I don't work at any outside job. I just wish one day I can get the temple that my master dreamed of, so we can help all these children.

My brother says, "Okay, we'll do it when we have the money. We cannot ask the people for donations right now." In the meantime, we work. The central idea that I have learned from my master is to make tools, so this is what we are doing right now.

The best thing about being here is I have more chances, more potential to do what I love. Also it is really good to see all the different people in this country. In my country, there is no chance for me to see black people, Indian people, Caucasians. I see more people, I understand more people. Now I have a Korean student and a Japanese student; I have various cultures coming together. I think this is a great country.

My two older brothers have finished college already, and the youngest one is still going. We took a test and are already American citizens. The one thing we have to be is American citizens in order to go back to our country or there is trouble.

Back in Vietnam

I'm going back to Vietnam to try to help them. I will try not to carry money back to the country, but I will try to bring knowledge that shows the common, good relationship of all cultures. It doesn't matter how bad the education in the countries is, how bad the economy is. We are just talking about human beings, and I think all the cultures of our world should move closer together.

Here in America

Most Vietnamese left the country just for freedom, and when they came over here and they made a lot of money, they forgot to give their children a good education. They work nights and they work days and they work all the time, and they have less time with their children. Their children are growing up with whoever is around the neighborhood. When the children grow up, fourteen, eighteen, nineteen, the parents are still work-ing all the time to buy a little house, then a big house, new car, but they don't take care of their children well. What happens if their children get a gun and do some stuff they don't like? Then they don't know how to deal with American culture or the situation. Their children speak English, so therefore they are disconnected; they do not understand each other well, and the children just run away and never learn the Vietnamese cul-ture. I feel bad about it. I'm really trying to make people spend more time with their children and not just make money to buy a big house. Success in business is good, but if you lose the children, it is not good. That is why I am trying to help the Vietnamese people, so they will have a strong community like the Jewish people or the Chinese. The young don't know their country. There is no school of Vietnamese.

At this point, the Vietnamese just work for their material goals. They are not yet working for the community. Now we must try to bring the people together to listen.

NINE

Rosemond Reimmer

GHANAIAN-AMERICAN

Rosemond wears an intricate hairstyle of thick coiled black braids with interwo-
ven golden extensions implemented in geometric patterns. The ends are capped
with beads. It is a splendid work of art. Weaving is a tradition for her people. Her
cheekbones are high, and she projects a strong white smile. If she had height, she
could be a model.

Immigrating to the States, Rosemond had to deal with many cross-cultural
adjustments in her own family as well as in the new nation. Besides having to
adjust to the differences between country and city living, she had to get used to
the presence of her previously absentee father and a half-sister from another tribe
who did not even speak the same language.

Her mother was a strong role model in independence. She worked hard at a
fast-food restaurant, and she noted that her mother came from a region where the
people were known for "speaking out." Rosemond said that she was from the Ga

tribe, "the best tribe," which only makes up 8 percent of the 99.8 percent black Africans in Ghana. The major tribe is the Akan, which makes up 44 percent (http://www.nationmaster.com/country/gh/people). Transporting the belief in tribal superiority and the concept that minority means special might have given her the inner confidence to leave home to go to boarding school with students of a different race and economic class.

Even in her adult life, Rosemond had to make additional cross-cultural adjustments to the father of her children. He is a Jamaican. She had to try to fig-ure out male/female differences, cultural differences, and the idiosyncratic details that make an individual unique.

Rosemond thought of her homeland in bucolic terms even though she sold items in the market at the tender age of four and had gone hungry when her father took off for America. When she spent the summer in Ghana, she could not re-adjust. At night mosquitoes buzzed in her ears. She could not get cold bever-ages when she wanted them. The bed that slept four people was uncomfortable. Nevertheless, she is now trying to buy land and build a house there for her future. Her mother and father have also purchased land to that end. This con-tradiction is evident in many immigrants' stories. They retain the goal of achiev-ing their initial fantasy of home ownership in their native land even though they themselves have changed.

In 1999, the Newark Museum showed a film of the populace of Ghana with their straight regal posture, dressed in their fanciful, colorful weavings. They walked as if they were queens and kings on their native soil. That seemed to be the key to Rosemond — she was a queen in exile.

The Crab Man Collects Bad Kids

In Ghana, if you're getting bigger and still wet the bed, they do something to scare you out of that habit. The family would get a potato sack, and they would put little creatures into it. I don't remember exactly what types of animals they were, but I think they might have been crabs. The little critters would be moving in the sack, and the adults would tell you that inside the bag were the little bad children who peed in their beds. Also, this peddler would come around to the village with a wriggling sack, and the parents would tell us bed wetters that this man collected bad kids.

Every time, as soon as I knew I had peed in bed, I would run over to my grandmother's house. I knew she would protect me. She didn't live that close, but it was within running distance when you were scared. Most of the houses were one story and were arranged in a circle with some land in the middle, which everybody shared. Everybody who lived in that area used one bathroom.

Behind the school was a cemetery. I was really petrified of cemeteries and death or anything spooky like that. In my country, they tell tales that normally have a lesson to them, and most of the lessons are to scare you not to do something. That is the whole point of our stories.

I never went to the outhouse at school unless I really, really had to because it was right behind the cemetery, and you could see through a hole outside to the graveyard with the headstones.

Collecting the Sister from Another Tribe

I lived with my younger brother and my younger sister. I also had another sister who was older than me, my father's daughter. She lived with her mother far away in another part of the country. They were from a separate tribe.

I don't remember ever seeing her in Ghana, but when we were leaving to come here, my new sister came with us. I remember my mother telling me that my father had to travel such a long way just to go fetch her so she could travel with us.

That union was never a marriage. My father was living with this woman. Until recently I never knew this, but my sister's mother was related to my father through marriage. It was only through marriage, but in my country, if you live in the same house—and they lived in the same house—it is really taboo. Because of that, they weren't allowed to marry, so when she had her baby my father had to leave.

My family is from the Ga tribe, and my sister is from "Aiebc" [pronounced with a click sound]. I really wouldn't know how to spell that, but it's like the "Aiebc" tribe. It's a different tribe, and all Ghanaians dislike that group.

The main reason why we disliked them was the simple fact that they were different tribes. I think this might have developed from the past as a survival of the fittest or something. Ghana people are very prejudiced, even though we're all black. They say the "clicks" [Aiebc] are evil, mean people, and they do a lot of bad voodoo. But they are also the recipients of good stereotypes. They are said to be very good at the wraps; when we do our hair sometimes, we wrap it with the cloth. They're known to be very good at making inventive styles with the hair cloth.

Since I'm from the Ga tribe, I don't know of any prejudice against my group, but Gas are the people who are most prejudiced against others, because they're supposed to be number one—the best. They believe they are the elite. But I know the area where my mother's mother is from is known to have "a lot of mouth." They know how to curse people and talk back to people.

My uncle lived in a house right next to ours, and I think there were like five or six families that used the one shower and the outhouse.

Most people have regular jobs in the city. We lived near Teshi [Kumasi], which is the main city, and it was not as agricultural as other towns. My uncle does construction. He just finished building his own house in Ghana. He mainly works making stuff from wood. When he was in Ghana, my father was a trash person.

My father has a degree from here, but my mother only went through high school in our country. My uncle, I don't know what kind of degree he had. For my country, he's pretty well off. He has two or three houses. He has a farm, and his kids go to boarding school. In Ghana, most of the people who have enough money send their kids to boarding school. Even the little kids go to boarding school. I went to public school. It was within walking distance. It was through the government.

My Wares Were Little Candies

When I came here, I didn't know one word of English, so because of that, they put me in first grade. I was in second grade in my country.

In my country we had to wear uniforms, and the girls had to cut their hair short; the guys had to wear their hair really short to the scalp. It's the style here now, but once upon a time, it wasn't. When I first came to this country, my hair was cut short like that. They used to call me Bald-Head. They teased me to death, and sometimes I would even wear a hat to school, and I would refuse to take it off inside.

Because of the culture and the society here, you can't really let little kids go out to the store alone, but back home, I walk to my grandmother's by myself. It was pretty far. Here you can't just walk to a certain place. You have to take a train or something. In Ghana we had the freedom as a child to walk anywhere.

Back home as a young child, I went to the market and sold stuff to make money. Mainly my wares were little candies or fruits or cakes or something you make in the house. There was one market where everybody went. Everybody goes to buy things you need for the house: foods, clothes, whatever. People from the different villages will come there. It's a central market. It is a very, very long walk from my village. Normally they have taxis that go back and forth. My mother did not go; I did. My grandmother makes her living by selling the hot peppers, the little red peppers, tomatoes, fruits, and other garden stuff.

My grandmother stayed on in Ghana when we emigrated. She just recently came to this country. She is here now, but she is returning this summer. I'll be going back with her.

America is like this big planet in the sky. It's such a wonderful, spectacular place to come to. America is everybody's dream. Normally one person will go over and get settled, and then they would send for the rest of the family. My father did that. He came and lived here for a long time. He was here for about seven years before we actually joined him.

I Am Not Going to Leave You with Anything

My father sent back some money but not very much. I remember my mother telling me that it was really hard for her when he left. He had told her before he left that he was not going to leave her with anything, and she thought he was joking. But when he did, he didn't leave one dime. Not one dime! It was really tough for us. I remember my mother telling me that sometimes she wouldn't eat; if there were food, she would just give it to us kids. I remember her always sending me to my uncle's house to get food for us to eat.

We never received any letters. But every once in a while, and not very often, my father would send a trunk with stuff in it such as clothes and shoes and other items that we could use. All the neighbors came to visit because once they saw that something came from America, everybody would come to the house. They would say, "Oh, let me see this," and everybody would take what they wanted, and by the time they left, there was almost nothing. Yes, because anything from America was like gold. Everybody wanted something from America, even if it was a piece of thread.

When we were still in Ghana, we didn't know the clothing was not new. They looked good to us. But when I came here, after a while, I realized the difference, that they were mostly used clothes from secondhand stores.

My family knew that my father would be going, but exactly when wasn't really planned out. When the opportunity came, he just took off. In the beginning, my mother hadn't heard from him, and she thought he had been killed.

Most likely, he had saved up some money, or someone sent him a ticket. He wasn't illegal. He had a visa. Now he is a citizen. I think that is when he sent for us, after he got his citizenship, and so we got our citizenship through him.

Where Did That Come From?

When we immigrated, I had never been to an airport, and I had never seen white people before, so I didn't even know they existed. At the airport, I remember seeing this little white girl. She had blond hair, and her skin looked so white to me, and I just remember staring and staring and staring at her, and I was thinking, "Where did that come from?" It was so amazing to me.

On arrival, I remember the bridges, and I remember going through this bridge with all the steel, and I was awed at that. Also, it was at night, so all the lights in the city were visible when you're driving on the bridge.

We lived in Harlem up at 133rd Street. It was weird, because we went to a supermarket right down the street. In Ghana, people travel to an outdoor market, but this was so different because in the supermarket in Harlem, there were lights, and it was in a building. I remember one time we went shopping. My younger sister was there, and my mother had asked her if she wanted something. My sister saw the cat food with the picture of the cat. She liked cats, so she wanted to eat that food. She didn't realize it was cat food.

We lived in a tenement. In the old days, apartments used to be much bigger than they are now. We had three bedrooms, a kitchen, a separate dining room, and a living room. It was pretty big. My father lived there with a man from our country. Most of the time people rent together and they shared. My father knew him from our country, and this guy introduced us to Chinese food. When I first ate the food with the little onions cut inside—and it had that fried taste with soy sauce—oh, it was so good to me. But now it just doesn't taste the same. I swear it!

She Would Shake Her Head from Side to Side,
Not Understanding a Thing

It was tough with my new half-sister. I didn't get along with her, or rather she didn't get along with me. I guess she felt sort of out of place. I think she was probably a bit jealous of me, too, because her mother wasn't there, and also, she didn't speak our language. She spoke her tribe's language and we spoke Ga, so she didn't understand us, and we didn't understand her. It was very hard for her and my mother to communicate in the beginning. She used to beat me up a lot. I was eight when we immigrated, and she was fifteen. She went to high school here. I started first grade in this country, which was really tough because the other kids beat me up. But it was really tough for her because she was in high school with the older students.

She didn't speak any English. If somebody asked her a question, she would say, "yes," and shake her head up and down, or say, "no," and shake her head side to side, not understanding a thing. Eventually she learned how to speak English, but it was really hard. She finished high school. We get together every now and then, take the kids to the zoo. Now we're close. Actually, she ended up moving out from my house when she was about eighteen because I don't think she was ever very happy there. My mother never treated her badly. My mother is the nicest person in the world. I guess my sister always felt that space between them, and I was always the number one daughter to my parents.

Even my younger sister was also a little jealous of me. In Ghana, when you are the oldest child, you get all the attention, everything. Even though my other sister was older than I was, she wasn't my mother's daughter.

I Wasn't Called "Baldy" Anymore

Once I started school and I got the hang of English, I wouldn't speak my language in the house. And I remember my father was always mad. He used to tell us, "Speak Ga, speak Ga. You shouldn't speak English in the house. You have to speak your language." I regret that now because now it's hard for me to communicate in my language. I get stuck on certain words. We wanted to speak English. We wanted to be like everybody else in school.

One way that I enjoyed being different concerned my hairstyle. Once it grew out, I wasn't called "Baldy" anymore. We wrap around the hair, so it looks like little trees. It's hard, and it sticks out, and you can twist it whichever way you want. And so my mother used to do my hair like that, and I used to go to school, and I used to always have crowds around me touching my hair. "Oh, how did you do that? Oh, wow." They were just in awe.

But She Never Really Loved Him

My mother told me that she married my father out of necessity because actually, they were very distantly related. She tells me that she never really, really loved him, but she married mostly because of her family, because I think, she came from a very poor family. She was the oldest daughter. Her mother had ten or eleven kids. My father's family was a little better off than her family, so she married him.

When we were first here, things were good for awhile, but then I remember lots of arguing at night. My father used to always think that my mother was cheating on him, and it wasn't a great marriage.

She left the marriage about ten years ago. In my country, once you're married to someone, you're stuck with that person, unless the two families come together and decide that they should go their separate ways.

When my mother first left, I was in boarding school because things were so bad, I couldn't take it being in the house. I had to talk my father into sending me to boarding school. He didn't have the money for that, but with help, I went to boarding school in Poughkeepsie.

My brother and my sister, they stayed there in the thick of things, and years later, my sister told me told me they were very angry at me because I got sent away, and they were stuck in the family mess.

When my mother left, she used to come over every week and cook food, and she used to give my brother and sisters money.

When my mother first came here, she worked at Church's Fried Chicken, and she was really good. I remember her telling me that she was the best person they ever had to clean the chicken, and she knew how to do everything. She would even train the managers, and one time someone told her that she should become a manager. She only had a high school diploma back in our country, so she couldn't move up after that because there was a certain class she had to take, and she couldn't do that.

My father was very mad at my mother, and he's still mad. He still talks bad about her. But I tell him, "Just stop it right there."

There was this program that helped minorities get into private schools. My principal from junior high school told me about it. The principal didn't feel that his school was a good place for me because I got into a lot of trouble. There was a lot of fighting.

Even though I got into fights, I never used to make trouble. It was as if trouble used to come to me. My junior high school principal knew my mother; he knew I came from a good family. I always got good grades, and so I guess that is why he chose me to go away to school.

He Didn't Want Me to Take the Children Back to Ghana

After I graduated from boarding school, I got a scholarship to the University of Pennsylvania. I went one year, and I had a few problems— I had a child. I came back to New York and lived with my child's father. I started going to the community college part time; in that way I could work during the day. Then I had another baby, and I couldn't handle it, so I wanted to send the kids back to my country. The guy that I was living with didn't want me to take the kids back to Ghana. Here the food and everything is abundant, but there the living is more conservative. My children would not starve or anything because I have money here to send to them. Whatever they needed would be provided for them. It is just that living there is on a lower scale.

The father, he is Jamaican. We are still living together but not for very long. I'm planning on moving out. I have an actual date. I just feel like I want to be on my own. I'm not married. We have two kids together, but we're like salt and pepper, or is it oil and water? We just don't mix. We don't agree about anything.

He likes to leave the TV on twenty-four hours a day, and I can't stand that. He loves to put the AC on, even though I feel like there's really no need for him to have it on. He has a little stereo in the bathroom that's hooked up to the TV in the living room, so he always has that on.

It's not cultural because in Jamaica I'm sure they don't have three TVs that are on all at the same time. I don't think it's a male thing either, but that's just the way he is. We've been together about six years. The kids are too young now to know what's going on between us. They are three and two.

I Couldn't Leave Them

I took them over to Ghana this summer, but I decided to bring them back because I couldn't leave them. It was too emotional, but they were sent back this past Saturday. A lady from our country was going, so she took them along with her by plane.

I let them go because it's just so difficult. I knew it was difficult before I decided to bring them back. I was hoping that somehow things would work out because I was planning on putting my son and daughter in day care. That wouldn't really work because I'm in school in the evenings. I don't get home 'til late, and daycare is open only until six o'clock. My mother works nights and returns home early in the morning to watch them. She also needs her time to rest. Before, when my grandmother was here, she was helping out by watching them during the day, but now she's gone back to Ghana.

Their father is also in school, and he would have been able to watch them after they leave day care, but he wouldn't have time to do his studies. That would have also made us argue more. It was just too difficult struggling with them and with my school and work, so I decided to send them back.

How It Really Was

When I went back this summer I saw where I grew up 'til I was eight years old. And I remember the house, the layout of the place and everything, but I really forgot how the everyday living was, and I had a hard time adjusting.

Here you can have soda anytime you want; the fridge is stocked with juice. There, you drink water. I don't like water. I always have some kind of juice or soda, so I couldn't have that there. I have American dollars. For people living there it's expensive, and I couldn't really just buy it just for myself. So that was one part of it.

Also the beds are different. My uncle is a carpenter, so he made his bed himself, and it's a wooden platform with beams going across, and then they have a foam mattress, so some parts were soft and some parts were hard, and it was just really uncomfortable. It was like a king-size bed. We all slept in it: me, my two kids, and also my nephew, because my sister sent her son over, too.

It was four of us in one bed. There were lots of mosquitoes. In the daytime it's not too bad, but at night, when you're going to sleep, even if there's just one mosquito in the room, it will just bite you all night or buzz in your ears. It was very uncomfortable for me at night. The whole house was crowded because my grandmother was staying there because she also had just come from America. It was her, my two kids, my nephew, my uncle, his three kids, his wife, and myself.

They Cut Off the Water for Three Days at a Time

My uncle had indoor plumbing that is called "self-contained." Your kitchen and bathroom are all in the house, but sometimes the government cuts off the water. My uncle didn't like to use the toilet that he had in the house. He had an outhouse, but you didn't have to walk too far. They cut the water off only one time while I was there, but it was really late at night when you didn't really use it anyway, and it was back on the next morning.

My uncle said, "You're really lucky because normally they cut off water for three days at a time." Most people store water in big containers underground. Those that can't do it have to buy water when the water supply is shut down.

They don't have lights on all the time like we do here; sometimes the government turns the electricity off because of the limited water supply. My uncle said we were also lucky when we were there because they hardly ever turned the electricity off. When they turn it off, we have to use lanterns.

I'm so used to the living here that when I went back, it was hard for me to adjust. Since the kids are so young, I really don't think it will make a difference for them. It is harder for me to change than the children. I was feeling for them when I brought them back, but they didn't seem to really get upset at staying there.

Building a House for the Future. That's Like the Thing

Years and years from now, I would like to go to Ghana and maybe set up a business. Right now, my uncle would like for me to build a house over there. Little by little, I'm going to start sending money.

He's building another house, right next to his house, and that one will even be bigger than the one that we were in. The one that he's living in now has two bedrooms. The one that he's building has six bedrooms and two kitchens. I would have my own separate house. My mother has land already, but she just needs to get more money to build on it.

My father, he's for it. He is building a house, too. That's like the main idea, that's like the thing for all Ghanaians when they come here. Their number one goal is to build a house if they don't have one already.

I think my father went back maybe two or three years ago. But the tickets are very expensive, and it's so far away. I've lived in New York City most of my life, so Ghana is definitely for country types. I mean, it's a beautiful place—the natural soil is red, and you don't see skyscrapers. It is definitely not New York.

They Arrested a Guy I Knew for Ringing a Bell

When I was home it was festival time called Homowa. A lot of people are Christian now, so some of them don't really celebrate it like it used to be celebrated in the old days. There is a law during that Homowa period that you can't play any type of music, but only special Homowa music. When I was there the police had arrested someone I knew because he was playing music, which wasn't Homowa music. I was like, wow!

When they're selling stuff on the street, they walk up and down the street, ringing bells, and they carry their things on their head, and this guy was selling something and ringing his bell, and they arrested him for that.

"Homowa" is translated literally as hunger—*homo, dowa*—*homo* is hunger. There was a time in Ghana when there was no food. There was a draught and famine, and Homowa celebrates the time when the food came back.

Last summer, people would laugh at me sometimes because it was hard for me to be understood since I stopped speaking my language when we came to the States. I wasn't as fluent as I could have been, and it was hard for me to communicate. Sometimes I wouldn't use the exact, correct word. Sometimes they would laugh at me because the English there is a British English, so they are pronouncing every little "t," every little "d." Sometimes they would laugh at me when I'm speaking English because I say a word differently.

There Is No Desire for Me to Find a Ghanaian Man

The Jamaican father of my kids doesn't like it one bit that the children are in Africa. He was dead set against it the first time, and he was still against it because as I mentioned it's just a whole different environment in Ghana, and the country is very conservative.

He says he's going in December to visit them. I'm sure he misses them a lot. He loves them. That's one thing I can say about him; he loves his kids, and he cares about them.

There is no chance or desire for me to find a Ghanaian man because I don't really associate with many Ghanaians here. I don't even go out to Ghanaian parties. I don't have time for that.

For Every Little Thing, You Must Bribe Someone

I spoke to my uncle this morning. He was telling me that I need to apply for permanent residence for my kids, because they're going to be staying there beyond sixty days, which is what they granted for the visa. If you extend the visa, they only give you another sixty days or maybe another six months, and then you have to apply for a permanent residence for them.

I wouldn't say the government is corrupt, but every little thing that you need to do, you have to bribe someone to do it for you. Here you can't do that. You could get sent to jail, but there it's standard.

Even if it is something straightforward, like getting a passport, there still has to be a bribe, and that takes a lot of money, and especially when they know that you're an American, or you have money. They know the people in America send back money. They really take advantage of that. If you need the service, you pay up.

I Have Been out of That African Sun

Everybody in America is considered wealthy over there. As soon as they know that you are an American, that's a big pot of money right there walking around—then the prices triple, quadruple. They even treat me that way. I'm Ghanaian, but I've been in the States for so long that when I go there, when they look at my skin, they know that I haven't been there for a long time, that I've been out of that African sun. I guess I could say that my skin has become Americanized just like the rest of me. Refrigerated drinks, soft beds, and a lukewarm sun have turned me into a guest in my motherland.

TEN

Edel Rodriguez

CUBAN-AMERICAN

Edel and his girlfriend Jennifer got married in Miami. The event was held at the Viscaya Estate, a fabled mansion on Biscayne Bay built in 1914 with a one-thousand-plus workforce by the rich American farm-machinery mogul James Deering. The young couple paid for the lavish event themselves. Ironically, the groom had arrived at this very shore, the renowned Florida Golden Coast, fifteen years before, as a boat person.

The State Department's official version of the Mariel boat lift is as follows: April 1980 entry: "10,000 Cubans storm the Peruvian embassy in Havana seeking political asylum. A flotilla of refuges (125,000) begins an exodus from the port of Mariel in Cuba for the United States. Many of these Marielitos turn out to be criminals or the insane, and the United States wants to repatriate these individuals" ("Chronology of Cuban Affairs, 1958–98," released by the Bureau of Inter-American Affairs, January 12, 1998).

Edel states in hindsight, "Everyone is a thief in Cuba." With the United States embargo, the planned economy of Fidel's Cuba floundered. People had to scheme for some of the basic necessities. Therefore, the term criminal showed inventiveness, "a capitalistic spirit."

Now, at the age of twenty-five, Edel is becoming very successful in the graphic art world. He is an up-and-comer at Time magazine's art department.

I was invited to an informal family gathering the night before the wedding. Food and drink were abundant. It was fun to be exposed to traditional Cuban family life. In Edel's sister's backyard, rhythms of meringues and salsa music sounded out under a full Florida moon. A circle formed as guests clapped their hands to the outstanding dancing of the father, an uncle, a sister, and Edel. An aunt tapped my shoulder and said in her broken English, "This is the family having fun."

Smaller Than I Ever Imagined

When I went back to Cuba last year, I saw that everything was smaller than I had ever imagined. The house was just a few tiny rooms. The backyard was only a patio, which connected to my grandparents' patio. My grandparents lived right next door. It was all sort of joined together.

My aunt, her husband, and her kids lived with my grandparents. They decided to stay because at the time my grandfather just didn't want to leave. The people who came to pick us up were from my mom's side of the family, and it was really funny because for years it was my dad that always wanted to leave. He was the one who was getting the paperwork for us to go. There was a list they had set up here, and my father, my mom, my sister, and me were on the list. Everyone knew that we wanted to leave. There were people in Cuba that knew that my dad didn't like the government. He thought we might be able to get to Spain and from there eventually the United States. Then abruptly this boat lift thing came up.

We were one of the first ones to leave. The week before, my aunt was scheduled to come to Cuba on a visit that she had planned for over a year. But then she said, "Listen there's this thing going on. Hardly anyone knows about it, but we're getting a boat together. Are you ready? We have this list made up of people we think would like to go."

My dad said, "Yeah, let's just do it now instead of dragging it out and spending so much money and going to Spain." Then he went out in his car and sort of advised everyone on the list that soldiers were going to come to their house and told them to pack up, so that they would be somewhat ready. Otherwise soldiers would be just showing up and saying, "You have to leave. There's a boat waiting."

Worm People

He had advance warning for a week and a half. My father did it secretly because if people knew we were leaving the country, the house would get egged or they would throw all sorts of old vegetables and tomatoes or have protests in on your street and call you "*qusanos,*" which means worm. It means someone that's in the system, underground.

I have one sister who is six years older than me. I think they probably told her. My parents told me the day before, sort of like, "We're going away. We're going on a trip." I had fishing poles that I had to give to the neighbors. I was wondering—What's going on?

I don't really remember how much I knew about what was happening. They told me we were going to see my aunt in the United States, and I thought, great! I didn't know we were going to leave forever. It was a fun thing.

Please Strip-Search Me

It was scary at times. We thought when we were leaving the house that we were getting on a boat and leaving right away, but instead they put us in this processing center for a week, where we had to live in tents. There were soldiers around with German Shepherds.

It was very scary. There was barbed wire everywhere. The camp was divided into sections. There was a family section; that's where we were. There was a section for prisoners that Castro was letting out of the country. Another section was for embassy refugees. For some time, Cubans had been rushing into the Peruvian Embassy and asking for asylum. They had these three sections: the embassy, the families that were being picked up by American relatives, and the prisoners.

When we first came in, it was a mess. The first night they let out dogs to push the prisoners this way and that to sort of make the divisions, and we were caught up in the middle. The chaos was the scary part because the government really hadn't planned it out, and the government didn't really care about us because we were leaving. Food was scarce. Eventually they got around to it and started to give people rations.

When we went in, they searched everyone. They strip-searched my mom and my dad to see if we were taking any gold out of the country or anything of value. I wanted to be strip-searched, too, but they wouldn't strip-search me. A lot of this was difficult for the adults, but I wondered why am I not being strip-searched. When you're a kid, this is kind of fun, the soldiers and all this stuff. At times it was scary, but at times it was fun. The first three or four days were difficult.

My dad didn't eat for seven days. He was just giving my sister and me his food. Then after a few days they got it together, and they brought in more secure tents, because we had very small tents, and we went through a storm while we were there and it almost blew our tent away. By the sixth or seventh day—I had made friends already. We were playing baseball in the camp. By the time they came around saying the ship was ready to go, I was like, "Oh, no!"

My dad was very worried. Recently, he explained what was going on. All the time my father had been putting pressure on the soldiers to call us because he wanted out of there as soon as possible. We got there on April 24, and May Day is on May 1. My father was afraid something would happen on May Day because that's when they celebrate Communism in Cuba.

On May Day, the soldiers go on parade and have all their guns. So he wanted to get out of there before that. My dad was always putting pressure on the authorities because he knew the boat was at the dock. He was always after them to find our files that they said they couldn't find. They were always giving us some story, and he was always trying to get them to get moving and call us. And eventually after seven days, they did.

The first few days I didn't know what was going on. But once you got used to it, you just sort of make friends. My cousin Armel was there. He's a few months younger than I am, and we sort of did everything together. He's my best friend here now.

You're Not Leaving until All This Stuff Is Back

My father did various things back in Cuba. He had a capitalist mind. He was always doing his own businesses. He started out in his twenties. In the beginning he was working in factories. But then he sort of moved into administration of restaurants owned by the government. So we always had food around because somehow he figured out ways to get us food out of the restaurant. Then he left that, and he became a photographer. He did weddings. He had his own photography business out of the house.

Maybe I got my artistic talent from him. He would also take his car to the city, Havana, and take tourists around for money.

There were rules he had to go by, and he was always hiding what he was doing. He was always pushing the rules a little more. I don't think he was allowed to rent his car, but there was no way of proving what he was doing. He was always tiptoeing around. That was part of the reason that he wanted to get out as soon as possible, because there were people that were already looking for him. We found out that there was a sort of a file on him. He was buying things on the black market. The only way to buy food there is to go to a farmer and buy from the farmer. But that's illegal. You can only buy in the stores. But there's nothing in the stores. So my father had to find other ways to get food and goods. He saw people watching him. Each block had the Committee for the Defense of the Republic. One person in one house was supposed to watch over the whole block, and he knew that person was watching him. When we did leave, my dad had given all his cameras and household effects to his friends.

A soldier came in and had a list of all the stuff my father owned and said, "Where is all this stuff?"

My dad said, "I gave it all away."

The soldier said, "You're not leaving until all this stuff is back here."

That same night my dad went out with my mom and got back all their possessions he had given to friends. Thank God, he didn't sell them or anything—he just asked for the goods back, and they put them in the house, and they sealed the house. They gave the house to someone in the party. Right now someone from the party lives in our old home, and they have our belongings. The government took his car and gave it to people that they thought deserved it.

In Cuba, Everybody Is Sort of a Thief

One day in the camp, they called our name, and we became excited and got in line. They put us on a bus, and from that bus they took us to the port, and a couple of hours later they took us out of the bus, and we got on the boat. That was about five or six in the evening and we left at ten o'clock at night. There were twenty boats in a row, so that we had company. Our extended family numbered twenty-seven, and we had thirty prisoners, plus we had thirty embassy asylum people. That's what they did with each boat. They just wanted to get rid of all of us.

So my dad became the boss and he said, "The families in the front, the prisoners in the back." Most of the prisoners were good. They just wanted to get out. They didn't cause trouble on the boat.

There were some characters. They were probably robbers. I don't know if there were any killers. But there were thieves. In Cuba, everybody is sort of a thief. All my friends were thieves because they had to be. They had to eat. They were always stealing bananas, going to some farm to steal this or that. Everyone steals, and everyone is doing the black market. If you're not a thief, you can't live.

We left at night, and we got into Key West about eight o'clock in the morning. It took ten hours. It was a pretty big ship. We didn't have any trouble with the seas or anything. It was a kind of boat that picks up shrimp. It's got these things with nets on the side, and it was about seventy feet long. It went very slowly. The trip was fine. I know people that went through storms. A couple of days before when we had that storm in the camp, people died on the boats. Thank God, the sea was very flat. The whole thing was pretty traumatic for my whole family because we had never done anything like that.

My mother was very protective of me. She was always grabbing onto me. My mother was the one who was taking care of us while my dad was running around the camp trying to do things.

My dad was in charge of everything. The people used to respect him, even thieves, burglars or prisoners. He'd say, "Do this. We're trying to get through this." And people just said okay.

We Started with Zero

My mother did sewing in Cuba. Actually she didn't do that many weddings or any big dresses. She just did sewing for my sister and me because clothes were hard to get. So my dad would somehow find textiles in Havana, and my mom would make us shirts or underwear. She was always a housewife, so I don't know if she made money doing that or not.

When she got to Miami, it became her job. When she got here she had to do some paying work. We came here with papers as political refugees. My mom started a week later sewing in a factory. It took my dad a few weeks to start working in a factory doing nuts and bolts, which was very different. He had never really worked for anybody. It was a big shock to him.

He has never resented being here. This is what he always wanted, but in the beginning it was very difficult for him to be away from his parents because they had lived together for his whole life. It was difficult for him to see his kids not have everything they needed. Because we had a lot in Cuba compared to the rest of the population. When we came here we started out from zero. Nothing. Someone gave my dad one hundred bucks.

We lived with my aunt, and he never liked living with anybody. He likes his house and his family. It was hard for him to live with other people and be so poor. And he worked at a factory, and he had never done that. He did a lot of odd jobs. He painted for some people, and then a year later or so he bought a truck and started doing towing for my family's used car business. Eventually that truck became a nicer truck and then two trucks and an employee that works for him. He's been pretty good for about eight years. We kept busy.

Bringing Baseball Caps Back to Cuba

Last year when my dad and I went back to visit Cuba, he brought back baseball caps saying "Cato." His name is Caesario, but everybody calls him Cato. Everyone wants a baseball cap with his name, and they think he's a big shot in the States.

It's kind of a small towing business. But he always likes to be independent. He never likes to work for anybody. Now that he's so busy and that business took off, my mom just works out of the house. She worked in factories for a while, and then she worked for some people, and then she got enough clients, so she eventually started working out of the house. She makes wedding dresses and all kinds of dresses.

School — An "A" Means Great

My parents were very funny about school. They both had about a sixth-grade education and lived on farms in Cuba in the 1950s and 1960s. So they didn't really study much. I went to school there. The school system was okay. The teachers were good, and we learned things, but it was only up to third grade, so I don't know how good it was. All the kids there wore patriotic uniforms in red, white, and blue. I was surprised when I came here and found that none of the kids had uniforms. My cousin, who's been all the way through high school there, is pretty well educated. But the only problem there is that the economy causes problems for people wanting to get to school. Teachers sometimes have a hard time getting transportation to school. Those kinds of problems get in the way of education.

When I came here I got into studying. Part of it was that I wanted to be the best I could be, thanks to my parents. I had to explain to them what the grades meant—that "A" meant great.

My dad was like, "Oh, okay."

They wanted me to be good, but they weren't that involved. They didn't go to open house at school or anything like that. At times I wanted them to, but I could see that it would probably be difficult for them to relate to and communicate with a lot of Americans. I ended up doing a lot of things myself.

They didn't push me to study one thing or another. They didn't even know what college was about or how to get into college. I had to do that myself. I knew I wanted to go to college because it was the next step. I just wanted to get the best possible education and get the most degrees.

My dad had a tow truck ready for me just in case. My mom just told me that.

I had a high school teacher who told me about Pratt Institute, and there was a previous student of hers that had gone there. He came in and talked to me, and I came up to visit Pratt during my senior year. I had gotten a full scholarship to the University of Miami and could stay in Miami or go to Pratt. I liked New York so much. I had never been out of Florida my whole life; I'd never been anywhere.

Once I came up here it was like "Wow!" I went to the museum, to MOMA [Museum of Modern Art], and there was the real thing. I was like, "Wow!" I just walked in there with the guys who were going to Pratt and asked them, "That's the real thing?" It was very hard when I went back to tell my mom that I wanted to come up here. It took forever just talking her into it.

You Know More than I Do

Then she said, "Well, if that's what you want, okay."

Her objection was that I was leaving. It wasn't even that I was going to New York; it was just that I was leaving the house. That just doesn't happen in most Cuban families. Kids stay near each other, especially in Cuba. It's always if you get married you live next to your parents. Never or rarely do you ever go to another town. Even in Miami, my cousins still live in Miami. The guy that came with me on the boat, he still lives there. It's something you don't even think about. For some reason I wanted to leave.

I had teachers in high school who told me, "If you want to do anything you have to get out of here."

Pratt was very expensive. Even though I had a full scholarship to the University of Miami, it wasn't up to my parents. They thought colleges were free. First I applied to Pratt and applied for all their scholarships. Then I got a Talent Search scholarship for a few thousand dollars. But it wasn't enough. Pratt's tuition is almost fifteen thousand. I had done a mock cover for *Time* in high school as part of a competition.

I won another one-thousand-dollar scholarship. So I got three separate scholarships. I would apply to a lot of things, especially those that were art related. Then in my senior year when I knew I wanted to go to Pratt, I called the national Talent Search person there who also handled financial aid and said, "I want to go but I don't have enough money. Can you find something?"

Over time I found out that Pratt had this competition between all the freshmen; they get nominated. If you win—they had two scholarships that cover the rest of your education; they had three, which I didn't know about. I was doing my work—because I really wanted to learn all about this stuff. I wasn't taught that well in my art class in high school. My art classes weren't as good as in Pratt. I had really good professors who said you should keep on going because they had this competition at the end of the year. So I kept pumping it out. I was nominated with twenty-five or thirty other people. They picked me and another kid, and we won the full scholarship.

So I called my mom and said, "You don't have to worry about the rest of my time at Pratt."

My mother always asked me, "If you study art, what do you do?"

I said, "I don't know; I'll figure it out."

She wanted me to be a dentist because she knew that dentists always make money. I said, "Mom I don't like any sciences. I would be lost." I said, "Art is what I always wanted to do."

And she said, "Well, I guess you know what you're doing." That's what she always ended up saying. "You know more than I do." Which is true. "I guess you know what you're doing but be careful."

Finding My Photo

Going way back to high school, I always liked *Time* magazine and had won a student contest to design a cover. When I was in English class at Pratt, the professor said that her husband worked there. After I graduated from Pratt, I was going all around interviewing. One day I was calling different magazines, and no one needed anyone. I remembered what my professor had said. I couldn't remember her husband's name, but I grabbed a magazine and went down their masthead looking for a name. I saw the name Steve Conley. I called and said, "I had your wife for English at school." Would he look at my work?

"Come tomorrow." He looked at my portfolio and said in his gruff way, "Can you start next week? Someone is going on jury duty." I only delivered copy for two weeks. I guess because I worked so hard Steve wanted me to stay, so he had hired me at first as a freelancer doing small design jobs and progressively he increased my duties.

Life is so weird. When I came to work at *Time*, my dad had told me that *Time* or *Newsweek* or the *New York Times* had done something about us when we came on the boat lift. Castro had thrown out a lot of American reporters, and they landed on our boat. There was a big picture of me in the *Miami Herald*.

So I'm here working at *Time*, and I went up to the library and went through the old issues. There was a two-column box by a writer who still works for *Time* about how he took this ride on this boat called *Nature Boy* (which was the name of our boat), and he described the whole thing, "We left at ten, we got in at eight."

I gave him a call and told him I was on that boat, and he was all excited. I told an art director, and the art director told an editor, and everyone thought it was great.

They said, "Why don't we do a piece about you."

I said, "Okay." They sent me to be photographed by the Statue of Liberty by this photographer named Mario, who is also Cuban.

When we were there, he said, "You came in 1980? What was the name of your boat?"

I said, "*Nature Boy.*"

He said, "I was on that boat." He was one of the press people that was put off the island. He was working for *Newsweek* at the time. "I remember the time we left; there were prisoners on the boat. We did all this." It was so weird. The picture that came out in *Newsweek* had some people in my family.

He said he had tons of rolls of this whole thing. He had about forty rolls about that trip to Cuba and we went through all the slides. Sure enough, he had a shot of the four of us, my parents, my sister, and me. There's one shot of just my head.

Slackers and Cuba — Part Two

I was thinking about how I'm pretty successful for a twenty-five-year old. I was reading that whole *Time* article about Generation X. I never felt like I belonged to any group either, Cubans or Americans. I just sort of did my own thing. I never belonged to the Gen. X. I had a lot of friends in college that were like that. They grew up having things, so then they didn't want to have things; they wanted to be poor—slackers with torn pants. I knew kids whose families had so much money, and they were total bums with crappy hair. I like the music, but I never wanted to be a slacker because I wanted my parents to be proud of me. I think a lot of people my age don't care what their parents think.

I wanted to be able to help my parents. Now sometimes I buy them a ticket to come up here.

They're doing all right, but they are still in Miami, and the economy is not that great. I had no problem living in Florida. I think it was probably more of a problem for American kids to integrate themselves. There are a lot of Cubans there. Miami is sort of like Cuba—part two.

ELEVEN

Kamal Patel

INDIAN-AMERICAN

One day Kamal appeared in my classroom with her hands intricately painted in an attractive reddish-brown lace pattern. I had heard about henna parties, which in Middle Eastern communities were like bachelorette bashes. I asked, "Is some- one getting married?" My guess was correct, even though European-descended girls in the East Village art scene had also adopted this practice.

Then I read about a convention where young people who had the same last name of Patel were introduced to each other in hopes of keeping the lineage intact. Arranged marriages in free-swinging America — what an interesting idea! I asked Kamal Patel if I could interview her to see what traditions she had retained.

The twenty-one-year-old Kamal had always seemed very "Americanized." Always clad in lean blue jeans and carrying a backpack, she merged perfectly with the other students on campus, with no hint of South Asian ethnicity to single her out except her graceful movements. Like a description of India, this young woman blends the modern and the ancient, the spice and the spiritual.

Five Families in One House in Texas

My parents had immigrated to England from India, and I was born in London. We were on welfare there. The government paid our housing, and we stayed in one of those box rooms with another couple and their three kids. My parents didn't have money at all, so eventually they had to move back to India.

While in India, my father got a call from his cousin, who told him to go to Texas; he could use him because he had a busy grocery store. We lived in Texas for seven years—five families in one house. There was not a big Indian community except in this one house where all of us cousins lived together. Basically, I grew up with eleven kids, we all became really close. We were all girls except for my one brother. I never really thought about being an Indian in Texas. I thought more of the differences when I later moved to New Jersey.

In Texas all the five mothers rotated staying at home and going to work in the grocery store. The one who stayed home cooked for all of us and cleaned the house. All the men rotated in the warehouse with the packaging and storage as well as waiting on customers in the grocery store. We children would walk to school. Everyone was older than me, except for one cousin who was my age. My cousin and I walked together; but it was her father that never wanted us to study that much. He would complain about education, but my mom was very strict as far as schooling was concerned. My cousin's father was the head, and he was definitely against schooling. He was the eldest and had the most authority. Whatever he said usually went.

While in Texas, I had to take English as a Second Language—which was the only thing that reminded me that I was Indian and was different. I don't know what they thought, but they wanted me in that class, even though I spoke fine.

We Were Held Up a Couple of Times

I remember one time no one was available to watch me, so I went to the grocery store with my mom, and while I was in the back playing with my friend, my mom was held up in the grocery store. She was giving the robber the money, and my dad walked in. My dad acted like he had a gun in his pocket, so the guy ran out. I don't know what my dad was thinking because he took off after him. Then my dad let it go and forgot about it. From then on we had a little bit more security in the grocery store. All the mothers were a little more hesitant to go. We were held up a couple of times.

My Mom Was the Valedictorian

We left Texas because my dad's cousin called and said he had a manufacturing plant, and my dad was an engineer. He sold my father the business. My dad left by himself for a year. He went back and forth between New Jersey and Texas. Finally we all drove from Texas to New Jersey.

From then we were always moving to a bigger and better place until eventually we got a townhouse. My mom went to the top university in India. She graduated first in everything. When she came here she studied more in her field and again graduated valedictorian. She was a chemist at Johnson and Johnson Pharmaceutical. She always wants to do better. On the side she taught dancing. Two months ago she left Johnson and Johnson to open up her own dance school. She always wanted to follow her hobby, which is Indian folk dancing.

Towel Head

I think I am still immersed in Indian culture, even though a lot of my friends and a lot of my cousins are no longer. The reason for this is because I dance. For me doing Indian dancing is a way for me to hang on to my culture. It reaffirms the values and concepts. Some of them are traditional, but it has to do with culture.

I definitely got teased a lot more in New Jersey than in Texas. People would always say something about curry or towel head—very rude remarks. I was always very shy, and the remarks made me even shyer. I was never the outgoing one. We kept moving a lot to many different schools. In high school I had only two good friends. Everyone else was just an acquaintance. I was never Miss Popularity. I think a lot has to do with how we were raised. My parents struggled a lot. I am sure most people's parents had to struggle to come here.

We were definitely poor in the beginning. Now I get teased—"You're so spoiled"—because I have my own car, and we have a big house. We definitely are well off; we have money. I'm not ashamed of it because my parents worked hard to get it. When we first moved to New Jersey we stayed in little tiny apartments; then the more money they made, the more they saved, and our living quarters got bigger and better. It is just my nineteen-year-old brother and me. Then my mom got pregnant again, and she had to have an abortion because she couldn't afford another kid.

You Have to Marry Someone with the Same Last Name

My parents' marriage was arranged. Mom didn't want to marry my dad, and my dad didn't want to marry my mom. My dad really didn't care as much, but my mom used to cry, but her parents kept on saying, "He's a good guy, he's a good guy." At that time he didn't really have money either. But he was Patel, and you have to marry someone with the same last name. It works by villages. There are six villages in our association. You are supposed to find your mate from one of these towns. It is also good for the girl to find a husband with the same or higher social status because she takes on the guy's name. If I married someone from a lower level, I would be in a lower caste system. Now some people believe it, and some people don't; the pressures are a bit less.

We do have these Patel reunions where we can meet who we want to meet. We can see them and talk to each other. It is a big convention, a big fete. There are parties at night, and we hang out and we can meet people, which is really cool. Some people in a certain age group are very, very serious, but other people just want to party. You tell who you might be interested in, like "person number 241," and then you meet him. If you like him, fine, and if you don't, you don't. Then the parents get involved. They meet, so it works out like that.

Some Young People Go to Have Fun

Patel actually means "farmer," but there are so many Patels. Patels descend from Vishnu. It is funny because my brother's standards are a lot different from mine. I am sure my brother could bring in someone else. My parents might fight with him, but it would be tolerated more than it would be for me, because I am actually going away to the guy's house. For us, when we get married, we don't get our own apartment right away. Traditionally and culturally, the daughter goes to the guy's house. I would live at his house for however long. Before it was for a long time, but now it is not quite like that. Nevertheless, you should stay about a year. Then you move on to your own place. When a daughter leaves, it is a big thing, but for a guy it doesn't matter because the girl is coming into his house, so for my brother it would be okay.

When I went to the Patel meeting, it was fun because you go with all your friends. My parents didn't go this time, but you are there with all your friends. Everyone is drinking. Some people think it's bad because some young people are going basically to have fun, and that's not really what it is about. It is supposed to be for marriage and for people who are truly serious. I have fun, and you go around and meet people. Basically it is a small world, even though there are about three thousand Patels at the convention. Somehow you are always meeting up with each other.

Isn't That Incest?

My friends always ask, "Isn't that incestuous?" But it is not like that. I am in my own particular village. I'm from Bhad Ran. There are five other villages, and I have to marry someone from one of the other five villages. Someone from my village is like my brother. If a marriage takes place with a higher socioeconomic level, it is good, but with a lower, of course, it is not good, especially since I'm a girl, and it carries on my name.

There was a guy who I met in New York who was interested. I met him at a Patel convention. My parents were in London at that time, and I was going to meet up with my parents in London. At that time, I didn't know, but my parents had already met up with his parents. My parents really liked this kid. That is where we got into a little conflict, because I liked him because he is a nice guy. I want to finish school, and this guy wants to commit now, plus there are some things that are traditional that I don't like. I don't like him looking at six other girls while he was looking at me. If you like me fine, but don't be comparing me. I don't go for that.

All that my mom said was, "If it is not in your heart, don't do it." It looks like this guy has everything, but if there is no love or personality, what you are dealing with is nothing.

But then my parents compare my situation to theirs, "We didn't have anything. We didn't even know each other." They grew together, and today are so in love. My mom always says, "Divorces always come from love marriages." She contends that when you are in an arranged marriage, the divorce rate is a lot lower. When it is arranged you have to get to know the person. You should meet someone and not really know him to get married, and throughout the whole marriage you get to learn so much about this person. It is not like you're going out for three years and living with him. My mom thinks that it is really ridiculous that people live together. She tells me, "When you are married you want that. What's the fun of getting married if you know all about the other person?"

You're Not a Born-Again Virgin

Premarital sex is a big thing. I am a virgin. I want to stay one and be one until I get married. My mom always said, "Sex is a gift. It is something that you can only have with one person." That is one of my beliefs. People are always surprised to hear me say that. I'm not ashamed that I am a virgin. I think it's funny that a lot of my Indian friends aren't. They don't care, but they won't tell their parents. I got a lot of culture shock from that alone. All my friends are no longer virgins, except for one of my roommates who is Colombian.

Some of my friends say, "I'm a born-again virgin."

I say, "No, you're not." This is a big issue for me.

In some ways my parents are a lot more lenient than other people but in other ways my dad is pretty strict about village marriage tradition because he is the president of the Six Villages Association.

He says, "What will people say if my own daughter won't abide and marry someone from there?"

I know when it comes down to it, they will be happy with whoever treats me well, but it definitely has to be Patel; I could go lower or higher as long as he is Patel. The Patels can trace their ancestry back to the first person, so there is a big pressure not to break the line.

My Parents Knew but Were in Denial

My cousin actually married a white man. The whole event has a double standard. Because she was never cultured, people completely accepted it even though they snicker behind her back. Her father passed away a long time ago. That was the guy who got my father the factory. The only reason she said she married him was because her father had met the guy before he passed away and gave his blessing. So it was a nice gesture. Everyone likes him because he is an amazing guy. He was a lot more accepted than if I brought in some outsider. My dad would have a heart attack.

I date here and there. I'm not supposed to. I'm open with my parents. They know what goes on. I think at times they are in denial. I was with someone for two years. We are not together anymore. He was a Patel and everything. I met him at one of the conventions three years ago. My parents knew, but they were in denial. They never said, "Are you going out with him?"

They were just like, "Oh, he called here."

When we broke up, they forgot it. A lot of my friends can't even have guys call their house. Some parents are very strict.

Traditionally, when I'm finished with college, I should go back to their house. Your own apartment is for after marriage. A lot of Indian parents want their kids to be doctors. It was a big problem because I was going to do physical therapy. At the last minute, I said, "I want to try out art school." It just came out of nowhere. This was six months before I was going to leave to go to college.

They said, "Try it for a semester." For them to say that was a big thing. My mother was in dance, but she was also a chemist. Dance was considered her hobby. Now they couldn't be happier. They tell me I had made a great decision.

I Could Never Live in a Third World Country

I went back to India at Christmas time. My parents wanted a family trip. We stayed there for three weeks. It still hasn't changed. Being in a third world country, I realized that I take things for granted. In India every other person is poor, while a few are very rich. In India my grandfather owned one of the biggest spice companies. It was a lot different on this trip because my grandfather has passed away. Now the whole family has separated and has gone their own way. We don't have our old house and had to stay with our other relative. I could never live there. Even my parents, who were brought up there, say they would never move back. There are not many opportunities there, and we have gotten used to the Americanized ways of living. It is amazing to visit India, but I am always happy to get back home, and here is home.

TWELVE

Jorge Murillo Meza

MEXICAN-AMERICAN

Wiry, with knotted stringy muscles and a weathered face, forty-nine-year-old Jorge showed a lifetime of labor under harsh conditions. He had combed back his thick black hair so that the part and ridges were in perfect alignment. For our meeting he wore a freshly laundered windbreaker. Smiling often without regard for a few missing front teeth, Jorge was charming without effort or affectation. This unschooled pruner of trees and clipper of brush followed the world news and could talk knowledgeably on current affairs.

At one point, we went indoors, where Steve, our host, teased Jorge.

"Could you manage without a cigarette?"

"It's true," Jorge said. "I'm not used to being inside. Usually I'm outdoors, filthy, with a cigarette hanging from my lip."

After some small talk, Jorge said, "All new immigrants have it hard, even maybe your people, Steve?" referring to our courtly host.

"My relatives had it really hard," Steve explained. "First, they were so starv-
ing that they ate all the animals, then each other." It was true. His family had
been members of the infamous Donner Party, who in 1847 had been trapped all
winter in the Sierra Nevada and resorted to cannibalism.

Jorge stared at the floor, fearful that his English had failed him.

I Was Seven Years Old When My Father Brought Me to Oregon to Work

Very, very poor people lived in the house that I grew up in. I had one
brother and one sister, all living. My father, he was a worker, so we
always had something to eat, although I never went to school, as we were
so poor.

I was seven years old when my father brought me to Oregon to work.
In those days, if you are the son, they put you on the same passport. I had
the right to pass, but not to work. To us, trees are like gold. He took me
to Oregon to pick apples and then cherries. That's all we did there.
There's nothing else to do. People left after the harvest.

My father, he would pick fruit up in the trees. He brought me everywhere. At night we stayed in a cabin. It was just him and me, but they
used to keep big families in there. Some Mexicans were born in those cabins. My father used to know all the runs. When the season was over, you
have to move on, but some people stay on there.

We'd go to a store that was for the workers. The guy who owned the
orchard was the same guy or same family who owned the store where
everybody went to buy food. They charged you whatever they wanted.
Let's put it this way—the money that we made in the orchard working—
it stayed there. We didn't have anything because we spent the money on
food and the rent for the cabin. We paid for the ride from there to the
orchard in the morning. We had to buy alcohol-can stoves called "smok-
ers." The last time I worked there, they were selling them for twenty-nine
dollars each to keep warm.

In those days César Chávez didn't care for us. He only fought for the
ones born here. That is reality. He fought for the rights of the Mexican-
Americans. He didn't fight for the immigrants from Mexico or any other
Latin-American immigrants.

My father would take me all over California. We came here to Fresno. We picked grapes. After we finished all the runs, we'd come back to Mexico. And this is how my father started saving money. When I was young, we got by, day by day, until he got the job in Mexico. That's when everything changed. But I keep the tradition. I don't fit in in Mexico. When you're Mexican, and you're born in Baja, you have more rights than any other Mexicans. When I reached eighteen, I went to the Immigration Department, and I got my passport by myself. And they told me, "Okay, you can use this passport to go visit twenty-five miles into the United States, but no more than that. Other than that, it's against the law. We strip you from your passport. You go visit parents, you have parents there or you have friends there, or whatever you have you have to go to the United States. You can go with this one, but you cannot go farther than twenty-five miles." So it's like I have a passport to go from Mexico to San Diego. They told me, "When you reach eighteen, you got to do service in the Mexican army. Then you can come and go."

No, No, No! That's My Father's Money

After a while, my father found a job in the water department, and he worked there for thirty-five years until he passed away. He left ten thousand dollars for my brother and me. He left my sister nothing, because my sister, she is married.

I put it in the bank. I don't want to spend one single penny out of that money because he worked so hard for it. In December we had a family reunion, and all my uncles and all my aunts were there, and they asked me what I'm thinking of doing with the money my father left me. One aunt has problems, and another aunt has problems, and another aunt and another, and now they want me to take my father's money out and give it to them.

I told them, "No, no, no, no, no! This money will not be touched whatsoever. That money is going to stay there. If I get sick, and I'm ready to die, maybe then. . . . Nothing, nothing, nothing is going to touch it. That's my father's money."

They have money. Why are they asking me for money? I don't know. One aunt is a retired nurse, and she has everything. Another aunt has a daughter and a son, and she has all kinds of money from the government. Don't take me wrong. I love them, and they love me. But I said no; it was his money and not mine.

I can support myself and I will work. I will never retire even if I had millions of dollars. I want for me to keep going.

So we have the little ones now, and I think they're okay. They've got it made. They're not going to suffer like I did. I have one brother and one sister. My brother is the one who doesn't want to come to the United States. He only comes at the end of the month to buy clothes.

My sister, she lives in an apartment. She's been living here all her life. She immigrated when she was fourteen. She worked in the plastic company for twenty years. My brother works for an American guy who owns a company in Mexico, which is against the law. As an American guy, he cannot own a business, so he's got somebody else to act as an owner, which is not a big deal. I mean, he helps people. He hires Mexicans, and he pays them American money. He doesn't take advantage of those people.

My brother has the most education out of the three of us. He was very smart, and he studied. He worked. He took typing lessons and moved up high in education. My sister and me, we didn't.

I'm very unhappy because I don't have an education, but I'm very happy with my little bit of knowledge that I learned in dealing with all kinds of people here. I have accomplished a lot of things—like my own house, which I built back home. It's not my father's, not my mother's, not my sister's, not my brother's. They didn't help me build the house. I built it by myself.

Now I'm working, so I'm forty-nine years old, and I'm going to try to save as much money as I can, so I can build another house for rent.

I'm going to live right and free. What I'm trying to say is that I will never try to be a rich person, but I will get involved in community service and well-being for my neighbors. I will get involved in things like that when I get older, not here in San Francisco but in Mexico.

I'm happy. I do not have any kind of remorse or any kind of rage. I don't have anything against the people of the United States. They always treated me extremely well. Really, this country is all about immigrants.

People put you in jobs that the white people don't want. They give you the hardest work, and they do the easier job. And they have more money, and we have less. Housing was terrible in those days. Living in those cabins, you don't have any water or a bathroom. You don't have any right to complain, like we have now. For example, if I have a headache or I don't feel well, I just go to the health department here. In those days, you didn't have health services, and if they had it, they would deny it to you.

In a lot of ways I suffered a lot of prejudice.

I'm Kind of a Loner

I cannot afford to live in this neighborhood on the kind of money that I make in a week. I did yard work for an older woman, and she liked me. She told me, "Oh, Jorge, I like the way you do the garden. Can you keep coming and do it once a month or once every three weeks or whatever?"

One month later, she asked me, "Jorge, where do you live?"

And I say, "I live in the Mission District."

"There's a room here. Jorge, how about you come, you live here, you pay me a little bit of rent, and you take care of the garden, and you can stay here?"

She had gone to see a family member, and when she came back, she had been robbed. She said they left "only the walls."

She said, "I will tell you when, when I'm ready. I have to do a lot of things to make room for you."

I tell her, "I do it for you if you want."

"No, no, no, I'm going to hire a professional guy."

She hired a guy to fix up a place for me. He took off a day when she had to go to see another family member. She said that when she came back, they robbed her again. She said that it wasn't the workers; they didn't have anything to do with it.

In her mind, she says, "Well, I'm a single woman, I'm living by myself, I'm seventy-five years old, I have a lot of family, but none live here. They are so far away, so now what I need is a man living here." She told me, "Now you won't leave. You stay."

That's the only reason; otherwise, I could not afford to live in this neighborhood. I've been living there now for four years.

She is a nice lady. Everyone I work for is nice. I work for John. He's a real estate guy, so when he sells a house, he hires me to do some of the gardening.

I don't have many friends. I'm kind of a loner. I liked to have friends, but I don't have many. I work every day. Sundays I take off. I go to church. I go to the mission. But other than that, by nine at night, I'm home. I don't like to be out at night. I don't like that.

But before I came here to this neighborhood, I'll tell you it was bad.

In those days I did the same thing. Work, home, work, home, work, home. We did what we had to. I started work at six in the morning. But in those days, it was terrible. And I paid four hundred dollars a month for a room in the Mission District that I can hardly see—four hundred dollars!

The Indians run those hotels. They don't own them. The real owners are the Americans up north.

There Might Be a Tunnel from Peru to Mexico

My brother stays in my home in Mexico. He doesn't like it here. He's a Nationalist. But he is the one who looks the most like an American. He's completely white, and he's huge. We have a white part from my mother. She never talked to me about it, and I never asked her out of respect, but I think she belonged to a Mexican family that was mixed. When the Spaniards came to Mexico, they made all kinds of interracial groups with the Indians. And I think this way, because my mother's white just like an American. My father was dark skinned, darker than me. Father had the green eyes of an Indian.

Murillo Meza is my real name. A lot of immigrants from other countries like El Salvador and Honduras change their name. They always deny their ancestry. Not me.

We have lived so close to the United States. It's like going from here to another state. We go and buy things in America, and we are able to live in Mexico.

We are the people born and raised in Baja. A lot of Mexicans that you see there, they come from the south, and they are telling you that they are from Baja. And they're not. We have our customs, our way of living, our believing, our everything.

The difference is *we're almost Americanized*. We work here, and we live there. And in the next generation, some of them will be born here. See, it goes back and forth: the United States, Mexico, United States, Mexico. Other Mexicans walk differently. You can put me on the sidewalk with one of those guys, and if we walk together, you will see the difference.

They are my blood, too, but I just don't like the way they behave in front of people. I don't like that. They speak to each other with no respect. They're too macho—Macho, macho, macho!

Incas and Mayas are the smarter tribes. But I think they built this huge tunnel connecting Mexico to Peru underground. Nobody knows, but some kind of train ran through Central America. That is my opinion.

Talking about Life and Talking about Family

My brother, he's single, so all he does is pay the electricity and the water for my house I own in Baja. He's the one who lives there.

I want to see my nieces grow up and see what they do with their life. The main thing for me is I want to see the family keeps going. The rest of us are very, very old. So the only things we have left are my sister's three girls: the eldest is thirty, the other one is twenty-eight, and the little one is seventeen now. She's doing very well, and I hope with all my heart that she goes to college.

The other ones I want to see grow up, they are the two from my cousin. She has one nineteen-year-old, and she has another daughter who is so smart. She's graduating already. So they're fine.

My aunt, uncles, sister, brother, and me, I think we soon will go. We're getting too old. You cannot go back.

I always go to Baja on Thanksgiving and come back in January. Everybody gets together talking about different things, talking about life, and talking about family. And I was so happy that everything's fine. I don't have to worry anymore if they don't have a house or don't have anything to eat or their well being.

I Have No Regrets

Today they say, "You have to hate white people. Do not do things for them. They make you slaves." Everybody was fine until each day in the newspaper, in the books and in school, they started giving children the history about their race. They told them that all the Spaniards killed you, and they killed your parents; they killed your ways of life. They killed your religion. They killed your children, and they killed everything. And then parents will tell them, "Hey, when you work in the United States, you've got to hate the white people. Don't get along with them. Don't do anything with them." My father never told me, "Hate."

I consider myself belonging in both places because my ancestors worked here in California. They helped with the land, and like every other race, they put a little bit of effort to make California what it is. I have no regrets.

THIRTEEN

Natalie Jeremijenko

AUSTRALIAN-AMERICAN

I first met Natalie when she came east from California to give a lecture on her techno-art at the Museum of Modern Art. Natalie spoke in an educated, modulated English accent without a trace of the outback "G'day" in it.

There is an obvious dichotomy between Australia's expansive land, the openness and hardiness of its people, its penal beginning and Australians who wish to fit in and belong to the larger world — in all this, a culture clash rises. This has become the fodder for Natalie, as well as for other artists, writers, and filmmakers.

She has moved to New York. Natalie commutes to New Haven, where she teaches engineering at Yale. Her career in techno-art has also taken off, and the Massachusetts Institute of Technology has named her one of the top one hundred innovators of America.

To the Place of the Toad Lickers

I was the odd one who was born up the coast. My father was in Mackay, Australia, doing his internship; he was a doctor. The other nine siblings were born in Brisbane.

That area had some very interesting history. There is a stretch of road just outside town where they have had a lot of murders. It has something to do with the fact that immigrant workers with their own tribal laws are brought in together to work on the sugar cane. Apart from that, it's just a place that's dripping with sugarcane and sugar and rum and all things sugary.

It's also one of the places in Queensland that demonstrates one of Australia's great historical moments. Settlers introduced a huge poisonous toad from Africa to eat the sugarcane beetle—which apparently they do, but they don't in Australia because there's much easier prey everywhere else. So they let these cane toads out, these huge creatures, they poison all the waters, and they kill the entire native fauna and flora as well. They are a massive, moving wave; they have cane toad reports. "Cane toads have got up to the crossroads. They're moving west, and they're moving north."

They're very poisonous. But they're also a hallucinogen, if you lick their skin. There are all sorts of cane-toad licking. Being accused of cane-toad licking is a big insult.

My father arrived in Australia from Poland when he was fourteen or fifteen. If you arrive when you're sixteen, you're put straight into a work camp. If you're under sixteen you can go to school. My father had not actually been to school because he had been at war all his life. He fled the Ukraine to Poland and basically walked across Europe to get out of there. He lied about his age. He went to medical school at seventeen. His father had taught him along the way. It was just him and his parents. His parents had been very well educated. So I imagine along the way they tried to educate him.

He was in various camps. They escaped several times. The story is quite unclear. Every time he talks about it, he gets very upset. He was run over when he was eight; at ten he was stabbed, and then he was shot at a couple of times as well.

These incidences happened in the Ukraine and Poland. They kept moving. He once traced out on the map where their family walked, and it seemed to me—I was very young at the time—it seemed to me that they walked the entire way across Europe.

My mother was a local Australian. It is hard to find out her history as she is an unreliable narrator. I know there was one grand house along the river. My mother lived in it with her six maiden great-aunts, my grandmother, and my grandfather. My great aunt Nora, the pianist, the oldest of the children, supported the entire family through teaching piano. Eventually Great-Aunt Nora got an OBE [an Order of the British Empire] as well as various colonial honors.

It Was Absolute Cacophony

I grew up in Brisbane in a little suburban house, which was originally a three-bedroom house, a nice little two-story suburban icon, white brick in a little cul-de-sac. But my parents kept having children until there were ten, so they had to keep building underneath the verandahs, building in the four-car garage, building in the basement, to accommodate the ten children.

We all lived there, the twelve of us, with one bathroom. When there were still eight children, four girls were in the girls' room and four boys in the boys' room in two sets of bunks. My mother would sit in between the boys' and girls' rooms and read aloud. And we would all throw dolls and stuffed animals at her because it's very hard to read one book to eight children of that age span. My mother had two more children, but she wanted more and more. She had two miscarriages; the last two children she lost. When she couldn't have children, and even when she was still having children, she collected cupids. So there were always little baby figurines everywhere. At the dinner table there were little silver cupids, and hanging over all the walls and down in the music room cupids would alternate with all these busts of Bach and Mozart, the three pianos, the twenty-seven violins, and the cello and the mandolin and the balalaika in the music room. We would all go down and practice at one time. It was absolute cacophony. There were little brass cupids on the piano, little brass cupid holders to hold back the music.

A Shrine to Jamba

Before I'd left Australia, I'd gotten a couple of university degrees and had a baby when I was twenty, a beautiful little girl named Jamba. The person I had the baby with was, in fact, unemployed. I realized I had to make some money. So I started a business. Expo '88 was happening in Brisbane. I did a big black-tie ball and said it was the official ending party. I just lied. It was billed as the Last Night of the Expo. It was a huge event. It sold out instantly. I made thousands of dollars.

With that money I put on a big rock music festival. Quite coincidentally, I had became quite a successful businesswoman.

When I was in Brisbane I lived in a big abandoned warehouse with seven stories. I had the office and my place on the top floor, which was about four thousand square feet. It had these huge windows all around with great views of the city. It was in this very dilapidated area. It had a gallery on the first floor and a dingy little club in the basement. All the floors in between were studios. In the true sense it was very grungy and industrial. My daughter and I lived on the top floor. It was a shrine to Jamba. This wild little three-year-old drew on the open areas of polished wood floors. Her swing was in the middle, and her bathtub was right in the middle of the big bay windows. It was really a wonderful place.

That was when I started having trouble with Jamba's father. Basically he had not played much of a role in her life until after she was two and a half. He had gone away for six months and had not contacted her at all. We had split up shortly after she was born, when she was about six months old. That's when I moved back to Brisbane. When I was studying at Melbourne, my daughter's father had said that he would take Jamba away for a couple of weeks for a vacation to what I thought was England. And I had sort of agreed.

The day that she left, I had sewed her this little black travel outfit. I had all these rationalizations in my head that I had a big festival going, and I had some papers to finish. I thought that it would be great that I could have some time alone and that she could reconnect with her father, Brad. It was the first time she was really away from me. We had made her a little suitcase and painted it ourselves and stuck pictures of her on the side, and I made her a little travel suit. I packed up her little bag, matching velvet jumper and skirt with pom-poms sewn all around, and black boots that were shiny, shiny, shiny. She was very thrilled and spun around in her skirt. She didn't understand what was happening and neither did I.

I remember on the day that she was leaving I had gotten her and spoken to her a lot, told her that I would miss her a lot, that I loved her, but I had never had such an incredible split between my rational head that said, "Oh, good! I'll get some time alone to do some work and to be very productive," and my emotions. I sent her off with her father for a two-week vacation.

I was a mess. I couldn't work. I woke up that morning, and I smashed three cups. I just dropped them. I was physically uncoordinated and shaking and just in a terrible state.

He Had No Intention of Bringing Her Back

And I didn't see her again for about a year. I didn't know where she was. For the first two months, I was ringing her most days and talking to her, and her father started saying that he was delaying coming back, a day, and then another day. Then he was suggesting that I come over. I explained to him that I wasn't going to come to England, and we had this fight.

I remember my phone bill that month was two thousand dollars. And I went to the airport three times to meet Jamba, who was then three and a half, almost four. So you have to organize an escort to accompany her on the long trip to Australia. And I didn't go over there and get her myself, which is one of my great regrets. The father kept saying she was coming. And I'd go to the airport, and she wouldn't turn up. I'd spend hours and hours waiting. In retrospect I realized that he had no intention of bringing her back and that he was trying to use my daughter to get me to England. He had this idea that we were going to start a life over there. His excuse for why he wasn't coming back kept changing. She had left in October of 1990. By May of 1991 I was getting very distressed and realized what was happening. I sent him over four thousand dollars, which was a lot of money for me, and he came back finally with my daughter. And so I remember going to the airport, and I was then down in Melbourne, and my little girl was in customs, and I was on the other side of customs. I pried open the sliding door. The customs officials came out and started escorting me, started grabbing me and pulling me back. I could see Jamba in her little travel outfit that I had made with little pom-poms. She screamed out to me and I screamed out to her. She was actually standing on the luggage turnstile. And the guards let me go, and I grabbed her. I thought I was going to squeeze all the toothpaste out of her.

Then started the most horrible month of my life where the father had completely changed his tune. He had gotten it into his head that I was an irresponsible mother. (He really had not much to do with her beforehand). He came and stayed. He didn't stay with me; he stayed with his sister. But he wouldn't let me alone with my daughter. He would follow me around and kept trying to pretend that this was a normal situation.

I also tried to organize counseling or mediation so that we could get a parenting agreement written up and signed, so I wouldn't go through this terrible torture that I'd just been through of not knowing when and how she was coming back. We could have it clearly set out. Those were the most horrible mediations I ever sat through, where they became forums for him to express this vitriol and hate and accuse me of all sorts of things. In retrospect I realize that maybe my daughter had said to him that one night she had woken up in the warehouse, and I was at the back working, at the end of the long space. She called out to me, and I hadn't heard her. So she walked out and down the stairs and out the front door and got all the way to the first floor and someone heard her. It's a traumatic thing for a kid. She had told the father that story. This was the thing he was using as the basis against me. Maybe he was genuinely frightened by that incident. He started a campaign where we would be walking down the street, and he wouldn't walk beside us but remained ten feet behind, always watching. It seemed very absurd and silly to me. I humored him.

He wasn't supposed to be there. I would say, "I'm taking my daughter out."

He would say, "You're not going anywhere without me to supervise," except when he wanted to play tennis. Then it was sort of a convenience.

That horrible, horrible month when I was studying, and I had my daughter at school, I was doing my honors degree in sculpture.

No One in His Family Knew Where He Was

I was full of anger at the mediators for not being able to resolve it. Well, that's not completely true. One of them said, "What you can do is call the policeman and get a restraining order on this man." I had no sense of being in a situation that required that sort of measure. It was so dramatic and irrational. It couldn't be a reasonable course of action because it sounded so absurd. I knew this person; I had known him for five years before I had a baby with him, and I just didn't think that police or courts had anything to do with this.

Then he said he was going overseas again, and he was taking my daughter. I told him, no, he wasn't going to. I kept telling him, "No."

He said he was just going back for a couple of weeks. His mother and sister and I kept saying he couldn't take her. His mother talked to him for two days. He took Jamba.

I followed them to the airport and stood there holding on to my daughter and saying "No, you're not taking her." Still I didn't call the police. I just couldn't believe that I was in a situation I couldn't handle, so intensely personal. He took her out of my arms and took off, and he said he was going back to England. But I called that number trying to track him down, and they weren't there. They had in fact gone to America, to Utah of all places. I later found out that he had met a woman, Susan, who is his wife—but now his ex-wife—and she was an American at that time.

When I was trying to find him, no one in his family knew where he was, and I didn't know where he was. He was in Utah for some time; he was in Indonesia, he was in Africa, and he was in England for some part as well. I eventually tracked him down almost a year later to San Francisco.

Get My Daughter Back

I had finally gone to a lawyer, and I said to him, "Get my daughter back." He said he couldn't initiate any sort of case or do anything without the child being in the country. He told me very authoritatively and totally straight-faced. Completely wrong advice. I had no idea how someone could do that. It had just been a series of bad advice. So I didn't think I had a legal position to stand on because, according to this lawyer, he couldn't start proceedings until the child was in the country, which was completely absurd, as I later learned when I studied the Hague Convention on international child abduction.

The thing that finally worked was an informal network of family and friends. Someone had run into Brad in the street in London. Then someone, his mother's friend's daughter's husband, had seen him in San Francisco. I found out where they were, and I flew over there, again thinking that I could negotiate or speak with Jamba's father, in spite of how many unreasonable things he had done. I arranged to meet them. He said he got so angry that he forgot to bring my daughter with him. Then he let me see her, but again he was there doing his supervising thing. While he was supervising me he was also putting his hands up my skirt and rubbing my legs and making these really offensive and inappropriate gestures, really sexual gestures in front of my daughter. Again I was sort of paralyzed by all of this instead of just punching him. I was just trying to be normal in front of my daughter. I was pushing him away. Quite amazing.

I stayed for a couple of weeks. I went to a lawyer in San Francisco, and I paid a lot of money to initiate a court case in America. He was the one who said that I had to go back and initiate a court case in Australia under the Hague Convention, which I flew back for.

Then I started this whole long year of flying to and fro, trying to see my daughter and trying to get her extradited to Australia. After the first big court case it could have been settled. In San Francisco Superior Court (and in courts all over America) they get normal attorneys who sit in as a judge when the judge is on vacation. Unfortunately, the judge was on vacation that day. An attorney sat there, who didn't know the law, hadn't heard of the Hague Convention. The defense Brad had at that point was jurisdiction. He said international law doesn't hold. The law was very clear, a completely open and shut case. The person sitting in as judge didn't know about this law and so deferred to a long hearing, which meant that it was calendared for a later time. It got postponed. Then this long series of judicial arguments: Jamba's father kept bouncing one jurisdiction off the other, Australian jurisdiction against California jurisdiction against international Hague Convention jurisdiction, until finally the Hague Convention jurisdiction, which is only valid for a year after the child is abducted, became invalid.

The Slipperiness of American Characters

After about a year of to-ing and fro-ing between Australia and America and spending a great deal of money on court cases and borrowing money from my parents and my brother and my business, while also trying to do my Ph.D. in philosophy, I decided that spending all this energy on the court case was basically not being a part of my daughter's life. I was only being involved with court procedures.

So I moved to San Francisco on a tourist visa. I advertised myself as a personal trainer in the local paper. I found very wonderful people who were interested in having a personal trainer. One was a wonderful old queen who retired so he could devote himself fully to being a drag queen. He wanted me to come every day and work out with him and help him choose costumes. We had a great time. He kept taking me out to bars, to all the gay bars in San Francisco. We talked about the job, about what I was going to do. The last time I saw him, we were at a bar on Market Street, and he said to me, "Girl, you could do anything you want. What are you doing in personal training?" He was very sweet. I never saw him again. This was my introduction to the slipperiness of American characters. He never gave me his number. He just disappeared.

I'll Show You a Good Time

When I first came to America, I had never been outside of Australia before in my entire life. In retrospect it seems silly, but it was cheaper to buy a ticket to New York than to go directly to San Francisco. I was quite thrilled with the idea of going through New York.

And so I put on my orange taffeta coat and got on the plane and arrived in New York. On the subway train, there were black people, and they were playing music. They were speaking so loudly. I couldn't understand why they were playing this loud music. I thought it was the funkiest, most fun public transport experience I had ever had, until the train master came through and told them to turn it off, and they started talking back to him, and there was this whole yelling fight.

And something about arriving in New York, I must have looked like I was just arriving in New York, the complete innocent. I looked on my list of things, and it said "coffee shop." This very nice Nigerian international student came along and was talking to me, saying that he could show me a couple of actual coffee shops. He offered to show me this very elite nightclub that had opened up the night before and had been in the news because Cher had been rejected. She was told to go away. We went into this nightclub. I had been in New York for three or four hours. I was talking to this very sweet Nigerian fellow, and I remember these two shoulders came closing in; I was trying to talk over them, but there were these two men. One of them was a very tall New York barrister, one of the best-looking men I have ever seen in my life, and they started talking to me. They were thrilled that I had only been in New York a few hours.

They said, "I'll show you a good time. I'll show you some sights." We talked for a while, and I completely lost this Nigerian international student who had been so sweet.

And so I jumped in the back of this little white sports car that was only a two-seater and there was snow all around, and all I had was my orange taffeta coat. I remember walking along at one point earlier when someone yelled, "Put some clothes on. Get some proper clothes on." I realized that I was underdressed. Somehow I wasn't cold. I sat in the back of this white sports car, driving across the Brooklyn Bridge, squealing all the way across it. Big thrills!

They took me driving all around, everywhere. At three o'clock in the morning they took me down to the fish market. The light was just coming up; it was still kind of dark. I couldn't believe everything in New York was on a scale of one to three in relation to Australia. Seagulls in America are huge compared to Australian seagulls. I was fascinated.

Then we jumped back in the car. As we were driving off I waved good-bye to one of the fisherman, and he threw a fish, and it landed in the car.

And then we went driving to this tenement building and found a bakery down in the basement that had very steep steps. It was a very warm bakery. Anyway, by seven or eight o'clock the next morning we had been driving around. Mark and the other fellow—I can't remember his name—anyway he had to go to work. He was going to drop him off and then drop me back to where I was staying. He dropped his friend off; and they had been just charming and lovely all the time, really great fun.

Maybe I Could Escape through the Window

Then we drove uptown to drop me off. It must have been about seven o'clock in the morning; there wasn't much traffic. He drove right past the place I was staying in. I said, "Mark, where are you going?"

He said, "Now I'm going to show you New York." He took me up to Harlem, and he turned nasty all of a sudden.

He had my purse.

He took me down to the ferry, and we were on the ferry. At this point I was panicking; I wanted to get away, and he had me by the wrist. I was saying to passersby, "Can you help me? This man won't let me go." They all walked past. No one would help. Here I was in the middle of this strange city.

I was forced to spend the whole day with him. He took me to dinner at this place where he was very well known. I remember going to bathrooms thinking I could escape through the window. While I was climbing out the window, the waiters came in and grabbed me. I couldn't get out. I had to go back to the table.

Then he took me for another drive out to the Bronx. About two o'clock the next morning, and I was still a prisoner in the car. Eventually he fell asleep on the side of the street. So I just quietly got out of the car with my money and my purse and walked away. I got home and told this whole story to the guy I was staying with. That was my first day.

Going to Stanford

I was still trying to finish my Ph.D. at Melbourne, but I wasn't getting much work done the first year I was in America. Basically, I was on a tourist visa, and I couldn't work. I was going to court every other week, being arrested by police on various trumped-up charges of child abuse, threats to abduct my daughter, and essentially being harassed by having to arrange people and lawyers to supervise my visitations with my daughter to take her to the park. So I didn't get much work done on my Ph.D.

I was looking for a job. I had to find a job with a company that would invest four thousand dollars in getting me a work visa. I went to a lot of design firms; I worked for free at IDEO, the biggest design consulting firm in America. And they would give me some consultant work and see what they could do. I was just knocking on doors trying to get a job. That first horrible year I couldn't find anything. Of course, there were little jobs like being a waitress that wouldn't pay for your working visa.

Eventually I sold myself to some people at Xerox Park, which is the corporate think tank in Silicon Valley. I told them they should employ me. It was the first time they had an employee who was an artist type. So I ended up in this dream job in Xerox Park, computing, and giving talks to visitors. TV crews came in all the time. This was where they invented the future. I worked there for a year. Then I realized that I had to finish my Ph.D., and I knew I had to stay in the area. I applied to Stanford. By virtue of the fact that I was working at this job at Xerox Park I could be accepted. I worked at Xerox Park full-time and studied for the first year. Then I realized that I couldn't do that effectively, so I spent the next two years at Stanford. I left my job at Xerox Park to work on my Ph.D. there in mechanical engineering, design engineering. I always say that Stanford is the only unstructured university I've ever been to. It's a funny place.

Marrying a Pushy Guy

In August last year, I met by chance a young fellow at an art gallery. I made a point to gain his attention by being dramatic and grabbing both ends of a techno-piece made with a Tesla coil, which produced vivid electrical sparks. The delivery system consists of a high-voltage transformer and a spark gap, and essentially it is a charge delivery system that keeps energy sloshing back and forth, but it won't electrocute you if you know what you are doing.

After I impressed him, he was very pushy, following me around asking me all these questions. He gave me his card, and now I was very impressed.

And to cut a long story short, I am marrying that pushy person in two days and having a baby, and I am living happily ever after.

FOURTEEN

Isil Gundes

TURKISH-AMERICAN

Isil is a fresh-faced twenty-year-old, high-spirited and always in a rush. Living in the present, she gets involved in what is in front of her and then is late for her next appointment or class. She dresses in blue jeans and backpack; her hair is long and loosely pulled back. She looks like a typical college co-ed. Her defining trait is the immediacy of her emotions. A therapist would never have to tell her to go with her feelings.

Time after time, her face grows red as she pontificates on the hazards for women in a marriage, using her parents as illustration. In Turkey, unlike a lot of neighboring Muslim countries where only men sit outdoors sipping their dark coffee and smoking cigarettes, a scattering of women sit at the tables with their uncovered faces tilted toward the sun. The Turkish government is fiercely secular, although Islamic fundamentalists have been trying to gain strength, and the

country is almost entirely Muslim. Isil knows the political and emotional risks
in a world where women are not valued as equals. However, Isil herself now has
the upper hand in her American "green-card" marriage, as the husband is now
smitten with her. Turkey's major city, Istanbul, is in two continents. A two-
dollar cab ride over a bridge that spans the Bosporus Straits takes a person from
Asia into Europe. Isil's sneaker-clad feet dance over the breach.

She Didn't Want to Let the Marriage Go

My mother probably never worked in her life. My father sells construction
materials to companies. My mom and my dad are two totally opposite
people, so they fight. While I was growing up, it was fighting all the time.
That's why I actually came here, because when I was in high school, it was
terrible. They fought so much, and I said, "No way," because I started feeling a change in my personality. I started being really aggressive.

So after high school, I went to college for one year in Ankara, and it
was still really bad at home. Everything would start a fight. "Why did
you put this there? I put that here."

This is how we ate: My father would eat in the living room, my mom
would eat in the kitchen, and I would eat in my room. Mom, Dad, everybody had different TVs, and it was strange.

Their marriage was arranged. At that time in Turkey, it was more
likely the man would choose the woman. What happened was somebody
saw my mom in the family, and they took my dad to see her, and they
arranged a meeting. My grandfather didn't even know that this was happening. My mom had no idea, but my dad knew that he came there to
take my mom. He liked her, so a couple of weeks later, the door rings,
and my father's relatives come in and say, "He wants to get married to
your daughter." And that's kind of what they do in Turkey. They check
out the guy's background, what's going on, and they find if he is coming
from a good family, and if they're rich. Everything checked out so my
mom's family was okay with it.

My mom said that my father was really nice in the beginning. I don't
know what happened after that. He used to drink a lot, and he would
come to the door around five in the morning, and we would not know

where he had been. My mother would not open the door, and he would stand there begging. I'd have to go to open the door, and it caused a big fight. "Why did you open the door?" He was not a family father. He should not have gotten married.

He worked for a company, and they sent him to manage a business in Istanbul, so he went away for about three years. He came home for weekends and often not even then. That was the time they were really separated, and my mom found out that there was another woman in Istanbul. Because she did not work, she didn't want to let the marriage go, because if she got divorced, my father would not take care of us. He would have gone to China or someplace—so I kind of understood my mom.

Eventually they came back together, yet they could never get along. I couldn't get along with him either, and neither could my brother. For too many years we had been separated from him, and then all of a sudden he came back into our lives and started telling us what to do. "You don't do that. You do this." I kind of hated my father at times.

If You Get Divorced, It's Not My Fault

When I was sixteen, I met this guy. He was really old. He was thirty-six, and I fell deeply in love. Not only that, he was married, and he had a kid. Nobody found out for three years.

All of a sudden, my mom heard it from somewhere, and she came up to me. She said, "I hope I didn't hear these things. I hope it's not true, but if it's true you go and arrange to finish it. I don't want to hear a word. If your father hears about it, he'll kill both of you."

This fellow would never let me go. I knew that. I said, "Okay, I'm not happy at home, and I'm not happy with this guy. I have to finish it, but I know if I stay in Turkey, I'm not going to do anything."

Then he *did* get divorced. I knew that he had relationships before, and he always told me, "If it wasn't you, it would be someone else because I'm not happy with this woman," so I never blamed myself.

I always told him, "If you get divorced, I won't take the blame. I don't want you to get divorced." He was not in my plans. I hadn't arranged my future yet.

My Brother Was Talking to Himself

So I came to America. My brother actually left home when I was in junior high. He came here to do his master's degree, and he never wants to go back. One summer after he came back, he saw my mother and father fighting, and it made him go crazy. Also my brother knew that he would do better here. He was in New Jersey working for a company when I came. He was sort of odd when I arrived. He was so crazy. He was talking to himself. I was like, "Oh, my God, who are you talking to? What are you doing?"

He had a hard time, because my father really didn't help him much, but he's the kind of guy who would tell us, "I'm going to be really rich when I'm thirty." He wakes up at five o'clock in the morning. He hangs out at home. He would make business phone calls to Europe at two in the morning, and then go to the office. He did well, although I couldn't get along with him.

When he found out about this older guy, he got really crazy, and we had a big fight. This guy actually came to New York for one night. It was really good to hear from him. He called. I had missed him, and I said, "You know, I'm staying with my brother. There is no way that I can see you for more than one night."

"Okay, for one night, what the hell. I'm coming."

But the bad thing was I had this conversation on the phone when he was leaving the airport, and I totally lied to my brother about that, and I said, "I'm going to a friend's house, and I'll stay the night with her." But I'm so stupid. When he called from the airport to say good-bye to me, the answering machine picked up part of our conversation.

My brother yelled, "You lied to me. I really don't want you anymore! I think you're a very bad person. You cannot lie to me about this. You're doing wrong, and you have one month to get out of my place."

Towels Don't Wash Themselves

I was nineteen. It was the first year I came here, so I didn't know anybody. I was looking for a roommate, and I met this Pakistani girl, and she was looking for a roommate, too. I didn't know her, but she kind of looked okay. And I moved into her apartment, and she turned out to be this really dirty girl. For a month the bathroom smelled really weird. I don't know what it was. I found out if was her towel. I'm like, "Noveli, do you ever wash your towel?"

She said, "Why, I always use it after I take a shower when I'm clean. You don't need to wash your towel."

I say, "Towels don't wash themselves."

She was the one who rented the apartment. Actually it was her uncle who had signed the lease, so she was taking the rent from me, but she wasn't paying it to the building management. I thought that she was. And one day I came to the apartment, and I find this note. "You have two days to take your stuff out of the apartment or they're going to come and take it out for you." I couldn't believe it. I have two days. I don't know anybody here. I have nothing. Where am I going to stay? Will I have to live on the streets or something?

She tells me, "Don't worry about it. I'm so sorry I did that to you. I'm going to go find an apartment for you."

And she could have, but the funny thing is, I met a guy a few days later. I'm crying on the phone. I'm telling him what happened, what she did to me, and he said, "Okay, come and stay with me for a week."

I don't even know the guy. What else can I do? I don't know anybody here.

I immediately started looking for an apartment. My phone bill came, and it was more than eleven hundred dollars. I couldn't believe it. They were all calls to Pakistan—on my phone she started calling Pakistan! I could never find her, never get my money back. I had to pay the eleven hundred dollars.

This guy turned out to be really nice. In New York, it's hard to find somebody, but he was really nice, and he offered to let me stay with him and share the rent, and I said, "Okay," and I stayed with him for one year.

The Easiest Way to Get a Green Card Is to Get Married

Actually, I have only one problem here. I cannot make friends. It's so strange. In New York, there are so many people from different countries, and American people should be used to it, but they're not, actually. So that's the bad part. I do not know why. I just cannot talk easily to any-body. Also, I'm not helping anybody anymore because of the experiences I have had. A Turkish girl stayed in my house, maybe four months, not paying rent, and I found her a job. I've done everything for her. She's not calling me now. That's what I mean.

People change when they come here. It's so strange. My brother actu-ally talks about the green card. He is telling me that I should get a green card. The easiest way is to get married. After I broke up with this guy that I lived with for a year, I met a new fellow. He needed some money. I knew that this guy needed some money, so I went to where he worked, and I talked to him. My brother was willing to pay anything. It was, "Get your green card. It's very important." So I talked to a guy and gave him seven thousand dollars to get married.

I married him, and he wants to stay married. He also turned out to be a really nice guy. It's like I'm lucky. We're married, and hopefully I'm going to get my green card. We got married at City Hall. I didn't tell that to my father. He would be so mad, yelling, "What are you doing!"

I went to Washington, D.C., this weekend, and my dad was screaming and yelling to my mom, "Why did we hide things from him?" He didn't talk to me because when he starts talking to me, he acts like he is going to kill me. I acted proper to my father.

Our family is not really religious. We are not that crazy about Islam. The guy I married, he doesn't believe in God. He was a philosophy major.

"There is no God." That's how he is.

I say, "What are you talking about? There's no God. Don't even say that there's no God."

He's nice, but he's not my type—so I kind of regret what I did a little bit. I'm just not sure.

I am trying to stay together another year, but I didn't tell him. It's not that I don't like him or anything. I will be a friend forever, but he's just not my kind of guy. He's too quiet. He likes me, but I don't think he loves me because our relationship went down a bit because we're totally dif-ferent. I think he's a little stupid, too. I'm not saying "stupid," but I think he's a little slow, mainly about relationships. If you gave him a book, he would read it, and he would tell you what it says exactly. He would understand that. But when you talk to him about relationships or emotions, he's a little slow. When you fight, he doesn't get it.

His background is American. I met his mom. He has a sister, but I have not met her yet, but probably I need to go over there and tell them techniques of the green card and about our green-card marriage. He is from Michigan.

I used to work at a restaurant, and there was another restaurant across the street, and he was bartending over there. He came east to open up an iron design shop. He's trying to save money to do that.

I just kind of regret it because I did arrange it. Now, I'm not fighting. I'm just agreeing, "Yeah, you're right." Because since I've decided I'm not going to be with this guy, I'm not trying to change him. I'm like, "Yeah, okay, you're right, whatever."

Actually, here's what I told him for a fact. I was going to get married with my ex-boyfriend. Because when I first met him, I was still seeing my ex-boyfriend, and I said, "I don't know if you want to be with me, but I already talked to my ex-boyfriend, and he wants to do this for a green card."

And he said, "No, I'll do it, right away," because he knew that there was money in it.

I said, "Okay."

I Got So Depressed That I Ate M&Ms, Candies,
Whatever I Found in Front of the TV

We're waiting for the INS interview. Probably that's going to be next year, and after the interview, I'll say, "Let's separate our apartment and everything." Our apartment is a one bedroom. It's kind of nice, but not my kind of place. It's a huge apartment. When I was with that first guy for one year, I was in a tiny room. Two people in that apartment. I was going crazy, and the worst thing happened to me. Oh, it was so bad. At that time I got pregnant. I couldn't have the baby, so I had to have an abortion. I paid so much money. It was a very expensive, nice place. I never had an operation. I was so scared, and I felt so bad about it. I thought about it.

What if I go to the place, what if something happened? What am I going to say to my brother? I told my friend, "My brother would kill you, you know. I'm telling you, it's like divorce, a bad thing."

"She died when she was getting an abortion," kept running through my head. I felt really bad. I paid two months rent, but after the abortion he paid the rest.

He would leave me at home to go out with his friends. I said, "I can't believe you're doing this. You know that I don't have any friends." Then I talked again to him, "You've got to do something. You can't just leave me alone. I don't know anybody. I just cannot be alone with this."

I never got depressed that much all my life. I didn't come to school. It was terrible. I got dismissed. When I wanted to return to school, I had to beg. I would not go out. I didn't work. I sat in front of the TV and ate M&Ms, candies, whatever I found. I gained like fifty pounds watching TV, fighting with everybody.

I talked to my friends on the phone all the time in Turkey. They helped me a lot. They would insist, "Get out of the bed."

People were calling at seven in the morning to wake me up. "Hey, you've got a call from Turkey."

Eventually I said, "I have to find a new apartment." So when I was trying to look for the apartment, I realized that I needed money, so I went to get a job.

I'm like, "Oh, God, I've grown up a lot."

During the time that I was young and at home, my mom was so unhappy so she often left me alone, so I know how to arrange things for myself. My brother cannot believe what I have accomplished for myself because he didn't help me with anything. I found my own job as a hostess in a restaurant. I found my school. I did everything myself. I found my own apartment. When he threw me out of his place that night, my brother told me, "You'll have to come back." I did not come back. I was totally fine. I can't believe myself that I did all this.

I finally got my own apartment. Oh God, I was so happy. I didn't have any work permission here, but I was able to wait tables. School was terrible at that time. Luckily, my father paid the tuition. That was the good part.

Hopefully, I have only one problem left—the green card. I still have to go to the interview. When I get it, that's going to make me even happier.

My mother knows about my life. I never like to hide anything from my mom, not anymore. She just came from Turkey to stay with my brother. I just promise myself I'm going to be so nice to my mother. I really feel sorry that her life with my father got so crazy. This time when I went to Washington, we were all together, and we were talking about how he got so crazy. He's really nuts. I thought that maybe it was because he used to drink a lot of alcohol. I don't know what happened to him. He screams, "Don't put it there." Everything from him is just yelling. My mother came here to talk to him in order to get a divorce. She says, "I'm getting a divorce. I'm going to talk to him about arrangements."

I'm like, "Okay." And then she comes, and she irons his shirts.

"Mom, what are you doing?" She promised herself that she's not going to do anything for him.

She said, "I feel so sorry for him. Who's going to take care of him? You know I'm a Turkish woman."

I'm like, "So what? If he needs somebody, he would have respect for you, he wouldn't scream. You know he would be nice to you if he needed you. He doesn't need you. He doesn't care. He just screams, yells, and tells you you're stupid."

She's like, "I don't know. Nobody would deal with your father; he is so crazy."

I'm like, "Why do you have to deal with it?"

I've decided that I'm going to be nice to my mom. She loves the fellow I live with. She loves him because he's so quiet. For me it's boring. I can't talk to him.

My mother is like, "Oh my gosh, he's so great, a nice guy. I can feel it. He's very nice."

I hadn't been to Turkey for two years, and I went last summer. I had the best time. I didn't want to come back. I was crying at the airport not to come back.

I have to be here because I'm going to school. If I go back to Turkey, I'd have to start school again. It's too hard to get into a college in Turkey, a lot harder than here. I did that once. I can't do it again. You take one examination in Turkey for the university, and in that one test, they ask anything that you learned in junior high or high school. They give you only one exam. I can't take that anymore. I've forgotten everything I learned in Turkey. But being in Turkey I have the feeling that the people are my brothers and sisters and that I am home. I don't have that kind of feeling here.

I called my first love, the older man, when I got my first boyfriend here in the States. "I cannot lie," I said, "I met this guy, and I started dating him." And he got mad, and he talked about it for about four more months, and then finally I said, "That's it!" I had been so much in love. I still think about it, about how stupid I was.

My brother is now nice. He bought a house in Washington, and he moved there, although he is still talking to himself. I think that once he has a million dollars, he'll be fine.

People Started to Cover Their Hair for Money

Turkey is such a strange country. I see these Muslim girls still covering their hair in New York. Who's going to look at your hair? The whole idea of covering your hair is from a long time ago, like thousands of years ago. Okay, it made the men get excited. That's the whole idea of covering your head. Who's going to look at your hair anymore? I don't care about that.

But in Turkey it's the same thing. The first year I went to high school, I really hated that. Because it was that time that Turkey started to change and go back. People started to cover their hair for money. The outside world doesn't know that a lot of models and stars do it for money, too. They get money from all these religious people, and it's like being a paid model. They have appeared in the last issue of *Playboy*, this issue of some sex magazine, and suddenly they are saying, "I found the way to Islam." She covers her hair in the toga. It's funny. She gets paid for that. They do for two years, and then they're bored with it. It's like, "Okay, I'm going back to *Playboy*. I'm sorry."

I used to fight against the conservative line. I would stop my classmates and say, "Why did you come to school like that?" I did that because I used to be scared where Turkey was going. But now I know, nobody's going to let Turkey be like that. I'm sorry, but I hate the other

Muslim countries. I hate them. I'm so scared of them because they're right on top of Turkey. They're trying to change Turkey, make women oppressed. I won't talk to anybody outside. I just stay away.

They're Always Like Working at McDonald's

I totally had a different idea about black people in Turkey. You think that they are real cool—musicians, athletes, hip clothing, and attitudes.

I really didn't know that they were in that bad situation. I didn't know.

I didn't know that there's that much of a big difference until I saw them. They're always like working at McDonald's because they are not allowed better jobs. I didn't know that. My brother used to tell me that there is so much racism in the United States. "Go and see what kind of people there are and how they are treated."

I saw it. I couldn't believe it. It's really different. I can't understand how if they were American and if they were born here, why are they just so unlike the rest of the people? Their language is different. It took me one year to understand at least the summary of what they are saying. I used to look at them, and they'd yell at me because I don't understand. "Oh, please don't shout at me." I really got shocked about that. It's a very different culture. They act that way because they are not in a good situation.

I Am Not Going to End Up Like That — No Way!

Right now I have to concentrate on my studies because it would be the end of my life if I don't finish school. I would have to go back and iron some guy's shirts all my life. That is exactly what would happen. I can't go back to school in Turkey, and I know that. One thing I am certain about—I am not going to turn out to be my mom. I am not going to iron shirts and have some guy screaming and yelling at me. I am not going to end up like that—No way!

FIFTEEN

Jacinta Jones

BRITISH-AMERICAN

I was to meet Jacinta at an Italian coffeehouse. As she came to greet me, her hips swayed to the live jazz. She paused in front of a mural of the canals of Venice. Supple and tall, with olive skin and her black hair in a bun, she could have been Italian herself. She had the looks that are currently popular with models in television advertisements: the semi-identifiable appearance that would appeal to all ethnicities and offend none. Speaking with her upper-class English accent, it was hard to place her inside of any country's border. She was raised to enunciate clearly and precisely in a "rain in Spain falls mainly in the plains" voice.

The clientele in this coffeehouse looked as mixed as she did. There were a few naval officers from an armada that could not be identified. There was a handsome Greek man and a heavyset American black man sitting together, each with identical long white silk scarves and jackets, as if they were mismatched twins who had just come from a separated-at-birth pageant.

It wasn't until she was eighteen that she discovered that her father was a black man from Trinidad. Currently Jacinta is trying to join a "black community" in a city that she asks that I not identify. She is struggling to find the manners and vocabulary that will help her gain acceptance.

I Started Wearing Nine Pairs of Underwear at Once

My mother sent my younger brother and me away to a horrid boarding school when I was seven. When I look back, I think, "God, she was desperate to get rid of us." There were other children who came in by bus every day from where we lived, so I thought, "Why are we boarders?" The first day of school, all the other children were weeping. My brother and I asked, "Why are you crying?"

They said, "We are homesick."

We said, "Homesick?" We didn't know what that was because our parents were never around.

Another girl at school could make herself cry at will by thinking of her parents dying. That would never occur to me. I never worried about my parents because they were never there for us.

We always walked past the bus stop where the kids from the public school waited, and we always thought we were going to be attacked because we wore these bright red uniforms, but when one boy called out after us he turned out to be the sweetest thing.

At that school my brother and I didn't spend a lot of time with each other because he was in the boys' dormitory with boys' activities, and I was with the girls. We had a housemother and housefather who were appalling. They would be all sweet and nice when our parents came to visit, but when the family left, they became ogres.

I remember once scrubbing the table, and the housemother came up to me and said, "Use some elbow grease."

I asked, "Can I get some in the village?"

I was keenly aware that my parents didn't know things about me, that I didn't take sugar anymore, or that I was considered funny. I got very phobic about my clothing. I started thinking if I took my sweater off and the sleeve was turned inside out, I might lose my arm. Or if I took my pants off and one was turned wrong, I might lose a leg. I started wearing nine pairs of underwear at once. I don't know why. I would rotate the one closest to me. I think I was trying to be in diapers as long as I could. I felt kind of lost. I tried learning the piano, and I had a very cruel teacher. She had been in the war and it had affected her mind.

My mother moved to a country house, so she came to pick us up. She had a tendency to move every year. So we left boarding school. My mother always had boyfriends. Previously we had lived with a boyfriend for two months in Cornwall in a hotel. I spent most of my time with a waiter. I would do that. I would establish these great crushes on people and spend all my time with them, and, of course, they would be monstrously flattered.

That Bastard Is Not Your Father!

When we were around ten and eleven, my brother and I were taking a bath together, and my mom came in and said, "How would you feel if your father and I got divorced?"

"No! No! Don't do it. We'd feel terrible."

She said, "Too late. We already did it."

Then there was the issue of whom we were going to live with. My brother picked my daddy.

She screamed, "You ungrateful thing." I wanted to pick my dad, too, but I was afraid to say so. I felt sad for her because nobody wanted to live with her. I guess my dad came and picked up my brother. The other complication was we went to visit Ernest, who had been a friend of my parents originally. There was a postcard from my dad that said he was having a marvelous honeymoon, so she was terribly angry. All the way home on the train she was crying. It was very rare to see my mother cry.

Then she said, "I have something to tell you." I always grew up thinking I had a tan. It seemed strange that I had dark hair and dark skin, and my brother was blond.

So I asked her, "Am I adopted?"

"No," she had said. "You are not adopted, but that bastard is not your father!" She told my dad that she had told me, but he never mentioned it ever. So that's how I found out that my dad was not my dad. My mother, the pathological liar, also said that my natural father was a Spanish doctor.

There was awkwardness regarding "my father" while I was growing up. You can sense it. I think you can tell that by the way people behave. "My father" was my favorite parent, but I felt I didn't deserve to live with him. So off my brother went to live with Dad. At that time I became crazy about horses. Every year my father promised me a horse for my birthday, but he'd say, "Next year." My mother said, "I gave your guinea pigs away six weeks ago, and you didn't even know." I think she could have asked me. She also gave my dog away. She said she gave it to a woman who liked corgis. It didn't get along with our other dog. But at least she should have asked me.

I took two days off from school and went to the town where she said the woman lived, looking for my dog. I wandered all the streets looking for my dog to no avail. My mother must have told another one of her lies.

My Mother Decided That She Would Never Get a Man with Me Around

I used to live at my girlfriend's house. Her mother would think I was an amazing creature. She thought I was fabulous. I asked my mother if I could live with them, and she went bonkers, which surprised me because she was never home. Every year we moved, so I went to many different schools. Somehow I became a Rasputin expert because every school I went to they taught it. I don't know anything else.

Then I developed into being the rebellious one. I got a lot of attention. I was always in the headmaster's office, which was great. I got a lot of attention by being naughty. I needed specs since I was eight years old but my mom was busy, and I never got them. One teacher made it her mission with her fists in the air shouting, "This child needs specs!" I never got them until I left home at seventeen, when I got them myself.

My mother decided that she would never get a man with me around, so she sent me to yet another boarding school when I was fourteen. This school had a very good academic reputation, but they knew I was a wild person. They were extra strict with me. It was like going to prison. It was awful, but I made millions of friends, which I still have. I was expelled because I had a boy in my dormitory. My mother begged them to take me back, but the headmaster said no, that I was too rebellious. I wouldn't wear my hair up because it made me look ugly, so I wore it long down my back. I didn't want to look like a pinhead. I would swing this big rope of hair, and the other students started to follow my lead. Also I was a rabid vegetarian. You were supposed to wear proper black shoes, but I wore rubber flip-flops because I wouldn't wear leather. I was only there eight weeks, but I was famous. Afterwards, people would write me fan mail, and I didn't even know who they were. When they expelled me they called my mother, and she wouldn't have me. They called my father and told him, "She will be on the next train."

I was sobbing. I had made so many friends. I was looking out the back window. We were all sobbing and waving handkerchiefs. It was devastating. My father wouldn't let me unpack because I had to stay in my stepmother's best friend's room, who had space in her house. I wasn't allowed to go to the local school. They thought I would get settled in if I went. When my mother resurfaced, they wanted her to take me. I got very depressed. I was lonely and bored. Thank God I had my brother, but he was in school all day. I read a lot. The librarian took a shine to me, so my father gave her a little money, and I went to live with her. My parents always fought over who should pay for my clothing, so neither gave me any frigging clothing. But this young librarian got pleasure in dressing me up.

My Mother Resurfaced with a New Guy and a Baby

There was a horrible time where we went to look for my mom, but we couldn't find her. Her landlady wouldn't tell us where she was. My father drove my brother and me to her district of England, but then we asked if we could hitch home. My stepmother went bonkers that we hitched back hundreds of miles. She was worried. My stepmother had normal instincts.

Then my mother resurfaced with a new guy and a baby. She said I could live with her again. After the first few honeymoon weeks, she went after me again. She didn't cook for me. I had a bowl and spoon that were designated mine. So when I made my porridge, I had to wash my own bowl and spoon. I was so jealous of my friends who had maids or whose mother made their lunch. I got all my attention outside of the home.

I was working for my mother in the café and watching my little brother, who I was crazy about, but it was hard to get along. Then I met this older guy. He was from South London and trendy. He was staying in this area to recover from his London life. My mother didn't like him because he was working class. Every week, we'd go shopping, and he would buy me some little clothing item. And his mom cooked. My mom couldn't. I would go there for dinner, and we ate like a proper family. He fell in love with me, and I thought I was in love with him, although I was still sort of in love with the boy who had been expelled with me.

Being Beaten Counts as Being Really Down

I found out I was pregnant, so we ran away from home together. I didn't know what to do. I was afraid they would take my baby away from me or make me have an abortion. I had millions of friends, but I lost contact, but fortunately I still had my brother. I went to Scotland, in the wilds. My boyfriend had some friends there. They ranged from twenty-three to twenty-six, and they looked on me as a baby or a pet. People would come over to the house to hear me sing because I had a good voice. I had a horrible time. My boyfriend started to abuse me. My father didn't believe in hitting, but my mother would hit us all the time. My father would say, "If your mother hits you, call the child authorities." My boyfriend would punch me in the arm, even when I was pregnant. That was a very vulnerable time when you have a baby. I was thinking of leaving him, but now I had a reason to stay with him. I had a wonderful baby who I was crazy about, my perfect child, who is now a proper man. So I stayed with this guy, and I married him because we were afraid of my mother. I got in touch with my father because I bumped into their best friend, the one whose bedroom I stayed in. "Please let me tell David. They are so worried." After the baby was born, David and my stepmother came, and they were very sweet and brought presents.

Then I got in touch with my mom. First she was cold. I said, "I called to tell you . . ."

"Yes?"

"I got married."

"Yes."

"And had a baby."

Then she got keen. "What did you have?"

She was very sweet then.

My husband kept getting more and more violent. About two years later my mother's husband died. I asked my mother if I could come back to live with her, and she said yes. I think if the chips were really down, like if I were dying, my mother would be there. But they had to be really, really down. Being beaten counts as being really down. Living with my mother was a year of hell. I had to give her all my welfare. Then I moved to a house they bought from money that they had gotten from an accident settlement from when my brother was hurt. They said they were going to sell the house because it wasn't covering the mortgage.

I said, "Don't sell it. I'll pay the whole mortgage payment."

Everyone said, "Look what you got." But I paid for the whole damn house.

I took the Oxford exams, but a schizophrenic woman living close by became obsessed with me and believed that my son was her child. She stalked me and said she was going to kill me.

So at the last moment I changed my university selection to go to the other part of England to get away from her. My parents sold the house without telling me. They made nine thousand pounds' profit. They said they were going to split the money, but they didn't. I thought it was very important that my son has a house, but they didn't give me money, just dribs and drabs.

After my first year, I transferred to London University and finished my degree there. Meanwhile, I met another guy, my second husband, who has a very controlling personality. One part of me hungered for that as someone who cared, but another part of me found it stifling. He was a very comforting person, and he was crazy about me. I love my brother, and I love my son, but it was hard for me to sustain a relationship. I had to pick for two people, my son and myself.

I'm Big and Black

When I first went to London, I was perusing the telephone directory, and I saw only one listing with the same name that my mother had told me was my father's name. I was amazed to discover this person was existing and living near by. I called him up. "Is this Gabriel?" Next I called up my mom, the pathological liar. "Mom, there is a man whose name is Gabriel Petitbone."

"It's a coincidence."

I called him again. "Is this Gabriel Petitbone and did you know my mom?"

"Yes."

I sort of hesitated, so he said, "Go on, darling. . . ."

"I might be your daughter as well." He didn't sound Spanish. He had an accent, but it didn't seem Spanish. I called my mother and said, "He knew you." But she kept denying it. I knew, but she was still so convincing. Right in my face she said, "It's a coincidence."

I said, "I'm meeting him next week."

She called me up, pleading, "Please don't go. It's him; it's him. He's into black magic. He will flirt with you, his own daughter. Please don't go."

Since that woman kept trying to attack me, I didn't want to get into a weird situation again. It was too late to call it off. I said to my fiancé, "You have to go." He was one of those people who preferred me to be neurotic. I was phobic and worried all the time, but it is unfair of me to blame him. He went, and I waited around the corner.

He said, "You'd be amazed." I was told that he had buckets of roses for me and I *wasn't there.*

Originally I had asked, "How will I know you?"

"I'm big and black, and I will be the best-looking fellow there."

My boyfriend reported back, "He was black."

"What do you mean by black. A person of color?"

"No, black, black."

"Why are you saying that?" A year later, I wrote to him, and I made my mom meet him with me. When I finally met him, I saw that he was very imposing, like Malcolm X. He shook my hand and crushed it. He was a very good-looking man, about seventy-five. He originally came from Trinidad.

He sang with the most beautiful voice. He wrote a beautiful song about their romance. We went to the café. I sat beside Mom and him. He was laid-back, and my mom said stupid things. He would say, "I know she is my child because she looks just like my other daughter."

My mom would answer, "But I bet Jacinta is much prettier."

It was fascinating. It's like when you have a baby, and you want to inspect it. I am a person who would invent guilt if it hadn't been invented. I felt like I was cheating on my other father. He knew I knew, and I knew he knew, but it was never mentioned. My biological father wanted to keep me secret from his family. He also had other children in Trinidad. I was so overwhelmed by it. He was supposedly dead and a doctor from Spain. I found out he was a conductor on the train in London. I also learned that he loved music and me. I think men often love their children immediately. I wrote him a letter and said I wanted to back off until I got used to it. So for three years I didn't see him, although I drove past his house.

One day I knocked on the door. I was in analysis. That was a great support for me. If it didn't work out, I could talk about it. I knocked on the door, and he didn't know me. I said, "It's Jacinta." Then he recognized me, and he was over the moon. "This is the best Christmas present. I'm going to tell my family about you." I went back to meet them, and they were very nice to me: two sisters and a brother. Everyone looked black, but this one sister looked mixed because the mother was German. I found her very controlling. She was crazy about me, but she wouldn't let me alone. My brother and I are very close, but we aren't stifling each other. This sister was in a weird way, she was like Cerberus, the three-headed dog who guards the gates. Sometimes I might want to go over and see my father, and she would say, "What were you thinking of." I just wanted to see him. She made me feel like I was intruding.

Another time she invited me over, but I had a prior engagement. This half-sister would yell, "But we are family." Sometimes she would invite me over to her house, and there would be my dad all spruced up, which was sad.

"He doesn't dress up that way for me," she'd say. She was saying, "Look, he likes you," but she was saying it in a way that made me feel sad. My relationship that I had with him was very infrequent. He looked over at my half-sister and me, and he said, "I made that."

My marriage started to go. My husband became quite successful and had tons of money. The more cars and possessions we had, the more I felt guilty. I felt I didn't love him enough for all this stuff. After nine years, we separated. My son was nineteen. He said, "Why don't you leave him with me?" I always liked my husband, and he wants to be seen as nice.

I moved to a terrible little residence in London, and I worked as a journalist. I was freelance. It was very stressful for me. I loved him but was not in love with him. He was not the right guy for me. He should be with someone who was the right person. It was like gnawing off your arm. I swallowed my pride to let my son live with him. He couldn't live with me, but basically I wanted them to get closer. I'm glad I gave it to my son. Since I was adopted as a child, I hated when people said, "That was nice of your father." I think he was damn lucky to have us.

I Used to Have Nightmares about Going Back

I met this marvelous man who I interviewed at ninety. He came over to London to accept an award. He picked up his award. He said, "Why don't you visit me?" I thought, Do I really want to be here and write about people or do I want to be written about? The magazine folded the week that I did the interview. It already was at layout stage. He said, "Darling you must come. I pay. I might die soon." I didn't let him pay, but I borrowed the money. And I went to stay with this guy in California. We slipped into a ritual where we had breakfast and bought the papers and did the crossword puzzles, went into town and had lunch, then did some gardening. "Stay, you don't have to go." Then I realized that I outstayed my visa. Going back to England seemed like taking a step backward. California was so big, so raw. I used to have nightmares about being back. When you get to California you can see why the Indians worshiped nature. It is the most beautiful terrain. I couldn't bear to leave. It's so common; people go for a holiday, then they volunteer at a homeless shelter, and people are so friendly on the street. You can be gay if you want to. I'm not, but it is the beautiful freedom to be. I was making a kind of living as a kind of ex-pat. I felt like I was doing it myself. No one helped. All the connections I made myself. I met gorgeous people.

I saw my biological father maybe ten times before I went to America.

He got Alzheimer's. It would get worse and worse. My half-sister called and said, "He's dying." I didn't want to see him diminished. I didn't want to see someone who didn't know me. I didn't want to see my memories crowded out. I didn't know what to do. I was in America then, and I never went back. She called me the other day and told me he had passed away. She said, "I know you cared about him in your funny way."

"Funny way! What the fuck! I was obsessed with this person." Of course, he was a Spanish doctor in my mind for a while. I asked, "Can I come to the funeral?"

She said, "I won't deny you that."

"Deny!"

She called me back and said, "My mom said no. It's not what I would have done." So I didn't get to go to the funeral. But then I found that there was an "auntie" in America. I was the love child. She is a beautiful, incredible person. I know I romanticize her. We are both glowing when we are together.

I Cleaned People's Houses

When I moved to California, I became very new age, which is to me—Be as nice as you can and be as kind as you can be and it will come back. I cleaned people's houses, that was how I got by. I met this very young couple. They had a little graphic design studio, but you could rent a computer there. My husband had state-of-the-art electronic computers, but I was the journalist with no equipment. Basically they would not let me pay, which was a nice thing. It was hard to write, and I was always broke. I used to fax from their place as well, and they wouldn't let me pay. I had to learn to accept. I was too broke to turn it down. Without them, I would have had to go home. Every little success, they were over the moon.

I can call my new "auntie" in America, and she is so kind. When my father died, she said all the right things. She talks about "all the opportunities lost."

I met this doorman, and I recognized his accent. I asked, "Where are you from?"

"Trinidad."

He even knew my father, even though my father lived in London for such a long time.

Now I Am an Exotic in My Father's World

I am staying in America, and I had a visa, which I stupidly allowed to lapse. I'm all up in the air. I don't know how to apply. I married briefly here out of love, but we separated. I don't know if I can apply as a divorced person. I have an interview in September. I have a million friends, and I mostly write for the English press. In England they have an expression called "Tall Poppy Syndrome." If you get too tall, cut them down. You get hated for success in England. The pressure is on you to fail. The ideal hero in England is Eddie the Eagle, who is very unattractive and wanted to be an Olympic skier but would fall down immediately. It is all about holding up people and then knocking them down. You couldn't be a singer; you couldn't be a writer. What do you think you are? They wouldn't even know. They just make that assumption. But Americans don't do that. "Jacinta is a brilliant writer." It doesn't cross their mind that I was a cleaning person. But in England I would have just been a cleaner. It's the way Americans treat their waiters. They might have been actors. Kathleen Turner was a waitress. Danny DeVito was a waiter. Sandra Bernhardt was a manicurist. In England you are looked down on. If you are a waitress, you have free hours to do other work, but I can't let my upbringing go. Everyone is in your corner here. That is an important difference. I learned a lot about black culture here, more than in England. That is because it is more divided here. No one would think it was politically incorrect. Here you don't have to be a rabid racist but still disapprove of mixed race. I now live in a black area, and I have people giving me dirty looks like, "White people moving in raising the rent." Another gave me a huge hug and said, "Welcome to the race."

Other people say, "Wow, I'd never know."

I am learning the politics of it. My son is into hip-hop and is a Sufi Muslim, which is more ancient. Now I make it my business to listen to that type of music. Now I make an effort to learn about racism, which I didn't believe in when I was white. Anything that is predominately black is underpaid, like jazz. Musicians work for next to nothing. White people who are very mediocre are very successful. Also I had an argument with a guy who said blacks do not speak different or have an accent. I'm still learning about race, and America has been my school.

In some way I was always an exotic in my mother's world. Now I'm experiencing that in my father's world. Perhaps I have been destined to be a metaphor of race and culture, to be a living link between nations, classes, and colors.

SIXTEEN

Oratai Nuchsombat Schwartz

THAI-AMERICAN

Thai-American Oratai could be described as a war bride, but she does not evoke the familiar image from old movies, which were usually comedies where a GI met an attractive blonde or brunette — an "enemy" from Germany or a saucy French girl — and brought her back to the States against his commander's wishes. This attractive war bride was usually a bubble-head and had to be shown the American Way of Life — from operating an automatic washing machine to preparing a proper Thanksgiving dinner.

After the Korean and Vietnam conflicts, Asian brides brought along their own stereotypes, either of being docile doll-women or conniving bar girls. Higher-ranked commanders still advised the GI not to marry these "foreigners."

Oratai had come to this country as a so-called war bride during the Vietnam War era. But, of course, she was not the Hollywood stereotype. She is called "Tai" — for Thailand and to help people who can't pronounce her full name. She has the luminescent face of the moon. She says she can only get shoes in Thailand, as she has the typical Thai foot: short and stubby. An outgoing woman, she makes good friends of a table of strangers before the main course is finished. It is hard to believe that this self-assured woman learned her English from watching I Love Lucy *reruns. The slogan for Thailand is "the Land of Smiles." Sometimes there are truths in clichés.*

My Father Had Been a Monk

My father had been a monk in the temple for years prior to meeting my mother. He had been planning to make that his life's devotion. Monks were not allowed to marry or to socialize with the opposite sex. My mother had accompanied her family to the temple to make some offering of food and little goodies to the monks. My father changed his mind.

I was born on a farm east of Bangkok. In those days, there was no transportation by land, only by ships. My parents had eight children. My twin died at three months from dysentery. My father became an elementary school principal. I don't think his formal education was higher than fourth grade, but he studied extensively. I am the youngest one in the family, so I don't know much of the family history.

The culture is different from the Western culture. Children usually don't socialize with adults, and they tell us only what they want us to know. We don't ask too many questions about our parents or ancestors, so I don't know too much about them. By the time I could remember anything, all my brothers and sisters were away in school.

Yet I grew up surrounded by other children because my mother and father owned eight pieces of property, farms and ranches, and we lived in a very large house. We were considered wealthy and prominent in the village because my dad was not only principal of the elementary school, but he also practiced what you would call "Indian potions," herbs used to make medicines. There were no modern pharmaceuticals available at the time, so the villagers depended on my dad to help them with their illnesses.

Stomping on the Stilted House

My father was very close to the people in the village—well loved and respected by everyone who knew him. My parents had bought a large piece of land that was surrounded by a canal. We had a lot of ranch hands that my mom and dad allowed to build huts at the edge of the property. They lived around us, and they worked for us, and their children always came to the house and played.

I had a very good childhood. We swam in the canals, and we climbed trees. We played house. We invented a lot of things. We used the coconut shells as the pots and pans.

We used clay and mud to make mud pies and meats, and we were really creative. We made dolls from old blankets, and we folded paper into little boats to float them down the river. We were allowed to run around the property.

I remember getting in trouble with my dad because we were not supposed to be running around the house. The house is built on stilts about ten feet off the ground, and we had what you might describe in the Western culture as a wraparound balcony. The house was all solid wood and had very few windows. People usually sat on the outside during the day because it was very warm over there, and you needed to be in the shade. The wraparound balcony provides you with shade all day long. You just simply moved around. You also get the nice cool breeze from whichever direction it comes. We were not supposed to run around on that balcony; since it's on wooden stilts, it sometimes shakes the house. My dad was trying to take a nap, I was running around, and I got in trouble with him, but often.

My Mother Bought a Couple of Trucks

My father died when I was three and a half, and after that I was under the supervision of one of my brothers or sisters. My life changed a lot because my mother then had to leave home to go to work. She got into the business of brokering fresh produce and fruit. My mother would contract the produce from the farmers. She bought a couple of trucks and had to go into the city of Bangkok, so she was constantly traveling.

My mother was always interested in business, and she ran the family farm while my father was teaching. My dad usually brought home his paycheck and handed it to her. But it was still very hard for her to have to leave home and hard for us children.

My big brother moved back home with his wife and one little daughter and mother-in-law. We lived in the old house on the farm together. One of my sisters moved to a small town nearby, and so I moved into the city to live with her and continue my education there.

By that time we had access to automobiles. Someone owned a little bus, and he would drive it back and forth from town to town to pick up passengers, so that we didn't have to walk. And I was there for two years, and then my sister married a Thai marine. When I was twelve, I moved in with a distant relative in Bangkok. My mother was in the process of building a house there for us children. One of my brothers was in technical college at the time when I moved into the new house.

There's really not that much choice of schools in Thailand. You can choose to go into vocational school, which teaches you to do carpenter work and sewing and cooking, which two of my older sisters chose. For me, it was more like a prep school, preparing to go to college.

I have a lot of good memories of spending time with my father as a young child. Even though I was a small child, my dad had told me that he wanted me to become a physician. He basically had a map drawn out for what all his children were going to do.

They didn't have very much choice when he was alive, but after he passed away, they went their own way. Nobody wanted to continue to farm, so they eventually left the farm and went into formal training in school.

By That Time Our Money Was Depleted

The idea of being a doctor sounded good, but I didn't feel like I was capable of handling the study. I'm just an average student, and people who are going into the medical field are so bright and have to have a natural adaptation to science and math, and I'm average with math. I'm more inclined toward art. But if my father was alive, I think I would have killed myself trying to do it.

I guess I was more fortunate than others were because my sisters took an interest in me, and they taught me English. And then when I was in high school, I went to after-school classes with an English instructor.

It really didn't enter my mind to leave my country. I wasn't really that interested in other cultures. I remember at the time that I was exposed to very little television. By the time I was in high school, television was still kind of new, even in Bangkok. Only the very, very rich had television, and by that time we weren't very rich. Our money was practically depleted, and we were struggling to try to stay in school. My mom and a couple of my sisters were helping me and my brother to stay in school by sending us a little money here, and so it wasn't a real good time. College was not even considered because when I finished high school, I needed to get a job to support myself.

I finished high school at sixteen, and being too young was a hurdle. The legal age in Thailand to work is twenty-one. Most people don't want to hire any office clerks or any workers or anything unless they are at least eighteen years old, so I met with a lot of resistance.

I Became a Singer with a Band

At the boys' school, they had the band, and my teacher got me a job singing with them. They played at weddings, promotion parties, and they also played at theaters or to promote museums. It was fun. There were times when we would travel to northern or southern Thailand, so it gave me the opportunity to see my country that I otherwise probably wouldn't have seen.

My uncle was not too happy with my singing position, but he didn't have very much to say. Singing in the band is considered show business, and society kind of looks down on show-business people as being shallow and promiscuous. For me, it was something to do, and I enjoyed it very much.

It was a big band, and it had been around a long time. The bandleader was like a father to us all. He formed a contemporary band similar to the Beatles. That type of combo band was very popular in Thailand. It was called Pocket Music. I didn't know there were so many people interested in what we were doing. We were just a bunch of kids. The girls and boys in the band were fifteen and sixteen years of age. Anywhere we went, we were received well and had good audiences, and I learned to work as a group. My social reaction to everything changed. You had to be cooperative because we traveled together a lot, and I had to learn to look at the other musicians like family.

Not long after I joined the band, I was offered several jobs at nightclubs. I was too young to go in there, but I wasn't too young to perform, and I got very busy and didn't have much time for a social life.

He Showed Up Wherever I Played

Then I met my first husband when we were playing at one of these promotion parties. A Thai general was promoted, and they had a huge party for him at his home. My husband was there as a guest. He was an American Marine stationed in Bangkok at the American Embassy. I was the only one in the band that could speak enough English to communicate with Americans. After that party, he followed us around, found out where we were going to be playing, and surprised us all the time by showing up at different theaters. I might have a luncheon engagement at a very big nightclub or restaurant, and he'd show up.

I got to know him and to visit with him. We really didn't date or anything. I guess I wasn't comfortable going out with him, because Thai women are generally looked down upon if they date Western men. If I agreed to go to a movie or go somewhere with him, to lunch or dinner, I walked five or six paces ahead of him. I acted like I wasn't with him in public.

He was much older. He was thirty-one, and I was only seventeen. We got married when I was eighteen.

By that time I liked him very much because he was always polite and proper, and my mother and my sisters liked him, too. Usually I would invite him to come and visit at my home rather than be seen in public. At that time, I lived with my sister, who has three boys. I helped tutor the boys, and he came to visit and brought the boys candies and played with them, and so my mother agreed to the marriage. She wasn't too happy with it since I had to leave the country.

Religion was not an issue. He's a Christian, was born and raised Baptist, but he is not religious, and we Buddhists are not that strict about our religion.

Buddhism is encompassing. All that's important is that he's a good person. My mom was concerned about his taking care of her daughter.

Thai people usually have a religious ceremony, and I don't know anything about Christianity, so it was just a civil proceeding.

No, It Can't Be Where I Am Going to Live

Two weeks after we got married, I left the country. We came to the United States. My husband had been ordered to report to the Marine Corps base in Twenty-nine Palms, California, and so we flew from Bangkok into Houston to visit his mother and aunts and uncle. His family was all in Houston. I was apprehensive, but they were very nice to me. I didn't speak very much English. I understood a lot, but I was not used to conversing in English.

It was strange, but I wasn't afraid because I was accustomed to taking care of myself, and so I figured I would survive this, and it would be okay. And it was. We stayed in Houston a month.

I thought that the people's homes were all very orderly, different than in Thailand. In the United States there are different areas for residential and commercial buildings, and that was not the case in Thailand. In Thailand, if you wanted to build a little hut, you built a little hut—no restrictions. Fortunately, I didn't have to learn all the customs in one day. I was shielded and protected, so I could absorb ways a little at a time.

After Houston, we went to Twenty-nine Palms, which was a desert town. I could not believe that people lived out there in the desert. My husband had shown me this spot on the plane. He said that's where we're going to live. And I said, "No. it can't be where I am going to live." I thought he was joking with me. I didn't want to believe it.

I Was Very, Very Lonely

It was quite a difficult adjustment to be out there in the desert. We rented a little two-bedroom house, and he had to go to work every day. I didn't drive, and there was no way to go to town or to the market. It was very, very lonely. I didn't have any friends. I didn't meet a Thai person until eight years after I had been in the United States. So I had to learn English very quickly, and during that time I watched a lot of television.

I learned a lot of my English from the *I Love Lucy* show. I used to watch

Lucy every day at nine in the morning. There was nothing to do, and it was winter when we settled in Twenty-nine Palms. It was very cold outside and dusty. There were a lot of sandstorms blowing around at that time.

My husband made sure that I wouldn't leave the house by telling me, "There are a lot of wild dogs in the desert, so don't go out and walk around."

At that time, I felt like he was trying to protect me.

I didn't drive when I was in Thailand because we didn't have a car, and there was no need to learn to drive. Even in Bangkok we used busses. I learned to drive in 1967. I got a driver's license, and that's when I started getting out and around and learning a little bit more by going shopping by myself instead of waiting to be taken to the store, and taking my babies to the doctor. By that time, I had two babies.

It was not difficult to make friends in the military because everybody's from somewhere else. Everybody's away from home, and you make quick friends. In fact, even until this day I still have two or three friends that I've known since 1964.

I Pulled Out My Gun

Our life was difficult because my husband had a lot of friends, and he liked to drink a lot, and there were times when we had pretty violent arguments. But he never really hurt me, and I think we had the last violent argument after my first child was born. She was about three months old. We had a really big fight, and he got a little violent. In my whole life, I've never actually shot a gun, but he had given me a gun as protection when he was not home and showed me how to use it. And so I think I had frightened him during that argument because I pulled out my gun and told him that if he laid a hand on me, that I was going to kill him. And so he was good after that. He had never seen me that angry before. I'm very easy going, and I'd prefer that we have a quiet and peaceful family than have a lot of arguments.

When he would go out drinking with some Marine friend after work, he'd come home and start to ask a lot of questions, annoying questions that I didn't want to engage in. I was very angry. My baby was three months old, and I didn't want to expose her to our conflicts. The gun stopped the disorder. He didn't do that again, and in fact, he was not a violent person, only after he drank.

I Had to Depend on My Mother-in-Law

He went to Vietnam a couple of times. My oldest daughter was only six months when he went on his first tour in Vietnam. I didn't drive at the time. In 1965 he left, and I was still new to the country, so I came back to Houston and spent a year with his mother.

We had our ups and downs, but his mother was very understanding, and she tried to help me in any way she could. She had a little garage apartment that I rented from her, and that gave my daughter and me a place of our own.

But I still had to depend on my mother-in-law to take me grocery shopping. She was very good helping me out with the baby. I don't have any complaints about her. She was probably the best mother-in-law anybody could expect to have.

He Was Adamant That It Was Nobody's Business

We got a separation in 1984. We had three children, and the oldest one was away at college, and three years prior to that we were having a lot of problems with our son. He was involved in drugs, and we were trying to salvage him, and we had to confront our own problems at that time. We lost our son. He did not die, but we lost him because he left home and continued on with his life. We could not help him, and I guess we blame each other a lot. I think the problem with our son brought the undercurrents to the surface. In my heart I felt like my husband had betrayed me. I had depended on him for support, and he was not there when I needed him.

We did some family counseling with the children, joint counseling between my husband and myself. That didn't work out. He was adamant that it was nobody's business.

"This is our family business. We can work this out. We can solve it."

"How are we going to work it out if we hardly talk?" He was so angry. Every time we started to talk, it was a lot of accusations and outbursts and bad feelings. Counseling didn't help, but I continued to go to counseling by myself and continued to take my son to counseling, but that didn't help him. In the end he turned his back on the family and went his way.

Besides my son, I had two girls. At the time the oldest girl was in college, and my young daughter was in middle school. They are fine today, but they were shattered for a while because of the family breakup. We lived in turmoil for three years, from the time that we discovered our son's problem.

At that time I was working at a real estate construction management company in Houston, and I continued to work there until 1991, when there were drastic cuts in the company.

And I Met Sid

While I was working, I was going to school part-time, but once I got laid off, I decided to go full-time and finish school, and I did. My major was accounting. And I met Sid.

We met at the Miller Outdoor Theatre. He was just newly divorced, and I wasn't divorced from my husband at that time. We didn't get divorced until 1995, but we were separated for many years. And Sid and I have been together ever since.

It has worked out very well. He's a good man, good temperament, and very sensitive. He and I talk all the time, and we go do things together.

We play music. He plays in a band, and I help him putting together his music. I help him with his office [Sid is an oral surgeon]. From time to time, if one of his assistants is ill, I will go in there and help answer the phone, and I do handle his paperwork, keep books for him—things like that.

My Daughter Is a Feminist

Both of my girls are in Houston. The oldest one has decided to go back to school after many years of working in the banking industry. She is now in law school, and my youngest daughter is married. She's been married about four years and works as a social worker. She is a feminist, and she's always telling her mother to stand up. She is working at the Houston Women's Center.

I enjoy going back to Thailand to visit. I go back once every other year to visit with my sisters. My mother died in 1993. After Sid and I got married, we went there to visit the family, and I took him to the little village where I used to live and showed him what it was like. There are still some traces of it. But I think he enjoyed that a lot, and it was a good experience for me to compare the two worlds.

PART TWO

Postcards from America

SEVENTEEN

Sam Lizarraga

BOLIVIAN-AMERICAN

When we met for dinner in Chattanooga, Tennessee, both Dr. Lizarraga and his wife had just lost more than twenty pounds on the grapefruit diet. I admired their accomplishment. After having discussed our respective diets, we all chowed down quite heartily, shoving calorie caution from our minds. Sam is shorter than his blond, Tennessee wife, who exudes the famed southern charm, calling various things "precious" and "darling." Sam's thick, dark hair is worn slicked back in Spanish fashion. When talking, he chooses his words precisely to avoid misinterpretations. Later that evening, Sam's demeanor changes when he shows photos of a magnificent carousel horse that he has carved in a sculpting school. "Now I am much happier than when I was practicing medicine, and my knowledge of anatomy is paying off," he announced, beaming.

He Publicly Threw All His Art into the River

My grandfather on my mother's side was a very accomplished Catholic artist. He had a lot of talent, especially in murals, and he made a comfortable living. He had copied the murals from St. Paul's Cathedral in Italy for the church walls in Potosi, Bolivia. One night he was coming home half-drunk when he heard people singing in a tiny church. They gave him a welcome, and he kept returning. Finally he converted to be a Protestant, but he made one big mistake. He publicly announced his conversion and the rejection of the Catholic faith. He decided that images were idolatry, so he loaded all his work on a wagon and threw them publicly into the river. After that he did not get any commissions.

Once he became a Protestant, and Bolivia being a Catholic country, he lost his livelihood. My parents were both Protestants; therefore we had limited benefit from society. When I was young, Protestants were only 0.5 percent of the population. I didn't have access to private schools, as they were Catholic operated. And even in the public school, I had to get legal and judicial authority not to participate in certain activities due to my religious background.

The Protestants Persevered

I grew up in a stable home because my grandfather owned his property. Eventually I ended up having three sisters and one brother. I am the oldest, and everyone is alive except my parents. My dad died in 1962, and my mother passed away in 1997. My sisters work as a teacher, a principal, and one is an accountant, and my brother is an engineer.

My extended family was divided into two groups: the Protestants and the Catholics. The Protestants persevered and encouraged us to improve our lives. My mother pushed us all. Thanks to her, we all have professions. That was the challenge—"Not to be like the Catholics."

My Father Never Made It Home

My father went to war in the Bolivia-Paraguay conflict called the Petroleum Wars. My father had become a prisoner of war. When he was repatriated, on his journey home, he stopped in a mining town where my mother lived, and they met in church. My daddy stopped in just for curiosity's sake. He had been going from town to town and working briefly in each community in order to earn some pay to get back. He met my mother, and he never made it home.

Growing up, I played a lot of soccer and chess with my father. I learned to play chess by watching my parents after dinner. I was an observer. Later on we had a radio, and listening to the radio was a family activity. The programs that my parents selected were either music or short stories.

My mother was educated, but my father did not have schooling. But after he was married he studied at night and got his equivalent of a high school education.

I went to the university for medicine for eight years. Being a Protestant, my first inclination in medical school was to be a missionary doctor with a Methodist church of Bolivia. When you finish your degree it is necessary to put in two years of rural practice. After that the government gives you certification and you can move to the city if you wish. The Methodist Church was already established with hospitals. On the staff were two American doctors and two local physicians. So I went to work in the mission field with them, and I had immediate access to a well-staffed hospital.

I Was Invited to Chattanooga

Just by chance, I met a team of Chattanooga doctors who had come to train in the hospital. These groups of doctors are the ones who invited me to come to Chattanooga. From that point, all I had to do was apply for my immigrant visa. I was lucky in that period of time because we had the Vietnam conflict, and knowing that I was a doctor, the government processed my passport expeditiously. Before I knew it, I came to Chattanooga, and then within months I was supposed to be on my way to Hanoi. It was part of my agreement. I saw it as an experience, but they had the truce in 1972, so I didn't have to go.

I thought Chattanooga was a very nice town. I didn't like the temperature. I came at a very, very bad time of year. I came in November. Even though I came from a mountainous country, it is dry; so if you are cold, you put on a sweater. Here you are still cold because it is damp. Chattanooga offered me the friendship of doctors. I considered myself lucky because I came to the home of one of the doctors, and I lived in his house for a number of months, and I felt like I was a member of the family, except I didn't speak English very well.

The only culture shock was language. One thing that gave me an advantage was that I went to work with the government. I worked in a nuclear plant and had to work with a workforce that was very diverse—from Boston, New York, Miami—so I had to learn the characteristics of each group.

My Wife's Mother Was My Patient

I met my wife—who worked across the street from the hospital—in a rehabilitation center. We met in the cafeteria. My wife's mother, without me knowing it, had been my patient. She had to have surgery, and I was in charge of that case. My mother-in-law and I had a very good relationship.

Their Behavior Is Like the Rest of the World

There were fifty thousand workers at the construction of one nuclear plant, and they needed a doctor for on-site injuries as well as regular illnesses. My practice was industrial medicine. In the beginning it was emergencies and admissions. The work involves litigation, injuries, heart attacks, and accidents. After that I dealt with worker's compensation. Working with that I have learned that people are dishonest. It has changed my perspective of the American people. Their behavior is like the rest of the world. They want something for nothing.

You see that the rules are designed to protect the employee, but it then becomes a golden egg for everybody, especially the lawyers.

Working in government you get a lot of animosity because you come from another country. What was interesting to me was that when you work with construction people, they think that there are only two other nationalities: Mexicans or Chinese. Since my hair is very black they thought I was Chinese or Mexican. People do not know where Bolivia is. By asking a question, they demonstrate their ignorance. There is some discrimination, and some subjective animosity is an everyday event. I had the opportunity to be promoted from an onsite doctor at a local nuclear plant to be an area supervisor. Instead they hired a brand new African-American who had no experience. When I questioned them they could not give me an explanation.

The Perception Would Be That I Was a Spy

I have no regrets coming to the United States. Occasionally I missed my family, especially my mother and my sisters. I can make myself comfortable here. I never went back because of political instability. There were two factions, pro-American and pro-Russian. Che Guevara, the Cuban revolutionary, was nested in Bolivia. Fifty-five percent of the population was pro-Russian. Political instability and attempts to overthrow the government occurred. Anybody who comes from the American establishment is suspected. For instance, if I went back, I wouldn't be perceived as a private citizen; the perception would be that I am a spy. Originally when I was ready to leave they held my passport and exit visa until there was a coup; then I was able to leave. With this experience my mother asked that I do not return in order to protect her and my sisters, because they might say that they were harboring me.

My mother discouraged me from coming home, and she never came here. Another perception of the cold war—everybody over here is a hippie who abuses drugs. That was the type of American people she saw visiting Bolivia, so her perception was that if she came here she would be mugged.

After All My Clearance Checks, I Feel That I Belong

My son was born here in Chattanooga, and he grew up in this community. He speaks Spanish with an American accent. He has no time to wander around. It was part of my philosophy to keep him busy and have no idle time, so he would not get into trouble.

I have my wife, and I have my son. This is the only family I have, so this is my country now. I have a nuclear security clearance, and also I have unescorted access to most federal offices.

I have had much more security checks than the average American. After I went though all my clearance checks, I felt I belong. The U.S. government has made me feel authorized to be here.

EIGHTEEN

Manuel Ortiz

MEXICAN-AMERICAN

The loamy, fluffy fields were harrowed as if into a soft chenille bedspread. "Look for a blue pickup truck in the field." Those were the instructions for finding Manuel outside of the agricultural town of Hollister in central California. The farm owner had continued, "He's not like most Mexicans. He's not in it just for the money." From the perspective of a car, the earth looked comforting, a cushioning mother.

Manuel parked his pickup truck and came into the office. He was a solid guy with an embossed hat that said "BOSS."

When the owners came through, they joked about the cap. "We'll have to ask him all the questions now. He's in charge."

Manuel smiled, good natured and stoic. He shook hands formally and nodded to one of the women at the desks. A solid, muscled man, Manuel could brace himself against the sandstorm that they had experienced that week. The idea that

"He's not in it just for the money" made a subtext in my mind when I saw pho-tos of that wind-whipped, biting sand and the immigrant workers who toiled during the height of it.

After a while Manuel loosened up and began to talk and gesture like he might with friends. At one point, he lowered his voice to say he preferred the company of Californians to Mexicans; he appreciated the schools here and the opportunity to make money. Yet the paradox was that he was building homes for each of his children in Guanajuato State in Mexico. This was another case of the United States of the World.

I Used To Sleep inside One of Those Tombs

When I first crossed the river to get to Texas, I lived in one of those trail-ers or semis, but it was on the ground, so we would go inside it and sleep in there. We would build a fire to cook outside on the ground. And we lived near a river, so we used to bathe in the river, and if the water were too cold, we would warm the water in buckets on the fire. And we would take a bath right there by the river with cold and warm water.

We were ten single men. We used to make three dollars a day. We didn't have any transportation to come into town or to go buy our own stuff, but the farmer-boss would bring us food and clothing and what-ever we needed.

He would give us the food, but clothing we would pay for. The farmer used to buy the clothes at the Goodwill, so we never had nice clothes from the store. They were always used.

I've been working in agriculture forever—since before I got married, and I continued after I got married. In the beginning, my wife stayed in Mexico, and I came over here by myself to the town of Dillard, Texas. I worked with a guy who had a chicken hatchery. He was working with eggs, and the guy was paying us really cheap, and he threatened us, "If you leave me to go work for somebody else, I'll call the Immigration Department to pick you guys up." I left anyway and met a guy who was growing cucumbers. He had a few acres.

He said, "You can work for me."

"But I don't have a place to live."

He told me there was a cemetery that was abandoned, that nobody was there, but some tombs were open.

So that's where I used to sleep, inside one of those tombs. I was more afraid of Immigration than ghosts. I didn't want to be deported to Mexico. I wanted to make money and go get my wife.

Calling Immigration for a Free Trip

At that time, agriculture was going to start here in California, and I knew that coming to California, I was going to make more money, so I didn't want to be deported.

At that time, I was working with the cucumbers. They had told me that that was going to end, so another guy and me had saved money because we had been told that we could get to California from Tijuana—a "coyote" would bring us for two hundred dollars. We had the money saved up, so we turned ourselves in to Immigration, so they could send us to Mexico. They took us back for free. Then we went to Tijuana and paid our two hundred dollars to get back to California.

I came to San Juan Batista and worked for Hanson Farms for twelve years. I started making two dollars an hour. And when the company closed their door, I was making over eight. That was good for someone with an eighth-grade education.

My father crossed the border as a "wetback," too. He didn't have papers. And he worked in Salinas with this farmer, and the guy helped him fix his papers. My father went back and started fixing papers for the rest of the family.

I have family in Mexico and some of my brothers are working here. Everybody has houses and cows in Mexico, and most of them come here temporarily.

She Decided to Leave Me Because I Had Nothing

My wife's family went to Chicago, and she was born in Chicago. When the parents returned to Mexico, they had a big dance, and that's where I met her. I also told her that I was coming to work in the United States. Then we went to several dances together, and then we broke up.

The reason that she decided to leave me in the beginning was because

I was poor, and the house belonged to my parents, and I had nothing. Then I said to her, "If we get married, we would start saving money and get a home of our own." She believed me this time, and that's why she decided to do it.

Now I own land in Mexico. I have built a home for each one of my kids. I say, "I'm not rich, and I'm not poor, but I'm in between. I have my own home in Mexico. That's why my six kids believe in me." I have bettered myself because I have worked here real hard and made good money.

My wife stays home in Hollister and watches our six kids. My kids were all born and raised here, and they have their friends nearby, and that's why I consider them Americanos, and mostly because they speak English. They feel that they know that their parents and great-grandparents are from Mexico, and that they need to know their ways of living, too. When I go over there, I bring them back videos of the family and show them, and I tell them the way I was raised, and they feel that here in the United States education is better than in Mexico.

I Am Ashamed to Say It, but I Think America Is Better

Everybody, American guys, are friendly and that is fine for me. All the time, "Hi, what's your name?"

"Oh, my name is Manuel, or my name is Williams or something." The Americans are good people to me. My children in school have no problem. Well, some problems from the Mexican guys, but not from the Americano guys.

I taught my kids, you want to meet friends, you look around for an American guy. For me, they're good people. In the school, the guys that got problems are the Mexican guys.

For one thing, my kids, they say, "Oh, one guy fought me for a blue jacket." Mexicans that work here are the problem. All the time, I'm telling my kids, "Hey, I don't like for you all the time to be with Mexicans. You tell the friends, 'Hi,' or 'Good Morning,' but do not look for problems."

They said, "Okay."

I ask the teacher, "Hey, my kids are okay?"

"Oh yeah, the kids are all right; your kids are okay."

The first kid went to grade school here and then high school and now to the university in Mexico. He's studying to be a veterinarian.

And the little one maybe will go to the university. The next is a girl, maybe one day she marries. My kids all the time ask me, "One day will you go back to Mexico?"

I say, "Maybe." I don't have money for doing a business here, no house, no business, no land. All the time I pay rent. That is okay for a working man. Over there I've got this house. Nobody pays rent. I've got the small ranch, maybe sixteen acres.

My brother watches the ranch over there. Now I plant alfalfa, corn, and onions over there. It's a good business. Here I work for six dollars an hour, but I like to stay here. I stay here to put my children in school. I tell my wife, every kid speaks English fine.

I prefer the United States because the poor person here lives like a rich person in Mexico. So that's why I like it here. Over there, the poorest people work every day and eat beef one time a week. One family, they've got six kids. They don't have money to buy things. Here, everyday you want to drink a beer or eat beef, you're able to do it, but over there, no. One guy works all day for twenty pesos over there.

I put in the application for citizenship. Immigration says they're going to give me another chance. They sent me an application for U.S. citizenship, and I lost it, so they're going to send me another one to reapply.

My heart is in the United States. There are more benefits for us here than over there. I feel bad saying that, but I feel that the United States has done more for me than my mother country. It is embarrassing for me to say this, but I feel more Americanized.

NINETEEN

Tatyana Lytkina

RUSSIAN-AMERICAN

It is said that Russians have a genius for suffering. That is what makes their literature and history great. Common Russians take this into their daily lives. A ready, visual example is their passion for fishing when it is twenty degrees below zero. Fishermen perch above a hole cut in the ice in their wind-chilled isolation.

Tatyana and her husband Sergey have the look of moroseness and suffering, but with a little prodding I found out that Sergey wrote witty poems and funny pieces on the Internet. Their sly humor is the secret part of them, but their disgruntlement they wear like a bespoke overcoat. A middle-aged woman, Tatyana has short blond hair and is bundled up — boots, mufflers, and heavy overcoat. She knows how to dress for the winter. The couple looks beleaguered. Sergey slouches dejectedly, but Tatyana seems feisty. My perceptions were borne out when I found that she divorced Sergey when at first he would not immigrate with her to the States. They then remarried.

Tatyana said, "Everyone thinks that it is only crooks and murderers that come from Siberia," but many millions of people were lured there to mine the region's fabulous natural wealth, such as Tatyana's father.

Wet Nurse for Czar Nicholas Alexander

My great grandmother was a very beautiful woman who was brought to the palace to be a wet nurse for Czar Nicholas Alexander. Her husband had been a palace soldier. Eventually he left the army to lay the railroad. They kept moving as the rail line progressed. They had ten children, all while they lived this transient life. They kept moving until one of the babies was stolen. At that point, my great-grandmother said, "Enough!" And they didn't move anymore.

They Think We Are All Criminals

My one grandfather was a builder. My grandmother and mother were doctors in microbiology. Their specialty was cholera and plague. They would get called to go to India and different places. I have my doctorate also in microbiology. I don't like to tell people that I'm from Russia. Their faces close up, and they stand away from me, especially if they know I'm from Siberia. They think we are all criminals there.

It is very dangerous to tell you about my father's father. He owned a gold mine in Siberia. He shipped a lot of gold bricks to London. He paid his workers hardly anything. When the revolution came, the workers said they would spare his life if he signed over the mine to them. He signed the paper, but then they killed him anyway. My father did not take his father's name because he was so hated. Even now I have to whisper it because it would cause us much danger if it were known.

My daughter got asthma from the severe cold. She had to stay home from school. An attendant stopped by each day to teach her. We all lived together in one apartment. We had no chance of getting another. Even when I married Sergey, we move in with my family. There is not even a list to get on.

They say, "Why do you need an apartment? You've already got one."

In Siberia there were lines for everything. We all went each day to work, so my grandmother was the one to stand in the cold. She had to stand in line for hours to get the one apple every day for my daughter. She had to stand in another line for the chicken for our household. Every six people get one chicken. That's two bites per person. Then she has to stand in line again for other items. People with lots of education make less money than factory workers. We all have lots of education—doctors and engineers.

When we were back in Russia, religion was practiced privately in the home. We are Christians, Russian Orthodox. But my sister, who is eight years younger than me, married a Jewish man, so she was able to migrate to Italy, and then she was supposed to go to Israel, but instead she went to the United States.

"Walk" and "Don't Walk" — That's All That I Knew

Once she got here my sister said, "Come to Brooklyn. I will sponsor you."

My husband Sergey did not want to go, so I got a divorce from him and came to New York with my parents. My sister signed a paper that she would take care of us, so we did not take a penny from this country. The first two months we lived in a hotel room on Broadway. Then we moved to Williamsburg in Brooklyn. When I saw Brooklyn for the first time I cried. So ugly—all the red brick buildings, no architecture, no lawns. Even in Siberia, the buildings are separated, and there are places for the children to play. And in Moscow there are great palaces and buildings. My mother and I got jobs as home attendants. Then my sister and I were going shopping in Brooklyn, and we passed a medical laboratory building. We just knocked on the door, and I got a job.

The first year, I cried and cried. Twenty-four hours a day I wept. I did not speak the language. I could not understand anyone. I could not understand television. "Walk" and "Don't walk"—that's all that I knew.

After a year, Sergey decided to leave his family and emigrate. Without me, he was lonely in Russia. We got remarried in Brooklyn.

Everything is strange for us. We go to a supermarket, Finast, in Brooklyn. Now I know that this is not the finest supermarket, but when I first saw all the cans and boxes, I did not know what to do. You can not see anything. You don't know what you are getting. In Russia, you go, and if you want to buy something, say, like yogurt, you bring your own jar and you look at it, and the lady scoops some out with a large spoon in front of you. In America you don't see what you're getting.

I Couldn't Live in New Jersey Because It's Like a Small Village

I'm still very lonely here, but I'd never go back to Russia. My sister is a medical resident in New Jersey. They accepted all her credits because she took her courses within the ten-year period that they required. My sister and her husband bought a lovely house in New Jersey with a lawn around it. But I couldn't live there, because it's like a small village. I guess I'm a real New Yorker now. My mother bought a two-family house in Brooklyn. We live on one floor and my parents live on another. My brother-in-law spends four nights a week in Brooklyn because he is a social worker there. My mother now spends five nights a week in New Jersey because my sister had a baby, and she watches the child while my sister is on duty in the hospital. Then they switch back for the weekend.

People from Russia Are All Crooks and Liars

Recently, they cut back, and I just lost my job in the laboratory. I want to be a physician's assistant. I went to the chairperson at Kingsborough College, and I told him I was a doctor in Russia.

He said, "Everyone said that they are a doctor or dentist in Russia. But when you check the records, you find out that they only assisted doctors and dentists. Maybe they might have held the clamps. People from Russia are all crooks and liars."

That's what he told me. Now I'm ashamed to apply elsewhere for my education. Americans look down on us. They think we are all criminals or communist terrorists, so I don't tell people where we come from.

My daughter goes to an all girls' Catholic school and does well there. She's popular and has lots of friends, but I'm not letting her go away to college. She can go locally and live at home. In dormitories, they have drugs and sexual abuse, and I'm terrified of AIDS. She will live only where I can protect her. I'm not ready to let go.

TWENTY King Chan

CHINESE-AMERICAN

A little Chinese storefront restaurant appeared recently in my hometown of Carbondale, Pennsylvania. In this economically depressed coal-mining area, only Caucasians had lived there since the time of the Native Americans. Some time ago, our Jewish family had served the role of "Other."

I had been happy to leave the small, isolated world of Carbondale. Years passed, and my husband and I returned to buy a cottage on a nearby mountain lake. When my daughter's dark-skinned Hispanic boyfriend visited, our car was stopped twice and checked out by a policeman. We all expressed outrage at the obvious racism.

I did not think there was any hope for this little coal town. But at the end of the millennium, Carbondale changed. An African-American family moved to town and the father was the cop. More African-American families followed. Then the Foliage Restaurant opened, and the town had a store run by Asians.

Most of the workers in the restaurant spoke little or no English, except for
King. He was clean cut, tall, mature, and at ease — an All-American young man.
With his sweet confidence, I thought he was older then his sixteen years. He was
the link between the Carbondale customers and the kitchen workers who had
been sent there for their first work experience in their new land. He was the one
who took the orders in English, then translated them for the workers, who only
spoke in their native tongue. His mother ran a second Chinese restaurant in an
equally small town about five miles away.

When I arrived, he graciously offered me a soda, and we took a seat at the
most private booth. Occasionally, he pardoned himself when he had to take a
telephone order. His maturity was tested when a group of high school cohorts
came in and sat across from us and teased him good naturedly. "Ignore them,"
he instructed, keeping the focus on me. Keeping focused and wanting to join his
buddies to go play basketball are the yin and the yang of growing up Chinese in
Carbondale.

They Are the Stupid Kids at School

We were not like the common families of China. My grandparents were
looking for a different life. My mother's father was a truck driver in
China, and at that time, not too many people could drive. My family did
well driving around China. Since my grandfather was a driver, he saw
many interesting things and tasted many different dishes.

When my mother, father, and I moved to the city of Hong Kong, our
first place was only a room. There were two couples in their seventies living there also, and we rented one room of the apartment. All we had was
a portable table and the TV on top of the refrigerator. Eventually we
moved from there to the edge of Hong Kong, and it was a bigger apartment of two rooms.

My grandparents, parents, aunts, and uncles moved to the coal region
of Pennsylvania to open restaurants in several small towns. They left me
in Hong Kong with my mom's mother for several years. I was a kid who
liked to hang out and play. My grades then were not too good, but now
they are better. I liked living with my grandmother because she let me do
anything. When I whined, she said, "Okay."

When I recently went back to visit, I found out that many of my old playmates are now in gangs or act tough like they are in gangs, so I guess it is good that I left in 1992.

After I had lived in Hong Kong for seven years I joined my mother in Carbondale. I moved here right in the middle of the school year, in the winter's cold and snow. Back home there might be frost on the mountain but not cold and snow like here. This was the end of my fourth school year, and they treated me differently. The teacher made me stand up and introduce myself. I was the only new kid. My school friends here are a little bit different. They don't see through people. They are easy to argue with.

When I was in Hong Kong, it was pretty international, but in Carbondale everyone is sort of the same. There are a couple of kids in the school who call me racial names, but I ignore them because it's only words. They insult you, and after a while they stop because I don't do anything back. If you try to take care of yourself, they'll keep bothering and bothering you. They are the stupid kids at the school. I am taking academic courses but not honor classes. I want to study the markets, understand why they go up and down. I am only a sophomore in high school, but I'll go to any college that will take me.

Some People Have Not Tried Chinese Food Yet

I work at my mom's restaurant after school, except during basketball season. At the beginning my mother argued because times are tight, but I always wanted to play basketball. I guess you have to do something you like. Some of the people who work here at the restaurants are relatives, and sometimes we call some job agency in Chinatown, and they give you information about people. Some workers don't have their papers in order. I know a girl whose father has cancer, and her mom is really sick, and she had to quit school at sixteen to work. It is so sad. She is at my uncle's restaurant in Scranton. In the little town next to us, the Chinese restaurant is our competitor, but I don't hate this kid. He is in the same grade as me, and I talk to him. We are here to do business and not to kill anybody.

I have a lot of responsibility for my mother, but I want to do something

I'm good at. I'm sick of the restaurant. When people order, they just give you a number, and there are three number "twelves" on the menu—but in different sections, so sometimes we get mixed up. Then they get angry with us.

There are some people up here who have not tried Chinese food yet, such as my music teacher.

Touched by a Ghost

My grandparents are Buddhist. They say when I was a kid that a ghost-like thing touched me because I had drops of water on my forehead. My cousin told me this a couple of weeks ago. My grandparents do rituals. They burn gold paper. They buy fruit and food for rituals. They tell me certain days are bad for getting married or opening a restaurant.

I Am Just a Normal Guy

I have a girlfriend who goes to Sacred Heart High, who I met at the fireworks at the park. We have only gone out for a month. She doesn't like to talk about her father, so I don't ask her. He's not around, but her mother seems nice. My parents are together, but they are separated by where they are. At the holidays, we see each other. Sometimes I go to Philadelphia to see my dad. I'm not sure, but I think he owns a percent of a restaurant there.

Living in Carbondale is not so great. You have to drive to get to any place, and this whole town is dead. When I am older I want to live for a few years in the United States and then move back home.

Maybe I won't. I have not yet been to very many places in the United States because my parents don't want to take me on vacations.

My girlfriend and I like to go to the movies on the weekend to the place next to K-Mart on Route Six. I have my license, but most of the time, I just go to the YMCA to play basketball. Many of my friends are on the football team, but my mother won't let me join.

I'm just a normal guy.

PART THREE Charred Portraits

AMERICA POST – 9/11

TWENTY-ONE

Zohra Saed

AFGHAN-AMERICAN

I Had the Idea That the United States Would Be a
Betty Boop or a Popeye Cartoon

All my poetry is based on trying to reclaim my connections. One thing that my father had told me is that wherever your umbilical cord is buried, you are always drawn back to that place. Since mine was buried in a lime orchard in Jalalabad, that is one direct link because I used to dream about Afghanistan. It's been a place for me to try to recapture in my writing.

I grew up trying to make stories about the postcards on the wall. See the postcard of the three men talking? I would try to figure out what they were saying.

We come from a long line of dentists. My grandfather had been educated in Hong Kong in the British system, so he brought modern dentistry to that part of Afghanistan. So everyone in my father's family is a dentist.

He had to go back to school, and it took a long time for us to get back on our feet. My dad did a lot of odd jobs. He worked in a gas station for a few months and then a pizzeria.

When I was in Saudi Arabia I had the idea that the United States would be a Betty Boop or a Popeye cartoon. I had this idea that it would be a comic-book land. I think the main thing I was looking forward to was going to school. My father had really talked up school to be this magical place. My father is a great storyteller. My mother is a great storyteller as well. My dad is more into historical literary figures and folktales that have been passed down, and my mother has all these family legends and these great magical female heroes. And so from both ends I get this idea if you were a woman, you would have these special powers and special energy. So from when I was very young my dad had prepared me to be this great person that I was supposed to be.

When I came to Brooklyn, it was just in time to be enrolled in the school. I remember the school being pointed out, and since I had been so jazzed up in my head I thought it was the neon-lighted Waldbaum Supermarket in front and not the brick building in the back. I said, "Wow, what a school, with all this lighting." It was brightly lit. When they took me to the other brick building I was very confused.

In kindergarten in 1980, I didn't speak any English. I had the alphabet down, which was good, but I couldn't speak it. I spoke three different languages: Dari, Uzbeki, and Arabic. My great-grandparents were originally from northern Afghanistan and so we spoke Uzbeki. Coming to America, no one understood me because we mixed all three languages.

I would climb up on the playhouse roof because no one understood me. I would talk in so many languages, and nobody got it. I got frustrated because here I was, and everybody was my age, and it was fun, but no one could communicate with me. I got so frustrated that I beat up a few of the students. I had this sense of poetic justice in me. The fog sort of lifts and you go, "Oh, I understand what people are telling me." I still see my kindergarten teacher.

It was winter, so the weather was shocking. When we came to the

United States my mom loved it because it looked like our country [before the Taliban], where you could wear pants and you could go out. In Saudi Arabia the women were completely covered. Sometimes when we were living there, my mother would fall down because when you cover yourself and you hold a baby, you can't walk. My mom would wear really high heels to make up for the dress restrictions. She just got used to wearing high heels, and her ankles hurt if she wore lower heels.

We Were Just Screaming into Space,
"Can You Please Not Bomb the Bridge until I Get Over?"

I was on a subway on the way to the graduate center in midtown when the World Trade Center first was hit early in the morning. I saw it burning when the train passed over the bridge, and for some reason the severity did not hit me. It did not seem like it would crumble. Nobody really believed it would fall to pieces. As New Yorkers we think we're invincible in a way that everything will be taken care of—everything will be okay. A lot of people were either staring or just reading their books on the train. I didn't know what to do. Then when I got to Thirty-fourth Street, I learned that a plane crashed into the Pentagon, and then everything hit me. It was a very frightening experience because for three hours I was just walking around with a student from the graduate center where I go to school, with a radio that didn't have batteries, and we weren't plugging it into anything, but we were carrying it around like a security object just in case we had to listen to the news, but I don't know where we would plug it in. It was very surreal.

I walked all the way from Manhattan to my home in Sheepshead Bay. I twisted my ankle because I walked in sandals all the way from midtown. I was afraid because they were saying there was no way into Brooklyn. I was having anxiety. When the World Trade Center crumbled, there were grown men crying out in the street. You could see the dust. I didn't have anyone to walk with me, but there was sort of a group of people migrating from Thirty-fourth Street. Some had walked from Harlem. When we reached Chinatown everyone was buying hats and flip-flops and water, so the prices all went up. Then we walked over the bridge. It was the strangest thing about being on the bridge and walking because we were covered in the dust and the concrete. Film canisters were all over the ground, as were little Red Cross cups. When I was on the Brooklyn Bridge I was in shock. There was all this paper and dust everywhere, and all our lives are so based on paper and concrete. We thought the World Trade Center was invincible.

I really was glad that no one could pick out where I was from when I was walking home. All the while, I was hiding my face under this fisherman hat with a New York Yankee sign in the middle.

I was definitely afraid. We were on the bridge, and everybody was praying together that no one would come and attack us.

"We are poor people. Can you please not bomb the bridge?"

We were just screaming into space, "Can you please not bomb the bridge until I get over?" And we are all aghast, "Please, don't bomb the bridge."

I didn't talk to anybody, but I knew we were all in it together. What was great was there were people offering bathrooms for our use. After walking for hours we needed them. People were asking how you were, and if you needed directions, or when people broke down crying, there were people there to help them. You realized that humanity didn't really fall apart that day. There was something.

When I was out in the street, I walked with a woman for three hours, and I had no idea who she was. We just ended up talking and walking. But my first fear was, of course, as a New Yorker, not as an Afghan. First, you start realizing how vulnerable you are on an island. You can't get out. You are stranded and not connected to anything else, and whatever bridge that you could walk over could easily be targeted. It was very scary. I don't think I thought of being an Afghan-American until later when people were starting to target us.

One of my students was wearing a veil when she was walking across the Queensborough Bridge. She said that vans were offering rides to people, but they wouldn't pick her up because she had the head covering, and someone called her a terrorist. A lot of my students who had their heads covered were facing severe kinds of abuse.

The issue for me was seeing the World Trade Center fall apart. That was probably the closest thing I have come to a war, and we were refugees. We escaped the war, and we came to this country for freedom, not expecting that something that violent would come here. That was furthest from Americans' minds and furthest from all our minds because this is the ultimate place of freedom and safety.

They blamed the Afghanistan people, but it should have been the Arabs. They used Afghanistan as a launching pad, with the bombing of the Buddhas and the destruction of Afghan culture, wiping out a whole nation's culture and nationalism. They used our country as a launching pad for a new, very scary cult. I would not call it Islam or the purism that they are talking about. There are no fundamentals about them. They have very specific rules on how you engage in war in the Koran. There are very specific rules for everything. They are not fundamentalists, but they are definitely a cult. Who else would do that? In our religion, one of the things is to respect other people's religion and let them practice their religions, and we respect this. And they respect your religion. It is a religion based on peace. I am very against this idea of calling it fundamentalism or purist because it is not based on the Koran.

After the day of walking and terror when I finally made it home, I found my mother praying and crying.

Then she said, "Can you go get me onions?"

I think it goes back to the idea of being sort of normal after all that panic.

He Was Trying to Get into Our Apartment

During the Gulf War my brother and sister had some slurs made against them in school. Sheepshead Bay is sort of a small neighborhood, and everyone sort of knows each other. Because we've been here for so long I think we have a lot of people looking out for us.

We had a few frightening incidents. Some guy was trying to come into our house with a package.

He said, "I'm going to leave it at the door."

I answered, "No." Luckily my neighbor was here. We have been neighbors for twenty years. I said again, "No, don't put it here."

He kept insisting, "I'm going to leave the box here." And he was trying to get into our apartment. He was really frightening. That was probably the most terrifying. We called the police.

On the flip side, there were a lot of neighbors coming and asking if we needed things from outside; they were very happy to get them for us. For a week we stayed home, but again this isn't as serious as incidents that happened to my students. Our neighborhood is safe because we know most of the people.

We did receive a Bin Laden flyer that someone stuck on our door. "You get ten thousand dollars and a free trip to go to Afghanistan." Something like that. I didn't see it but my mom ripped it up. We received a lot of phone calls, from midnight to four in the morning they kept calling and cursing.

Maybe they found our name from the phone book. Maybe some were my friends or some of my brother's or sister's friends. I do know that a lot of firemen died from around here. A lot of neighbors lost people. It was younger people calling. It wasn't adults. We had to change our number. We got called specifically; they said we were from Afghanistan. People had done the research in order to call us, "Afghanistan." It wasn't like they were saying, "You Muslims."

People were not going out of their way to come and physically attack us. Whereas in the Queens community, older women who were wearing traditional garbs had their windows broken. People were actually being beaten up in elementary schools for being Afghan. Even though they are Arab, it's recognized as Afghan. That was probably the first time because we're not so well known. We became more visible in American consciousness.

It Was This Mute, Mute Place

A week later I was in the Wall Street area because I went to do a reading on a Muslim radio show. It was very scary.

It was very chaotic because I think that was the first time where I was encountering all the kinds of questions from people, and I didn't know how to answer any of it. I didn't even know how I fit in. I was reading poetry about growing up in Brooklyn, and I didn't know what that had to do with now. But the radio host had wanted me to read, and I didn't feel comfortable. And seeing Wall Street at the time, there was dust everywhere. It was heartbreaking. Everyone was just trying to be normal, but it wasn't. It was too quiet. It was very sad. And you could still see the smoke. It was just a war area.

People were together in clusters, but they weren't speaking. It was very surreal. It was as if it was a silent movie. The only noise was from a generator outside a building. And we were wearing gas masks and the surgical masks in case the air was bad. My mom gave me a mask. There was South Street Seaport on one end and just this mute, mute place on the other.

But the Best Part Was I Didn't Have to Wear a Mask

My school had been a little nervous about me coming back. "Why don't you take a week off?"

I wanted to come back and see what the climate was. My students were great. I had to deal with three hundred students, and I had specifically chosen an Arab-American course. It's actually a requirement class. Some of them were like, "What am I doing here now?"

What I had were students who were confused. They just wanted to talk about it. And they used the classes. We talked about the other side. We talked about the actual issue. We all got it out. This was only my second year teaching, and I am only twenty-six, so I'm no expert. I don't know how to deal with this, especially a crisis like that. My God, I didn't know if I had the tools to handle something like that. So we started with, "What are you hearing? What do you think?" And then a week later, "I think everyone should listen to alternative radio news. I think this is what we have to hash out first." We took it slow, and the classes became sort of looser after that.

Then I decided to get more speakers to come in because I didn't feel like I could really handle all the kinds of questions. So I brought more of the poets in, and also I wanted to give a personal face to these Arab people that are shown in groups and clusters, sweaty and all angry. So I just sort of wanted to give the students different people and, of course, the different cultures within the label "Arab-American." In the end it worked out really well. We became famous as a class. It was the first class in CUNY that had dealt with Arab-American issues.

But the best part was I didn't have to wear a mask. I came in and said, "What do you guys think? I'm scared." And I think that is what created this dialogue that we had.

Someone called the FBI on the father of one of my students because he owned an Arabic store. The father was held for forty-eight hours, and their house was searched. In the end there was nothing, and they apologized, and my student was crying, and he said, "I understand because I know terrorists from our region did this. I understand but still I have to tell you about it." He had this way of saying, "I understand we are being targeted. But this is my daddy who was taken away."

A lot of my Middle Eastern students who were still covering their heads were so great and so outspoken. I think having them in the class worked a lot for my other students who were just curious.

"We didn't know that women chose to cover their heads."

It was interesting because of the makeup of the class. They were ethnically diverse, but more Muslim and Arab and South Asian students came in because of the topic.

They definitely felt it was a safe place, and I think the fact that they were interviewed and talked about made them feel very good.

It is important for the Afghan community to come out and be part of mainstream multicultural America. It is important to be part of American history.

TWENTY-TWO Ibrahim Mojaddedi

AFGHAN-AMERICAN

If You Accept Me as a King, Then I Accept
Mohammed Zahir Shah as My King

My last name is Mojaddedi, and Mojaddedi is a very well-known family in Afghanistan because they were influential clerics and politicians. As a matter of fact, my great uncle is the one that made Mohammed Zahir Shah the king.

My uncle was a powerful religious leader and had a lot of influence. People came to our family to request favors on a regular basis. During the war between the British and Afghanistan, our people were the top soldiers, and they were the ones who gathered all the Afghans together to fight.

King Nadir Shah ruled for four years, and then he was assassinated; nobody wanted to bury him because they were afraid. My uncle stood in front of the coffin and said, "He died as a king, and he will be buried as a king."

Later the powerful people gathered again. My uncle spoke, "The king is dead, but according to all the rules and laws of this country, his son should be the next king." Zahir Shah was only a boy of twenty at that time.

The people said, "No, we don't want him, but we accept you as our king."

My uncle replied, "Well, if you accept me as a king, then I accept Mohammed Zahir Shah as *my king*." That is how Zahir Shah became the king for over sixty years.

At one point my uncle was prime minister. He was asked to go on the radio and announce a holy war against the government of Pakistan. My uncle asked, "How can I go and call a holy war against another Muslim country?" After that he was not treated so well, and our family became divided.

My father did not work a regular job. He basically oversaw the land and had an import-export business. My father sensed political danger, so he rushed my brother and me out of Afghanistan to the United States.

We Had Our Pride

We arrived in Manhattan and rented a hotel room. We'd say, "Okay, let's go out to eat now." When we went out to eat, we saw the same amount of people at nighttime as in the day.

In Afghanistan, there was no such thing as twenty-four hours of work, but here we saw people even at midnight, and they were still working. I had turned to my brother and said, "Are you sure we can work like this?"

My brother and I used to go for breakfast every morning in the same coffee shop. And every morning we went, and we had the same thing because we could only say, "Cinnamon roll and coffee with cream, and a pack of cigarettes."

One of my uncles was teaching medical school in Canada, and we really wanted to go there. Because of the political danger my father had hurried my brother and me out of Afghanistan. Once in the United States, it was necessary to go to Washington, D.C., to get a visa to get to Canada.

I had a cousin in Washington who said, "No, you're not going to

Canada. No way. You're going to stay right here with me, and you're going to start working, and you're going to go to school."

He showed us how to work, because we didn't know how to do it. I had worked for the government in Afghanistan for nine months. While I was there working, I was running the mechanical department of a bus transport company, just like the Metro, straight out of high school. Fifteen hundred people worked for me.

Our cousin showed us how to bus tables, and then he talked to his managers. In the Washington area, he was working in two different hotels. My cousin took me in the morning with him to Holiday Inn and took my brother with him at nighttime to the Sheraton.

We had our pride, and when somebody would tell us to do something, we would say, "Wait a second. Why are they talking like this to *us*?" At that time, it was a little bit shocking to be addressed roughly as a busboy as compared to our former lives in Afghanistan.

She Was Very Young and Had Long Red Hair

When my younger brother decided to move to Denver, I told him, "I'm not going. If you want to go, you go." I was working as a room-service waiter, and the money was good. A bunch of us rented an apartment together. We knew fifteen guys from Afghanistan. We would get together on Sundays, cook, socialize, and play cards.

It was the first time that I was separated from all of my family, so I decided to follow my brother.

When I was working at this Denver steakhouse I saw a young woman enter. I just stood and stared and could not move. She was very young and had long red hair. She was with her sister.

My boss sat them in my section, so when I went over there I asked, "Would you like anything to drink?"

My future wife was the one who said in a heavy New York accent, "Yeah, can I have a cup of coffee?"

I said, "I bet you're from New York."

She said that she was from Brooklyn. We served Turkish coffee, which is very thick and strong, and you can have only one cup. She had about four or five cups. Her attitude and looks impressed me. I asked, "What do you guys want to do later on?" I started going out with her. Within three months, we were married."

She was a college student, and her sister was taking belly dancing. That night it was her sister's birthday, and so she was taking her sister out. We used to have a belly dancer in our restaurant, so that's why she brought her there.

From Our Immediate Members of My Family,
We Are Missing Seventy-two People

Immediately after I met my wife, the Communist government took over Afghanistan. All the members of my family were put in jail—the women, children, servants, dogs, everything. The women and the children spent nine and a half months in prison. Life got harder and I was worried about my father.

After I got married, and my wife was pregnant, I had called home to Afghanistan. I found out that my father had suffered a stroke. I said, "I want to come back."

He said, "No, don't come, because you know, look what happened to your brother." My younger brother and my uncle, who was a professor in Canada, were among all those men that they took in 1978. Even today, we don't know if they're alive, dead, or what happened. From the immediate members of my family we are missing seventy-two people, my younger brother included.

"Middle East Peace in Denver. Muslim and Jew Get Married"

Then my own personal life changed. I became a father to a little boy. Right after that, we had a little girl. There are only sixteen months between the two.

I was a Muslim, and I came from a very religious family. My wife was Jewish from Brooklyn, so it was kind of a shocking story at that time. Some people found that really interesting. A lady wrote an article in the newspaper, which said, "Middle East peace in Denver. Muslim and Jew get married."

When I wrote to my father, everything was fine about our marriage. In my religion of Islam, we are allowed to wed the people of the book. A

Muslim man is allowed to marry a Christian or a Jew, but we are not allowed to marry a Hindu because they don't have a holy book. We're not allowed to marry a Buddhist because their book is not considered a book of God.

At first my wife's family was not happy. I told her personally, honestly, I don't mind if we have to have an Islamic ceremony, and then we can do a Jewish ceremony for your parents. We were afraid that her parents might not come to our wedding. The rabbi told us that the only way he was going to marry me was if I converted to Judaism, and I said, "No." We ended up going to the justice of the peace.

In the early months of our marriage, her sister's husband got killed in an explosion. He was working with Conoco Oil Refinery in Denver. Three weeks after he died, I was going to go with my sister-in-law to help her buy a car. When I went to her house, another gentleman came out from her room, and then she came out. I said, "Wait a second. Your husband died three weeks ago. Already you have a new man."

After that, I did not speak to my sister-in-law. I did not go to her house. I just lost respect for her, because I wasn't brought up that way.

When my father died in 1980, until today, my mother has never looked at another man, so I am looking at this a little bit differently.

My daughter and my son are Americans, but the values I have taught them are Afghan—that is to give respect. My father-in-law noticed that at dinnertime, we let the elder go first. If they are men or women, and then the young ones, they go afterward. So he's really impressed by that. He said he has never been treated that way. If my wife's parents walk in the room, we stand up in front of them out of respect.

I was working hard jobs here and there, and my son was a year old when my father passed away. Because he was very sick, my father was under house arrest, but not in prison. My father wrote me, "I'm telling your mother and sister to leave, and they're not leaving, and the situation is getting worse here."

My wife and I borrowed money from the bank, because at that time the family's land was taken, the stores were taken, everything was gone, and they were living off of whatever they could find to make it in the day-to-day life.

We sent them tickets, but they couldn't come. The tickets had been at the offices of Pan Am Airlines for almost eight months, and then my father died.

I started writing a letter to the State Department and asked them for help, and they were kind, but there was nothing that they could do for me as long as my family was in Afghanistan.

I contacted an uncle who was a rebel leader against the Russians, and somehow he helped my mother and my sister get through the mountains to Pakistan. When they arrived in Pakistan, we transferred the tickets from Kabul to Karachi to New York.

Afghanistan Is the Size of Texas

My little girl had developed a croup, and we had a very hard time because the Denver air is very thin, and we used to take her to the hospital on a weekly basis. After suffering many nighttime horrors, we talked to the doctor.

The doctor said, "The best thing for her is someplace humid."

When I was a young boy in Afghanistan, the only place I really wanted to live was Texas. When we studied geography they would say, "Afghanistan is the size of Texas." Texas also had the cowboys and the Indians. I knew who John Wayne was, Kirk Douglas and, of course, we all knew Raquel Welch.

At first my wife did not work because I was still old-fashioned, and I said that the woman should raise the children, but she helped out. She became the manager of our apartment complex, but she had an assistant in each building, and they gave us an apartment. When an apartment became vacant, they cleaned it up and got it ready for the next occupants, and she collected the rent. But she didn't go *out* to work.

They Pulled Me Out of My Car and Beat Me Very Badly

In Houston I worked for a Mexican restaurant chain, then a supermarket. In 1992, a big change in my life happened when I began volunteering to help Afghan patients who were brought back to America for surgery. They needed a home, and they came and stayed with me. I would take them to the doctor and take care of them until they got better and left.

Most were young children. One adult man had a bomb blow up in his face, and Dr. Schwartz worked with him.

Since the World Trade Center disaster happened, I feel really bad because it was an unfortunate thing to happen, and, of course, my country got involved in this, but my country also wasn't involved. Sometimes I sit down and tell everybody, "Show me one person in these hijacked airplanes that was Afghan." None of them are. But unfortunately, they took harbor in my country.

People don't treat me different because I sit down and talk to them, because I'm the kind of person who sees something is wrong and I tell them it's wrong. It doesn't make any difference who did it and why, if it is wrong. Right now, I work for a grocery chain, and so I know a lot of people, and they know a lot about me because they know I am from Afghanistan. They show a lot of sympathy. Of course, I get asked a lot of questions.

"Tell me about your country." My store director makes me sit in his office and questions me. "Tell me about your country. Why is this?"

The worst part was at the time during the Iran crisis when I got beat up in Denver. I had my windows of my car down while I was listening to the Afghan music. These four guys thought the music sounded like Persian music, so they just jumped out of their truck at a red light and pulled me out of my car and beat me very badly and left me there. There was nothing to do about it but go back home and change my bloody clothes and return to work.

As a matter of fact, since the World Trade Center disaster we have gotten a lot more sympathy than anything else. Some friends sent us a card, "I hope you and your family are doing well."

The Name I'm Giving You Is a Pure Name

At this time, I really want to go back to Afghanistan. I am working with this woman to open a nongovernmental organization for orphans. I told my wife and my kids. I said, "I want you to finish your education here. I will be back." This is a second home to me.

If we counted, I've spent more than half my life here. But because of my belief of who I am, I still haven't become an American citizen.

My kids are American. They were born and raised here. My wife is an American. She was born and raised here, so this is their country. Once my wife's parents saw how we lived our life and saw the way I treat their daughter, they are very good concerning our marriage, although my wife has converted and is now a Muslim.

I have a green card that allows me to live in this country. The only difference is I cannot vote. I don't vote, but I can express my feeling and my vote through my kids and my wife. I am a partner in this. I told my kids, "Okay, I'm going to go to Afghanistan now, and I want you guys to go. Are you guys going to go?"

My daughter said, "Well, whatever you say, Dad." For an American kid to come in and say that shows that she is close to me.

My son is a very secure person because I always talk to him about my family. I told him, "Son, I don't have anything in life except the name I give you. And the name I'm giving you is a pure name, and I hope you won't mess it up." And he lives by that.

TWENTY-THREE

Irfan Malik

PAKISTANI-AMERICAN

High-Class Stationery Mart

My earliest memory was about my father's Vespa scooter. I remember my mom would sit in the back seat, and he would be riding the scooter and I would stand in between his legs on this little platform, and we would go to the bazaars, and I would read the signboards on the stores.

And the funny thing is that now I look back, and it was really . . . it's hard to read those because usually the store names were in English, but it's so different than Urdu script. So it would be like High-Class Stationery Mart, China Crockery Store. And he would correct me. And I also remember reading newspaper headlines for his friends, and he would very proudly present me. It was before I had even started school, so he was very happy about it.

My dad has a collection of old literary journals, and very early on I started reading them and was fascinated by the literature. We didn't have libraries in the way we have libraries here. Lahore is a large city, but we used nickel storefront libraries. Somebody would buy one thousand or two thousand books of different genres and start a library, and you could borrow the books from the library for a nickel a day. I was born and raised in the old section of Lahore. My father's family was in the spice, oil, and grain trade.

My parents would not let me go to the parks like other kids. I liked to sit alone and read books, so basically I didn't miss anything.

I Thought My Father Had Ideologically Betrayed Me

When I was around twelve, there was this huge political movement of populists started by Zulfikar Ali Bhutto, the father of Benazir Bhutto.

My father was fascinated by his populist blend of Socialism and Islam, and he called it Islamic Socialism, and all my life I remember my father as a secular person. He was secular and a kind of national, democratic kind of person. My father was a person who I later understood had seen colonialism and all that. In my house there were two pictures hanging on the wall. One was of Gamal Abdel Nasser, the Egyptian president and the other was Sukarno. These were the people who helped their own nations get out of colonialism, and I remember never going to a mosque. My father was very much against mullahs and ridiculed them, and I remember just going once a year to a mosque. So I grew up in a secular, liberal milieu. Bhutto inspired him because of his ideas. My father got immersed in politics and started a children's wing, and he got me involved in it. I became a kind of leader. We kids would have our meetings. I would address big public rallies and became the star kind of person. In addition, men could not go into the houses, so as young people we were allowed to go into houses and talk to the women in a very simple way and we would basically tell them where to put their stamp when they vote.

I remembered what Bhutto had promised and then what he actually did when he got into power. That disillusioned my father very much. He was brokenhearted. At that time my father was in his late forties. He went on a pilgrimage and from that point on, he never drank, and he never smoked. He became a devout Muslim. But socially he is still liberal.

I thought my father left me, and I felt ideologically betrayed by him. That was a period of my life when I got very angry with him.

At that point he went to religion, and I went toward left-wing politics, which was critically opposing the government. I went into a very active political life when I was about fourteen.

I had already published as a short story writer. It was in a very big, very popular journal, which was not like a literary journal. It was more like *Esquire* or the *New Yorker,* and I was very proud of myself. I was still in high school at that time. And they published two more of my stories, and then another journal published another two stories, and I totally immersed my life in the literary world. I started a group for young writers called New Horizon. In a very short period of time we were a group of about forty young, mostly young teenage men. We were all aspiring writers, and we met weekly in the downtown city of Lahore, and those meetings were open to the public. We would read our literature and present it for critique. This is a big tradition. Usually only established writers did that. Slowly, we won some respect.

They Sentenced Me in Absentia

But when the military took over, they banned all kinds of culture and political activities, and so I felt very angry, and I felt that this was unjust. I remember telling my friends that I don't feel like writing literature anymore. This was the time when we needed to bring democracy back and needed to work some political action. It was not the time to write poems.

I look back, and I feel like writing poetry would not have been a bad choice at that time. Most of us got involved in different kinds of political movements, and I basically got very much involved with the student movement against the military.

It was a very dangerous thing to do. I was secular, and I was democratic, and I didn't want theocracy in the country, and I didn't want to militarize it either. Very soon I realized that I could not live a normal life now because I was politically active, so I had to leave home at the age of sixteen. I moved from place to place, staying with people who supported us.

Occasionally, I would go home and spend a few days, but then the police started coming to the home and started asking about me; I could not do it anymore. It is very unusual for a young man in that culture to grow up so independently. I was not a big gun, but I was active enough that I would make a statement, and sometimes it would appear in the daily press, so my family would know I was fine. And I would tour the country and go to different cities.

They sentenced me in absentia, but I was never arrested. I made a speech at a university in another province. When you make a speech at a university, it is very hard for the police. They can't come in. If they come in, they have hundreds of students to deal with, and they just don't make that kind of fuss. They like to arrest people when they are alone. The art is that you never give them a chance to do so. I guess I was good at it, as I never got arrested. I did that for a long time.

There was one close call. People were being killed and tortured and jailed, so I felt it was necessary to remain out if I wanted to make a difference. There was the cultural heart of the city. Everything happens there. That was my favorite part of town, too. There was this movie theater right opposite to it. And I think there was a movie, which I really wanted to see. I don't recall correctly, but I think it was either a movie about the Algerian resistance or it might have been *The Last Picture Show*.

I recognized that there was an undercover policeman standing outside. I just walked past, and he called my name. If you respond to it, it's over because then he knows that he is correct. Somehow I managed not to respond, so I kept walking, and then he called my name again. Then I heard steps, hurried steps, and I did not turn back. I did not look. I just kept walking. And then he touched my shoulder, and I stopped and looked at him and acted in a very surprised manner. "What is it?"

He asked, "Irfan?"

I said, "I'm sorry." And I could see this uncertainty on his face.

He said, "Aren't you Irfan?"

"No," I answered.

He said, "Who are you?" I gave him some name. He said, "Where do you live?" I managed to give out an address. And I could see that he was really struggling. I think the whole thing came out of my mouth so naturally and in a way that made him think, "Oh, okay, I'm sorry." And I started walking, and then he came back and said, "I'm very sorry I stopped you. I'm a police officer, and can I do anything for you?"

I said, "No. I'm fine."

And he said, "All right." And I was walking and knew that he was standing there still thinking about it.

About one hundred yards from there, there was a big road crossing and a traffic light. When I got there, I walked normally, and I turned left so I could get out of his sight, and I knew that he could not see me. I just ran.

They Put Me in a Rubber Suit and Placed Me in a Big Tank Full of Chemical Waste

I was living in the semi-underground when I happened to meet a Swedish girl who was working for the nongovernmental organization in Lahore. And in fact I needed a place to stay for some time, and somebody took me to her place, and I thought that could be a good place because nobody would come looking for me there. We kind of fell in love and got married and after another two or three years of that, we moved to Sweden.

When I moved to Sweden, I felt that this was the kind of society I was probably trying to bring. I was young. I didn't have any particular ideology in all that. I was inclined to envision equality and a vague kind of Marxist idea of society, but I never really understood Marxism enough. I was not an intellectual. I was more like a doer. Another thing that was very important for me was the gender segregation in Pakistan. I hated it. Men and women couldn't interact. It seemed so natural to me. I was delighted that there was a setting that was not segregated because of the gender lines. This was a social democratic society that took care of each member in a way that I had never seen before.

I moved from a very hustling, bustling town of five or six million to a very small town in western Sweden about one hundred kilometers from the Norwegian border. It was predominantly a farming community, and I was probably one of two non-Swede or non-European persons in that village. In addition, I didn't know the language, and being without language is a very interesting experience.

It happened to be the coldest winter in Sweden since World War II. I would walk one kilometer in the morning, at a quarter to six, to go to a certain spot where somebody would pick me up, and then we would drive about thirty kilometers to another town where I could go to a school to learn Swedish. The temperature would be minus thirty-six or forty degrees Celsius. And so I took a sudden plunge from forty above to forty below zero. It was just like, "Wow!" I think I learned language quickly because I was very curious, and I was not ashamed of using it, no matter how bad I was. And I didn't mind people correcting me. In fact, I liked it so I could learn more.

I had a very tough life. We left Pakistan because my wife got pregnant, and I became afraid. I became afraid that if I got arrested, who knows what would happen, and would I ever see my child? And she would never see her father. I thought that at least I wanted to see my child. The idea was to be in Sweden for about six months and then come back. Obviously, I never went back. Basically a month after we arrived, we had a daughter. We had no jobs, no money, and we got an apartment. There was this system; my wife did not know that her employer had not been paying her what is called social taxes, so she was out of the system. We were not entitled to get any kind of support, which we were expecting. I started getting stray jobs I had never done any physical activity in my life. In my first job, they put me in a rubber suit, which covered my body up to my chest, and they sent me in a big tank, which was full of chemical waste. I was shoveling it out of a small hole. There was another guy outside, and we would switch every half-hour, and I would shovel chemical sludge out of that hole. After that I got a funny job; in that particular part of Sweden they were building a museum. The king was supposed to come and inaugurate it, and at the last minute, they needed people to finish it up. I went for a job, and they gave me the task of building a fisherman's hut typical for that area. I was there in that country for a couple of weeks, and I had never even used a hammer, much less knew what a "typical" hut looked like.

In Pakistan men are not handy because you only do what is your profession. You hire other people to do that: Labor is not that expensive. So I quickly learned, and they gave me designs. Somebody cut the wood for me and said, "Okay, this is how you build it." I built it.

When my daughter was about a month or so old, my wife got a night job at a resident school for socially disturbed girls—young women who were addicts and prostitutes. It was very tough. I would leave home about quarter to six to go to my school, and I would come back at five. By that time my wife would have left my daughter at the neighbor's, and I would pick her up. My wife would pump the milk, and we had the milk. I would be with my daughter all night, and my wife would come home about fifteen minutes before I would leave.

We were both exhausted.

Suddenly after being someone who said something, which would be reported in the newspaper, I became nothing. I had enjoyed that role very much, in fact, because in Pakistan I felt that I had to do it because it's sort of a national-duty kind of thing. I was relieved in a way that I got out of it, but on the other hand I had made myself proud. I never took any money from my dad. And he regretted it. It's the big regret in his life. Parents are proud to support their children to go to school and stuff like that. I never did that. And here I was, I was totally dependent upon everybody else. I could not even . . . and without my wife I couldn't even go to do anything because I didn't know the language, and I couldn't understand the newspaper, radio, or television.

It's a very monotonous society in one regard. Everybody is blue-eyed and, at least at that time, blonde, and everybody speaks one language, and if you don't know that, you are in tough shape.

The hard life, in fact, it never ended. It was suspended with the separation and divorce. When we separated, I knew that being a person from a Third World country I would never get a visa to come back to Sweden, and I could not stand the idea that I would not see my child again. Therefore, I had to make a decision, and I decided I couldn't leave my daughter, so I decided to stay permanently.

I remained in Sweden and took a job as a cleaner, as a janitor at Stockholm University because that was the only job I could get. To this day, I haven't told my parents that I worked a year and a half as a janitor. It was a hard job. There I learned some Swedish, and my colleagues were mostly Greek peasants. They were economic migrants who came in the 1950s and 1960s, and so they had their families and the Greek community and most of them hadn't gone to school, so their repertoire of Swedish vocabulary was about fifty words. And they had been living there for twenty-five years. They were beautiful people, generous, happy, but usually the only words they knew were about sex and gambling.

There was a new policy in Sweden that the mother tongue of the students should be taught in the schools. And so they needed people who could teach these languages.

I am very proud of my language and my culture. Since I had no degree as a teacher, I got a temporary certification and was able to obtain more jobs than I could handle. I did that for about five years or more. At some point, I decided that I needed to study myself since I had a minimal formal education from Pakistan. I left my regular job, and I started studying at Stockholm University.

There Was This American Woman in the Front of the Line
Who Had So Many Questions

During that time I translated an anthology of modern short stories into Urdu. The Swedish Cultural Ministry somehow got to know about this project. It had not been published at that time. Business deals were going on between India and Sweden; therefore, Sweden was very eager to do some Indian cultural festivals and music and dance. The Swedish Institute wanted to publish my book.

Around that time, I was expecting some friends to visit from Germany. In the heart of the town is a tourist information center where tourists are able to get maps and directions and hotel information. I stopped there to get some brochures for my intended visitors. I was waiting in line, and there was this American woman in the front of the line who had so many questions, so many detailed questions that it amazed me how thorough she was. By then, I had traveled some, but I had never gone into a tourist bureau. Somehow I was taken by her questioning. Nobody else was able to ask a single thing because this American woman was taking up all the time.

By the time she was done, I had given up my idea of asking for information. After observing this American woman all this while, I obviously felt that she was also good looking and attractive. She happened to look at me and smiled, and I thought, "All right." I was divorced and single and around thirty years of age. When she went out, I ran after her and stopped her. I said, "Are you satisfied now?"

She looked at me, and she said, "Oh, wow! A man has never asked this question to me before."

I asked, "There is a very good exhibition of photography around the corner. Do you want to go and see it?"

She said, "Yes." And that was it.

Toni was an American teacher and had taken a job in Finland to teach for a semester. She was visiting Stockholm during spring break. After we met, she came back to visit me. When she went back to the States, I remembered her visiting me very often.

She would just call me, "What are you doing tomorrow?"

"Nothing, I'm just studying."

"All right, I'm coming tomorrow."

I used to call my age as minus twenty-nine. I was releasing the frustration in my life of growing up in a gender-segregated culture. I was with a lot of women. Other than writing and my studies, I would just meet women. If I was born in Sweden, I would have gone through that stage at seventeen. I thought that this American teacher was another one of those cases, but it was not.

I absolutely did not want to leave Sweden. First of all I was fine there. I liked it, and I had a daughter. In addition, I also felt that since everybody else wanted to go to America, I really didn't want to go to America. Toni thought it was really unfair, and so we decided that I would come and visit, so I traveled to the States, and I liked it. It was a surprise. Then we decided, "All right, I'm not moving anyhow." She would move to Sweden. We would try it for a couple of years, and if she didn't like it, then I would move to America and see for a couple of years, and that's how it turned out to be.

Toni moved there because I really didn't want to leave Sweden, and I had no desire to live in America. She most definitely did not like Sweden and was very, very unhappy there. She moved back, and for another two and a half years I traveled to the States. It was so costly, and it affected my studies profoundly. So I gave up everything, and also I felt my daughter, who was eleven at that time, would be able to handle it better than when she was younger. Since we were married, I also got a green card. Since 1993 I have been teaching creative writing in a private summer school.

When I moved to Boston I had a social circle in place; I had friends, and I don't think I had enemies. But that is also important to have.

I had stopped writing when I became political in Pakistan, and when I moved to Sweden I would sit and try to write, but I could not. It took a very huge effort, but I wrote a story. And after that I could not write short stories anymore. Then suddenly I discovered myself writing poetry, and so in 1992 my first book of poetry came out. Now I have five books published.

A Wal-Mart Type of War

After September 11, I noticed two things. One is that people were awfully nice to me. People sent me messages. One writer gave me his house keys, "If things get hard, you can just come and bring your family and live with us." People are concerned about me and my safety and my family. It was really touching.

The second aspect is that for some people who are very dear to me and who I love, the act of terrorism and the subsequent action in Afghanistan brought out sides of them which I had not been aware of. They became very angry and nationalistic. They had indiscriminate kinds of feelings against the Muslim population. This horrible terrorist act, the killing of three thousand people, is very sad and contemptible, and I have no sympathy whatsoever for it. It is a very emotional problem for me because these people are so dear to me, but somehow they don't deplore the large amount of people in Afghanistan and India that died as collateral damage. And that is totally acceptable. I'm living this dilemma day and night, and I don't know how to deal with it.

America dropped a fifteen-thousand-pound bomb outside of Kandahar. It has several detonators and different kinds of explosives in it. I am surprised people have not objected to it. I can bet my life that there is nothing in that country militarily that deserved this bomb.

On CNN a bomb will also come with graphics and specifications and a price tag. How much does it cost? It's like a Wal-Mart kind of war.

I don't want to hurt their feelings, but I'm also a principled person. I'm a pacifist. Life is very important. I don't see that killing people can be equivalent in any regard. I can't really understand it. How can somebody deplore one death and not deplore another one?

My problem is that when I was young and politically active I stood with people who thought things were either right or wrong. That is a very George Bush-ian kind of idea. "You are with us or with them." With age and with experience, I have understood that this is bullshit. It is not like that. But still it hurts me to see some of my most dear friends here not making that distinction. In some regards, I know that they would probably give their lives to save my life. They would do it on a personal level. But on an impersonal level, they have no sympathy for anybody who is in their way. This is a very human situation in a way, and with all my experience, with all my life living in two, three different continents and countries and all this, I suddenly feel very helpless, and I don't know how to deal with it. They are still my friends. I meet them as I was meeting them before.

I have gotten into heated discussions, and right now I have just refused to have any political discussions with them. I know this is temporary because this is not a solution, but I feel angry in a way about this incident because this has put me into this kind of situation. In a way September 11 has brought this dilemma to me. I hate it because it's a violent act, because of so much human life that was taken away. And suddenly I realized that some of my best friends . . . some of the people I felt were the reason I decided to live in this country, who I felt at home with, suddenly felt that violence was a legitimate act for them. And they don't mind it at all. It is very disturbing to me. It's a big dilemma for me. And I don't know what I'm going to do. I don't know how I am going to come out of it. I haven't a clue.

They are intellectuals. They are scholars, they are writers, and they are the people whose company you delight to be in. They are people you can have interesting conversations with, talk about philosophy and literature and culture and politics. These are people who have seen the world. I have no nationalistic feelings about Pakistan at all. I feel like the world is my country. They are the same kind of friends I had in Pakistan, they are the same kind of friends I had in Sweden, and they are the same kind of friends I have in this country.

In the beginning I did not take revenge talk seriously. I thought it was a big shock, and this country has never been physically attacked and so many people have never died within one hour. I had all this respect for them and all that. This was understandable.

But I think it has gone beyond that point. There are countries on the waiting list to be attacked. I remember just laughing when I heard on television that the Taliban command and control center was destroyed, and I thought that must be two donkeys. It's as primitive a country as it can get. But suddenly my friends felt that bombing Kabul was a legitimate target and if some people died, they died. This is a war between us and them, and that's how that particular person used the words, and I thought, "My God, this is the person who had shared so many nice things with me." He is still my dear friend, and I think that's why it hurts, because I think I have learned one thing is that you just don't walk out. You build relationships, and they are there for a very long time. That is how relationships should be.

Ask Grandfather to Kill All the Muslims

All my life I have been a secularist. I have been, politically speaking, anti-Islam—Islam as a political power in Pakistan. I surprised myself that for the very first time I said to somebody that I'm a Muslim. I really felt very strongly that I need to say this.

I had never said that before in my life, that I am a Muslim. Now I have repeated it so many times. In a way, culturally I am, but it also breaks my heart because this is not what I stand for.

On September 11 my son had just started his very first day at school, and he came home and said, "I want you to go to Pakistan and ask Grandfather to kill all the Muslims."

I said, "Killing is not a good thing. You should not kill anybody. You know what? I am Muslim, too. And Grandfather is Muslim, too, and partly you are Muslim, too." I felt bad because obviously it's very confusing because I have never talked to my children about religion. Also his first fieldtrip was to walk into a neighborhood and find the largest

American flag. After that, he would come from school and make statements like, "I want you to kill them." He precisely used the words "us and them."

I said, "Who are them?" And he couldn't explain it.

Friday of last week, he said, "Afghanistan is our enemy." So obviously he is American. He lives here. This is his country. This is his language. This is his culture. But these should not be his values. They should not be American values, and this is what he is getting.

My son will be six tomorrow. He is trying to make sense out of it himself. He loves his grandfather. He wanted Grandfather to take care of the situation. Culturally I cannot deny that I am Muslim. I am a product of that culture.

Compositor: BookMatters, Berkeley
Text: 10/14 Palatino
Display: Univers Condensed Light, Bauer Bodoni
Printer and binder: Maple-Vail Manufacturing Group